THE HOLY TERROR: CAPTAIN WILLIAM NICHOLS

A True Story

Dr. G. William Freeman

authorHOUSE®

AuthorHouse™
1663 Liberty Drive
Bloomington, IN 47403
www.authorhouse.com
Phone: 833-262-8899

Published by AuthorHouse 08/03/2020

ISBN: 978-1-4969-5933-1 (sc)
ISBN: 978-1-4969-5931-7 (hc)
ISBN: 978-1-4969-5932-4 (e)

Library of Congress Control Number: 2014922745

Other books by author:
Jehu Stage Driver: Benjamin Hale (2016)
Journey to Survival: From Lymphoma and Heart Failure to Remission (2019)

Captain William Nichols, Jr.
Custom House Maritime Museum
Gift of Eleanor Baumgartner Leninger

To my maternal
grandmother, "Gramma Baum,"

Genevieve Hale Baumgartner,

great-granddaughter
of Captain William Nichols

Contents

Illustrations

Acknowledgments

I am indebted to the following people for their assistance with my book:

To my wife, Dr. Juliette Z. Loring, who read my manuscript and who aided, counseled, and supported me at every stage of my research and writing.

To my son, Benjamin Hale Freeman, who photographed all images for the book, did the photographic editing, and provided valuable computer technology assistance in the preparation and submission of my manuscript.

To John Green, Newburyport, historian and former teacher, who read my manuscript and whose comments were instrumental in the development of the book's presentation.

To Michael Mroz, executive director, and Kevin MacDonald, curator, of the Newburyport Maritime Society, for their assistance in locating important research materials and for permission to photograph artifacts at the Custom House Maritime Museum.

To Margaret P. Motes and Jesse H. Motes III, Newburyport, who located important historical material and photographic images.

To Jay Williamson, curator, Historical Society of Old Newbury, who provided access to historical research materials.

And to the staff of the Archival Center, Newburyport Public Library, who provided valuable assistance in locating records and historical information.

Preface

Captain William Nichols was an intrepid privateer captain during the War of 1812. He captured twenty-eight British prizes, or vessels, during the war, even though he was a British prisoner for more than half of the war. He was captured six times, escaped three times, and was twice put on parole. The British Royal Navy referred to him as the "Holy Terror".

Nichols story is one of endurance and persistence, a story of determination and courage, and a story of bravery in the face of adverse odds. This is about the life of Captain William Nichols, a privateer in the War of 1812.

Nichols Portrait

Captain Nichols is my sixth-generation ancestor. As a young boy living in a large Victorian home with my grandparents and mother, I recall seeing a portrait of him every day. A large painting of him hung just above the second-floor landing of a winding staircase.

See Frontispiece

I could always feel his dark, intense eyes staring at me as I went bounding down the stairs every morning. A watercolor painting of his three-masted vessel, the *Harpy,* hung alongside his portrait, and together, they seemed to loom larger than life above the stairway.

I was not quite old enough to understand Nichols' connection with the family, but I referred to him as my "great-long-granddaddy." Initially, I did not fully understand how important Captain Nichols had been within the family, but my grandmother often spoke about him. She was Nichols' great-granddaughter and had grown up in his stately Federalist-style house in Newburyport. I often wondered, as I would pause to gaze at the paintings on the stairway, what it would have been like to be in command of a sailing ship like the *Harpy*.

My grandfather died just before I was ten years old, and the family homestead was sold. It had been my home for most of my childhood and was in the family for more than a quarter century. The paintings of Captain Nichols and the *Harpy* were given to my Aunt Eleanor, who lived in the Midwest. I missed the family home and those two paintings that reminded me of Captain Nichols. They had made him come alive for me as I grew up. I felt an affinity toward him and seemed to have some sort of connection with him.

Nichols Five Shilling Coin

When I was nine years old, my grandfather gave me a unique British coin, that he said came from Captain Nichols. He simply said, "Here, you should have this," and he offered it to me with no further explanation.

It was a five-shilling English coin dated 1804. Nichols possession of the coin represents the exploits he had with the British during the War of 1812. On the obverse side, there is a circular engraving emblazoned across King George's profile emphatically stating, "William Nichols Junr." The reverse side reads, "Bank of England – Five Shillings Dollar – 1804". There is also a small hole that was drilled at the top center of the coin, where Nichols used it as a fob attachment to a watch chain for his waistcoat pocket. I was enchanted by the coin.

British 1804 Five Shilling Coin
Circular Engraving Inscription
In possession of the author

When the British released prisoners during the War of 1812, they were each given a few shillings for the time they spent in prison with enough to return home. This five-shilling coin may be the coin Nichols received when he was released from the *Nassau* prison-ship in 1814, after more than one and a half years of British imprisonment. The circular engraving and the hole drilled at the top are symbolic of the deep anger and resentment he felt for the cruel and prolonged treatment he received from the British during his imprisonment.

By wearing the coin as a watch fob, Nichols sent a distinct message to the British that demonstrated his avenging spirit for what was done to him during the War of 1812. An antique appraiser assessed the coin and explained that circular engraving was very rare during that time period. While that coin has numismatic value, it doubles in historical value as a significant artifact related to Captain Nichols. That coin continues to remain in my possession.

When I was twelve years old, my uncle Donald Baumgartner gave me a brass telescope that Captain Nichols had used during his cruises. It was fascinating to see how carefully Uncle Don took apart the telescope to clean and polish the five lenses. He showed me how to use caution when reassembling the telescope so that the thin, brass threads were not forced and did not become cross-threaded. That telescope has been donated to the Custom House Maritime Museum in Newburyport.

Nichols Research

During my adolescence, my mother showed me a family tree that traced my lineage back to Captain Nichols. That opened a new world to me and kindled an interest in wanting to know more about him. In addition, my grandmother gave me a fourteen-page unpublished manuscript by Sidney Marsh Chase that described Captain Nichols' adventures during the War of 1812. As I read through the pages, I became captivated by Nichols' story.

As a young adult, I learned how to do genealogical research and was able to unfold his life story. Various writers collected and reported a wealth of information, and I was able to put the pieces together about his history. I also discovered new information about him that was a surprise to the family. No one else knew that there had been two Captain Nichols, father and son, both of whom had been privateers and in wars for this country.

Speaking with various librarians and museum curators, I was surprised to discover that many people in Newburyport knew about Captain Nichols. They continue to regard him as a hero in the War of 1812, more than 200 years later.

An interest in writing Nichols story began to germinate. My research discovered that a number of people had written newspaper articles or referenced him in books. At least eight different authors had written lengthy articles describing his exploits during the war, with a number of additional references made about him in various history books. It was repeatedly noted that Nichols left no papers or memoirs about his experiences and that he had destroyed many of his logbooks and records before he died.

From the genealogical and historical research that was being done, no single source related his complete story. I felt that the chronicle of Captain Nichols needed to be told. My interest in writing his story was galvanized when my son, Benjamin Hale Freeman, was asked by his fifth-grade teacher to have a parent speak to the class about a family history story. Ben asked if I would talk to the class about our ancestor Captain Nichols. He had heard me speak of him, and Ben knew that the Nichols' story was an important one.

The process of putting together a brief presentation of Captain Nichols story for Ben's fifth-grade class created a desire within me to write his complete story. The result of that effort is this book. It has been a long time coming, either because I have not been able to get to writing it or because I felt that I would not be able to do justice to the legacy of Captain Nichols. It has been an exhausting process but an exciting, obsessive, and productive one.

Frequent research visits were made to various places, including: Newburyport Public Library; Newburyport Vital Records; Custom House Maritime Museum in Newburyport; Historical Society of Old Newbury; Essex Institute and Philips Library at Peabody Essex Museum in Salem, MA; Massachusetts Archives in Boston, MA; Salem, MA, Registry of Deeds; National Archives in Waltham, MA; and Massachusetts Historical Society in Boston, MA.

The information about Captain Nichols was collected from a wide array of local, state, and national archives and newspapers. When conducting my research, some librarians indicated that, "you're looking for a needle in a haystack." I am not a historian, but I had to give myself a history lesson to fully understand what Captain Nichols was experiencing before and during the War of 1812.

During my research, a statement made about Captain Nichols by Editor Ephraim Allen of the *Newburyport Herald* became especially intriguing for me. When Nichols sailed out of Newburyport Harbor in August 1812 on the *Decatur* after war had been declared by President Madison, Allen commented in his newspaper,

> **"This town is disgraced with but two privateers –
> one of which is the *Decatur* - fitted out by Democrats,
> Captain Nichols, master - and they are not likely to
> ever 'set the river on fire'."**
> *Newburyport Herald,* August 11, 1812

That statement was perplexing, because Nichols was held in such high esteem in Newburyport. However, Allen was a Federalist, and Nichols a Democrat-Republican. But within two months, Nichols invalidated the editor's predictions.

Nichols Family Background

Regarding the family, in 1805 Captain Nichols married his next-door neighbor from childhood, Lydia Balch Pierce, the daughter of Captain Nicholas Pierce. Nichols was twenty-four; she was twenty-one. They had five children, two before the War of 1812 and three afterwards. Lydia, their third child, married Benjamin Hale Jr., the son of Benjamin Hale Sr.

NOTE: See Appendix M: William Nichols Genealogy

The elder Benjamin Hale was a prominent businessman in Newburyport and had been a close friend and associate of Captain Nichols. Nichols daughter, Lydia, married Benjamin Jr., the son of one of Nichols close friends. The marriage between children of friends was not uncommon in Newburyport during that time. The Nichols-Hale family became one of the wealthier families in Newburyport.

Benjamin Jr. and Lydia had one child, George Edward Hale. George married Emma Wells, and they also had one child, my grandmother, Genevieve Hale. She was the only child of an only child. Genevieve grew up in Captain Nichols' homestead on Harris Street in Newburyport in the late 1890s. She was raised in an elegant and refined manner in the Nichols' family home.

Genevieve married Robert Mark Baumgartner, and they had five children. Nance, their fourth child, was my mother. I recall "Gramma Baum" often sitting very proudly at Captain Nichols' desk in an erect and dignified manner as she handled the family finances. Nichols' ships-clock and barometer set hung over the desk, and she sat in Nichols diagonal sword chair. She frequently spoke about her great-grandfather. He had a strong presence in the family home, as Gramma always spoke of him with pride.

It is an interesting note that while Captain Nichols was tall and slender with black hair, Genevieve was quite short with bright red hair. She would often bristle, stand straight, and purse her lips whenever my Aunt Janet, the youngest of Genevieve's children, would refer to Captain Nichols as the "family pirate" and was derisive of his achievements.

Wildes Tribute to Nichols

Many accounts of Captain Nichols precarious adventures are in a paper by George D. Wildes with detailed descriptions that he presented at a meeting of the Essex Institute in Salem, Massachusetts, in December 1864. Wildes wrote the memoir as a tribute to Captain Nichols the year following his death in 1863.

Rev. Wildes was born in 1818, grew up in Newburyport, and was the son of Attorney Asa Waldo Wildes, Esq. Attorney Wildes had an office on State Street and was a contemporary of William Nichols in

Newburyport. As a boy, Rev. Wildes recalled seeing Captain Nichols, as an older man, at church or when he was taking walks in town,

> "Nichols was distinguished by something of the warrior's port and step."
>
> Wildes, 1864, p. 236

In the preparation of his lengthy paper, Rev. Wildes was indebted to George J. L. Colby, Esq., a later editor of the *Newburyport Herald,* for use of his extensive notes that documented the personal history of William Nichols. Colby had been a close friend of William Nichols, and "Colby had the highest regard for Nichols' character and admiration of the brilliant exploits of his venerable friend" (Wildes, 1864, p. 230). Even though Nichols did not keep any of his records, he did share a great deal of information about his encounters with Colby, who, in turn, related many of the adventures in the *Newburyport Herald.*

Chase's Unpublished Manuscript

Sidney Marsh Chase, in an unpublished fourteen-page manuscript, provided similar material to Wilde's paper, but he also included many additional details about the naval encounters of Nichols. It was the manuscript that my grandmother had given to me as a young boy. I had long wondered about the background of Chase and how he came to know so much about Captain Nichols.

Chase was born in 1877 in Haverhill, Massachusetts, and graduated from Harvard in 1899. As an adult, Chase was an illustrator and writer and had been a close associate of Wyeth.

He continued to reside in Haverhill, where he knew my grandparents, Genevieve and Robert Baumgartner. From his discussions with them, he became intrigued by the story of Captain Nichols. He did some research and prepared the manuscript about

Captain Nichols. He presented a copy to my grandmother, which she in turn gave to me. Chase died in 1957 at age eighty.

Of special note is that Sidney Chase also wrote a short story about Nichols that was published in *Scribner's Magazine* in May 1913. The twelve-page story about Nichols is written in the vernacular of the early nineteenth-century period and is entitled "A Yankee Privateer." It includes seven illustrations Chase drew as part of his magazine article. While it is a fictionalized story of Captain Nichols, it related many of the factual accounts of "Cap'n Bill" and his two privateer ships, the *Decatur* and the *Harpy*. Chase had surely developed a strong interest in the adventures of Captain Nichols.

Family Notes

A number of artifacts from Captain Nichols remained within the family, as they have been inherited by the generations that followed him. The artifacts were passed onto Nichols daughter, Lydia Hale, who in turn gave them to her only child, George Hale, who was one of two grandsons of Captain Nichols. My grandmother, Genevieve Hale, as the only child of George and Emma Hale, received those artifacts, and she later distributed them among her living children.

Captain Nichols amassed considerable wealth from the prizes he took during the War of 1812. However, his grandson, George E. Hale, who inherited this wealth, depleted the family fortune. George never had to work, and he became an alcoholic and remained living in the Nichols' homestead. Whenever he needed cash, he sold some of the real estate properties that Captain Nichols had acquired in Newburyport.

In 1994, my cousin, Dr. David Buzzee, and I made an effort to gather as many of Nichols artifacts as possible from family members and donate them to the Custom House Maritime Museum in Newburyport. Captain Nichols had worked at the Custom House as the Collector of Customs for four years from 1845-1849, when he was appointed by President Polk.

Author's Notes

This is a narrative about the life of Captain William Nichols. His story needs to be told for Captain Nichols, for the family, and for myself. The scattered articles and references about Captain Nichols have made him appear as somewhat of a myth, but he was indeed a "man of his time." My effort has been to accurately describe his experiences and to explain his place in the history of the War of 1812, of Newburyport, and of our young nation.

In recent years, we have celebrated the two hundredth anniversary of the War of 1812 that extended from June 1812 to February 1815. As I was writing the first edition of this book in early 2014, my thoughts went back two hundred years to the time when Captain Nichols was considered 'The Holy Terror' by the British, and was kept in a cage on the deck of a British ship, and then in chains on the *Nassau* prison-ship in Chatham, England. He was thirty-two years old at the time, but he was able to persevere and survive that ordeal, and he lived another fifty years and died at age 82.

It is documented that Captain Nichols was one of the most successful privateer captains in the War of 1812. It was during the "Age of Sailing Ships" when tall ships dominated the ocean. Nichols has long been remembered in Newburyport history for his bravery and daring on the high seas.

Nichols true adventures rival those of fiction writers about sea captains, such as Patrick O'Brien with his *Master and Commander* and Jack Aubrey series, and C.S. Forester's *Horatio Hornblower* series. Those stories are about fictionalized British sea captains.

While there have been references to Captain Nichols and other privateers in various historical accounts of naval encounters, Captain

Nichols story is the only one that fully details the exploits of an American privateer.

His story is a gripping true account that needs to be told. Nichols was an extraordinarily determined man. It is at times a dynamic and explosive story in his encounters at sea, while at other times it is emotional and touching with his family.

G. W. F.

Overview

Captain Nichols deserves to be
known in the history of this country
as one of the privateer heroes.

"Memorabilia #7"
Newburyport Herald,
August 1, 1855

Captain Nichols had an imperishably
record of his heroism.

D. Hamilton Hurd
History of Essex County,
1888, p. 1765

The extraordinary exploits of Captain Nichols
of Newburyport, a privateersman in the War of
1812, are not so widely known. They read like
fiction instead of a true story of a dare-devil
Yankee skipper.

Sidney M. Chase
"Captain William Nichols and
the Privateer *Decatur*
"ca. 1920, p. 2

William Nichols, Jr., was born in 1781 towards the end of the Revolutionary War. His father, William Nichols, Sr., had been a privateer sea captain during the Revolutionary War who was part of the infamous Penobscot Bay incident, but he died when young William was only three years old.

This is the true story of Captain William Nichols Jr., a commissioned privateer sea captain during the War of 1812. While the story relates his experiences throughout his lifespan, it focuses on the naval encounters and adventures he had during the War of 1812.

The War of 1812 is frequently referred to as America's Second War of Independence and is considered one of our "forgotten wars" (*Great Ships: The Frigates, DVD, 1996*). It was derisively called Mr. Madison's War, but it was truly the war that won our independence. Many issues had been left unresolved at the end of the Revolutionary War, as Britain still wanted to maintain some control in America. There was a lingering fear that Great Britain wanted to reclaim America (ibid.). "Would England ruin the shaky American republic? … it was a strange and illogical war" (Taylor, 2010, p. 10).

This narrative also includes a backdrop of events that were happening at that time in the nation and around the globe when the world was in turmoil; it was "A World Gone Mad."

NOTE: See Appendix A: A World Gone Mad

The tapestry of this chronicle weaves a thread into his life of those national and world events and the conflicts in his hometown of Newburyport, Massachusetts. It is the story of one man who was part of a larger national and world picture.

Daniel Boorstein, in the forward to Henry Cole's 1965 book, *War of 1812*, explains that history books about America have two approaches. The first provides a coherent, chronological narrative of American history. The second deals with significant aspects of American life. This book blends these two approaches by providing, not only a chronological description of events, but also how those events influenced the life of Captain Nichols.

Chapter 1: Introduction

William Nichols became a hero during the War of 1812. He is considered to have been a significant player in the naval war between the United States and Great Britain. Numerous articles have been written and references made in history books about his exploits in the war.

At least eight authors have detailed the naval encounters of his two privateer ships, the *Decatur* and the *Harpy*. Many of the authors' descriptions and comments have been included in the narrative of this book. However, some of these authors did not have complete or accurate information about his experiences. The present narrative is comprehensive in covering all that has been discovered to date about Captain Nichols.

Chapter 2: Nichols Early Years: Captured on the Rose

Very little information is available about Nichols's youth. He left few papers upon his death. He had an aversion to publicity, and he destroyed many of his records. Much of the material about him comes from those who knew or witnessed him in Newburyport or who were onboard one of his ships.

Some reasonable assumptions can be made about his experiences of growing up only two blocks away from the teeming waterfront and active downtown center of the seafaring town of Newburyport. Life on the high seas began for him at an early age, where he was exposed to the dangers and thrills of nautical life. Nichols learned to become an independent and self-motivated man. He developed the skills of seamanship as a youth, and he quickly learned to become a survivor in a tough and rather foreboding world on the high seas.

There was considerable apprehension whenever a ship would leave Newburyport Harbor and go out onto the high sea, because of the fear of impressment. Impressment is the forcible seizure of able-bodied men into military service that is authorized by a nation. Americans despised impressment because it violated the individual rights of a sailor. The practice of impressment inflamed Americans: "They had an ingrained hatred of the practice" (Jenkins & Taylor, 2012, p. 13).

See Appendix B: Historical Perspective: Impressment

Nichols was first captured and impressed at sea at age eighteen, and he was taken to Guadalupe. However, he escaped, and found a way to return home to Newburyport. Observing the naval battle and seeing for the first time, other seamen wounded and killed, and being forced to be on the crew of an enemy ship was a traumatic experience for him. However, he remained steadfast and did not allow the experience to affect him. His intelligence and perseverance enabled him to adapt and survive at an early age.

Chapter 3: Shipmaster of the *Sally Ann*

As a merchant trading mariner at age twenty-six, Nichols was captured twice when he was master of a neutral merchant ship, the *Sally Ann*, first by the British and then by the French. The *Sally Ann* was first taken to Bristol, England, and was released a few days later. Soon after, Nichols' ship was captured again by the French and taken to Amsterdam, where the Dutch government took his cargo.

He spent considerable time attempting to have his vessel returned to him, and he travelled to Paris to make a plea to the Council of Prizes for the *Sally Ann's* return. However, it was a futile attempt, and he returned to Amsterdam, where his ship was sold at auction. He obtained passage back to the United States, feeling frustrated with a sense of injustice. He began to develop a strong underlying resentment against both the British and the French.

Nichols was away from home for more than two years in his attempt to have the *Sally Ann* returned to him. During that time, from 1807 to 1810, events were occurring that escalated the tension between the United States and Britain. President Jefferson had proclaimed the Embargo Act in 1807, preventing any trade with foreign countries, and the Federalist Party had developed a stronghold in Nichols' hometown of Newburyport.

Chapter 4: The Alert: Captured and Retaken

A series of adventures unfolds for Nichols during this chapter. He was now thirty years old and was shipmaster of the *Alert,* another merchant commercial vessel that was claiming neutrality. It was prior to the War of 1812, but a British frigate captured him, and a prize crew was placed on board the *Alert* with orders to take the ship to Plymouth, England. However, the intrepid Nichols developed a plan to recapture his vessel, and he singlehandedly overcame the nine sailors of the prize crew.

After setting some of the prize crew afloat near the French coast on a long boat with supplies and a sail, he continued on his homeward voyage. However, another British frigate soon captured him again. Captain Berkeley of the HMS *Vestal* boarded the *Alert* and discovered the remaining captive crew members. Nichols and his ship were taken to Portsmouth, England, where Nichols was confined to a prison-ship. While awaiting trial, he managed to escape his Marine guard, and after some adventures returned to the United States.

Nichols had sailed from Newburyport in early 1811 and was not in town at the time of Newburyport's Great Fire in May 1811. He arrived home in late 1811 to see the devastation of the entire downtown area. Shortly after returning home, he again set sail on the *Dolphin* but was captured again by the British and taken to England.

Because of his reputation of having recaptured his own ship, he was treated well by the British captain who captured the *Dolphin*. However, his ship was sold in England. Nichols was able to obtain passage home on the *Aurora*. On the trip back to America, he was a fellow passenger with the infamous Aaron Burr, who was sailing incognito under an assumed name as he was returning to New York.

Chapter 5: The *Decatur* Enters the War

Shortly after the declaration of war, Captain Nichols became a commissioned privateer captain on the *Decatur*. Before the war started, Nichols had always been on the defensive, trying to elude both the British and French ships. He was always apprehensive about the possibility of capture of his ship and impressment of his crew. He was now able to turn and go on the offensive, seeking British ships to capture.

His first cruise as a privateer captain was an exciting one. He was first chased by the British frigate HMS *Guerriere,* but he out-sailed her. Later that night, he was chased by a large frigate that he mistakenly thought was the *Guerriere.* He threw most of his cannons overboard to gain more speed, but the frigate overtook him. To everyone's surprise, it was the United States frigate USS *Constitution*. Captain Hull of the *Constitution* had been searching for the *Guerriere*, and Nichols told Hull of the chase he had experienced the previous day with the *Guerriere*. Nichols provided Hull with the location of the British frigate, and Hull was able to pursue and engage the *Guerriere* in the famous battle that was victorious for the United States. If Captain Nichols had not given Hull those directions, the famous battle would never have occurred.

Immediately following the USS *Constitution* incident, Captain Nichols then had to deal with a mutiny on board the *Decatur*. His crew refused to obey orders, because the *Decatur* had been left defenseless with only two guns on board. There was a brief altercation where Nichols leaped below deck and fought the leader, and order was once again restored. This action won the confidence of his large crew of 150 seamen. Later the same day, the fortunes of the *Decatur* changed.

Chapter 6: Battle of the *Decatur* vs. HMS *Commerce*

The *Decatur* started capturing a number of British ships on a daily basis. He captured seven ships in five days, and his conquests on the "Atlantic lottery" continued. He took a total of ten British vessels in ten days. On his return trip to Newburyport, he engaged in an intense battle with the *Commerce*, a ship of the British Royal Navy.

In that battle, Nichols made use of his first rule of naval warfare, **"keep the helm clear."** Marksmen from the *Decatur* repeatedly shot sailors on the *Commerce* who attempted to take the helm. After a fierce battle, Nichols succeeded in defeating the *Commerce*. Nichols then continued with his return trip to Newburyport. As the *Decatur* came up the Merrimack River, followed by three of his prizes, hundreds of townspeople cheered him from the banks of the river. Nichols had indeed become a "Holy Terror" to the English.

Chapter 7: The *Decatur* Captured by the British

The second cruise of the *Decatur* was in late 1812. Nichols was successful in capturing three more British vessels, but in January 1813 he was captured by the British frigate HMS *Surprise* and taken to Barbados. Initially, Captain Thomas Cochrane of the *Surprise* allowed Nichols to be on parole in Barbados, until Captain Berkeley, master of the frigate HMS *Vestal*, arrived in town.

Captain Berkeley had maintained a long-simmering resentment towards Nichols as the captain who had singlehandedly recaptured the *Alert* two years earlier before the War of 1812, and who had attempted to deceived Berkeley about the incident. Berkeley ordered a cage to be constructed on the deck of a prison-ship in Barbados where Nichols was kept for thirty-four days. Nichols was eventually transferred to England where he remained chained on a prison-ship in Chatham.

During his imprisonment, a great deal happened at both national and international levels in the war. Napoleon lost the Battle of Trafalgar, and he had a disastrous march into Russia. America had experienced some victories at sea, but the war was not going well in Canada and the West. Nichols also received bad news that his father-in-law, shipmaster Captain Nicholas Pierce, had died shortly after Nichols left on his second cruise with the *Decatur.*

Chapter 8: Imprisoned on British *Nassau* Prison-Ship

Conditions were terrible, and there was cruel treatment of prisoners in the prisons and prison-ships of Great Britain during the war. The journal of Nichols younger brother-in-law, Nathaniel Pierce, who was imprisoned by the British, describes the terrible conditions at the Dartmoor prison.

Nichols was waiting to be hanged for the alleged murder of sailors of the British prize crew from the *Alert* incident that occurred before the war. However, those sailors had survived, and Nichols was eventually released from prison. Nichols was imprisoned for one and a half years, from January 1813 to June 1814, more than half of the War of 1812.

Chapter 9: Prisoner Exchange: Nichols for Two Shipmasters

A behind-the-scenes battle occurred regarding Nichols' imprisonment while he was in chains on the *Nassau* prison-ship. This was not a battle on the high seas but instead a war of words. Sharp and terse correspondence transpired between the prisoner agents for the United States and Great Britain, which is recorded in Volume III of the *American State Papers.*

President Madison ordered that two British sea captains be held in close confinement in the United States for the cruel treatment that Nichols had endured. This infuriated the British, but their charges against Nichols were eventually dropped. Nichols was finally released from prison in exchange for two British officers.

Chapter 10: Nichols Master of the *Harpy*

Following his imprisonment, Nichols immediately went to sea as the captain of the privateer *Harpy* in November 1814. He was seeking some vindication and retribution for his cruel treatment by the British. He had two successful cruises, captured fourteen British vessels, took many seamen and British officers as prisoners, and seized some valuable cargo. He was preparing for a third voyage on the *Harpy* when news of the declaration of peace was received in February 1815, and the war came to an end.

Chapter 11: Brink of Secession in Newburyport

The Town of Newburyport voted to separate from the United States in January 1815. The Federalist Party had developed a stronghold in Newburyport and New England. There was a threatened rupture of the United States, as New England came to the brink of secession at the Hartford Convention. The secessionist movement ended abruptly when peace was declared the next month in February 1815.

Chapter 12: Later Years: Merchant Mariner, Politician, and Customs Collector

Following the war, Nichols returned to foreign trade as a merchant mariner with his brother in Newburyport for the next fifteen years. He retired from naval service at the age of fifty-one. He then entered political life in Newburyport, as a state senator for two terms and a town Selectman for three terms.

During this time, his young daughter died as a child, there was a murder trial of his son, and then the sudden and untimely simultaneous deaths of his son and son-in-law.

Appendices:

Four historical narratives are presented in **Appendices A, B, C, and D** as background material to explain what occurred on a broader scale at local, national, and international levels that impacted Captain Nichols. These four appendices discuss, **(A)** the confusion and turmoil in the world, **(B)** impressment, **(C)** privateering, and **(D)** Newburyport, Massachusetts.

Additionally, transcribed letters and documents are included in the eight **Appendices E–L.** These documents are instrumental in portraying the unfolding story of Captain William Nichols. Each document describes its relevance to the various events that occurred with Nichols.

Appendix M provides the genealogy of Captain William Nichols through six generations.

Appendix A: Historical Perspective: A World Gone Mad

The world was in turmoil. There was ongoing confusion about the shifting alliances among nations in Europe. It was a dangerous time to be at sea. There was a complex series of events that were happening at that time in the world, in the nation, and in Nichols hometown. One event often led to other events, all of which had significant effect upon navigation on the high seas. "A World Gone Mad" describes the turmoil and madness during Nichols younger years that led to the War of 1812.

Appendix A is divided into three sections:
   Part I: Prior to War of 1812
   Part II: Foreign Wars
   Part III: War of 1812

Appendix B: Historical Perspective: Impressment

Impressment is a word that is rarely used today, but it is a highly emotionally-charged term that created a firestorm of reaction in early America. Needing thousands of men for their huge naval fleet, the British started capturing American ships and impressing sailors into service with the British Royal Navy. This was done under the pretext of locating deserters from the Royal Navy. Impressment is no longer used in warfare, but it was a major cause of the War of 1812.

British press gangs would arrogantly board American merchant ships, kidnap sailors, and force them into manning their naval fleet. The press gangs were also raiding coastal towns in America and impressing young men there.

Dr. G. William Freeman

Appendix C: Historical Perspective: Privateering

Commissioned privateers were licensed by the United States government with a Letter-of-Marque. There has been some confusion and misperception about privateers as pirates. Privateering had been used by countries for centuries, but the practice ended with the close of the War of 1812. American privateers were very successful in the War of 1812, because they had faster sailing ships and were more easily maneuverable. They became the scourge of the British Royal Navy.

Appendix D: Historical Perspective: Newburyport, Mass.

Newburyport, Massachusetts was a unique American town and had a golden age of prosperity just prior to the War of 1812. While it was a strong Federalist town, Nichols remained a Democrat-Republican. Newburyport actually voted to secede from the United States just prior to the end of the War of 1812. This waterfront town is where Captain Nichols was born and resided throughout his life.

Chapter 1

Introduction

During the war, he captured 28 prizes, though more than a third of his time, he was in prison, earning for himself the name of "Holy Terror", wherever seamen gathered.

Bayley and Jones
History of Newburyport Marine Society
1906, p. 371

Those who are still alive of the seamen of that period, well remember how the name and deeds of Captain Nichols rendered him a living terror at the time to all foes.

Rev. George D. Wildes
"Memoir of Captain William Nichols
of Newburyport"
1864, p. 235

Nichols story is one of endurance and persistence, a story of determination and courage, and a story of bravery in the face of adverse odds. This is about the life of Captain William Nichols, a privateer in the War of 1812.

Nichols met many challenges in his life and suffered through numerous hardships. His perseverance and fearlessness during repeated naval conflicts in the War of 1812 earned him the moniker the "Holy Terror," bestowed upon him by the British because of his success against them on the high seas. This lionhearted and audacious man had developed strong survival skills that enabled him to make rapid decisions with sound judgment when facing the enemy.

Nichols Seafaring Family

Nichols started as a merchant trading mariner and shipmaster before answering the call of the U.S. Congress, when he became a commissioned privateer captain during the War of 1812. A history of sea life permeated throughout Captain Nichols' family. He followed the example of his father, Captain William Nichols Sr., who had also been a merchant mariner and a commissioned privateer during the Revolutionary War.

His younger brother, Captain Samuel Nichols, was also a successful merchant mariner and captain, and his father-in-law, Captain Nicholas Pierce, had also been a privateer captain. All these men earned membership into the prestigious Marine Society of Newburyport, having been successful shipmasters from Newburyport.

William Nichols only son, Captain William Wallace Nichols, and his son-in-law, Captain Francis Todd Jr., were also sea captains. Nathaniel Pierce, Nichols younger brother-in-law, was a British prisoner at Dartmoor as an adolescent during the War of 1812, and he later became a shipmaster himself.

Nichols Captured Six Times

Nichols' shrewdness confirmed his reputation as the Holy Terror. While he was captured six times at sea, he was able to escape three of those times. He was first captured by a French privateer as a seaman aboard the *Rose* when he was eighteen years old. He was taken to Guadalupe, but he managed to escape being seized and impressed by the French, after which he was able to get to St. Thomas Island, where he hid in the mountains before securing passage back to New York.

He was later captured twice on a voyage as a merchant shipmaster on the *Sally Ann* when he was twenty-six years old. He was first seized by the British and taken to Bristol, England, where he was released, then soon after was again captured by the French and taken to Amsterdam. After a long delay, he returned to America, frustrated and angry that he had been unable to recover the *Sally Ann* from the French or Dutch governments.

Three years later, Nichols was again captured by the British while in command of the *Alert*. However, he was able to singlehandedly recover his ship from the British prize crew. The *Alert* was seized again a few days later by another British ship, and Nichols was sent to England. He found a way to escape from his Marine guard while awaiting trial, and he returned to Newburyport. Shortly after his return, he sailed again with the *Dolphin* but was soon captured and taken to England. However, he was not imprisoned on this occasion, and he obtained passage back to the United States.

All of his captures and escapes mentioned thus far happened before the War of 1812 while he was a merchant mariner. When President James Madison declared war in June 1812, Nichols sailed from Newburyport on the *Decatur* as a commissioned privateer captain. He had a very successful first cruise but was captured on his second cruise in January 1813 and taken to Barbados.

He was then transferred, sent to England, and imprisoned on a prison-ship docked in Chatham, England, for one and a half years. Upon his release from prison, through a prisoner exchange of two British officers, he immediately sailed out of Portsmouth, New Hampshire, as the captain of the privateer brig *Harpy,* upon which he completed two very successful cruises against the British that concluded with the end of the war.

Nichols Character and Appearance

Over the years, a number of writers have been intrigued by Nichols' story and have expounded about him when he was in command of the privateer ships *Decatur* and *Harpy*. They have extolled the bravery and fearlessness Nichols demonstrated in his naval battles. While it has been reported that Nichols left no papers, he has been remembered well by those who knew him or knew of him.

Regarding his appearance, there is only one known painting of Nichols to survive, which has been donated to the Custom House Maritime Museum, but more details about him can be drawn from those who wrote about him.

Sidney Chase, an artist and writer and friend of Nichols' great-granddaughter, Genevieve Hale Baumgartner, in the early 1900s wrote about William Nichols' escapades as a privateer. He also wrote a fictionalized account of Nichols in an article "A Yankee Privateer" for the May 1913 issue of *Scribner's Magazine*. He described Nichols from his portrait as,

> "a straight, slender man with black hair and dark piercing eyes".
>
> Chase, 1913, p. 2

Rev. George D. Wildes was the son of a Newburyport attorney who had been a close associate of Captain Nichols. Rev. Wildes wrote a "Memoir of Captain William Nichols" shortly after Nichols' death, which he prepared from extensive notes of George J. L. Colby, editor of the *Newburyport Herald*. Colby was a close friend of Nichols. Wildes was indebted to Colby for sharing his notes about Nichols.

During his boyhood, Wildes had occasion to observe Nichols and described him as being "lithe, with a compact and muscular build"

(Wildes, 1864, p. 233). He recalled that Nichols conducted himself with an intense focus and concentration that appeared in his eyes and in the set of his shoulders. Wildes related,

> He had a countenance marked by a bold, square forehead, piercing eyes, and the strikingly defined lower face of lion-hearted courage … he was quick in all his movements, even to old age, and his strident walk was distinguished by something of a warrior's port and step… his heavy brow would often lower above his flashing eyes
>
> Wildes, 1864, p.233

Wildes said of Nichols, "I think I never looked upon a face, which seemed to me so complete a reflection of thorough pluck combined with an iron will" (ibid., 233).

Chase reported that children would often become afraid of Captain Nichols and would run away whenever they saw him on the street (Chase, ca. 1920, p. 2). Boys in Newburyport were always curious to see "the man utterly without fear" (Wildes, 1864, p. 230).

Regarding Nichols' character, he appears to have been an intrepid and fearless man possessed of no self-doubt. By all accounts, he had an independent, bold spirit, daring courage, a strong will, and a determined and serious manner. His was the heart of a warrior.

In a letter written in September 1813 by Captain Benjamin Pierce, owner of the ships *Alert* and *Decatur*, which Nichols commanded, to the US Commissary of Prisoners John Mason, Esq., advocating for the release of Nichols from prison, he states:

> Touching the character of Captain Nichols as a citizen, a man, and a neighbor, he is modest and unassuming, yet brave and decided; warmly attached to his constitutions, federal and state, of his native

country … As a man he is strictly moral and sincere, as a husband, parent, and neighbor, tender, indulgent, and affable. His connections are highly respectable, and are among the first of our citizens. Universal assent among all classes and parties may be had, that Captain Nichols is truly and honest, brave, and useful citizen.

Captain Benjamin Pierce
American State Papers, p. 650.
(see Appendix I)

Richard Henry Dana, maritime lawyer and author of *Two Years Before the Mast,* when taking exception to the leniency of a judge regarding charges against a sea captain for cruelty at sea, explained that in order to insure the success and safety of his ship and its crew, the power of the captain on board his vessel must be maintained, but the exercise of it must be done responsibly (Dana, 1840, p. 104). Nichols was not imprudent with his power. For all of his aggressive and warlike activities during the War of 1812, he did not lack empathy and was not indifferent to others. He did not have a pervasive pattern of reckless disregard or violation of the rights of others, as some other shipmasters had been reported to have.

One hundred and forty years later, Charles Somerby, when reviewing Nichols' achievements during the War of 1812, reported in an article in the *Newburyport Daily News,*

"The ship commander (Nichols), although of rough exterior as master of a privateer was of tender sensibilities, always exhibiting the greatest affection for his mother and family".

Somerby, *Newburyport Daily News,*
March 5, 1952

Nichols Achievements Reported

Nichols cruises during the War of 1812 were dutifully noted on a regular basis in the "Herald Ship News" of the *Newburyport Herald*. In 1854, E. Vale Smith wrote in detail about the exploits of Nichols in her *History of Newburyport*, and in 1855, the *Newburyport Herald* had four lengthy "Memorabilia" articles about his life. Captain George Coggleshall also wrote about Nichols in his 1861 book, *History of American Privateers*. Nichols was elderly at this time, but he did have the opportunity to read how others described his naval encounters.

Shortly after Nichols' death in 1863, Rev. George Wildes wrote a lengthy memoir about him in 1864 and presented it at a meeting of the Essex Institute in Salem, Massachusetts. In addition, D. Hamilton Hurd included a lengthy reference about the naval encounters of Captain Nichols in his 1888 two-volume set, *History of Essex County*.

John Currier wrote a well-known, two-volume set of the *History of Newburyport* in 1906 and 1909, in which he made numerous references and provided a number of images regarding Captain Nichols. Also, in 1906, Bayley and Jones in their *History of the Newburyport Marine Society* wrote a long tribute to Captain Nichols.

Since then, there have been a number of additional articles, references, and papers written about Nichols by Maclay (1899), Chase (ca. 1920), Labaree (1962), and Coffey (1975).

When discussing privateering captains in Newburyport during the War of 1812, Lorraine Coffey in her dissertation, "The Rise and Decline of Newburyport, 1783–1820," described the qualities needed for a shipmaster as "perceptiveness, enterprise, inventiveness, daring, and sometimes ruthlessness, together with an ability to assume responsibility" (Coffey, 1975, p. 86). Nichols surely had those skills, as well as superior navigational ability and seamanship that were essential for a sea captain. He was audacious in his actions, and he demonstrated leadership with his crew.

Captain William Nichols was a fearless and dashing privateer in the War of 1812. He was an unassuming hero of the war and continues to be highly respected by those who know of his story. His courage and good judgment merit a more prominent place in American history, as Hamilton Hurd states in the beginning of his tribute to Nichols in his 1888 volume, *History of Essex County,*

"The career of Captain William Nichols deserves a more extended mention".

Hurd, 1888, p. 1764.

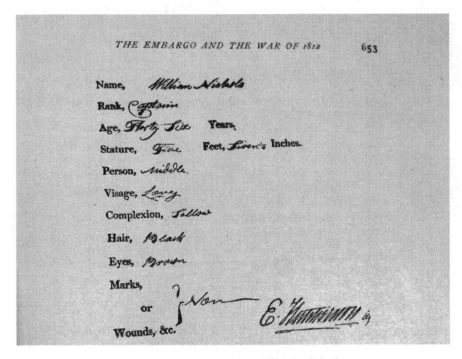

Description Captain William Nichols
from Certificate of Prisoner Release
Custom House Maritime Museum
Gift of Eleanor Baumgartner Leninger
(See Appendix K)

Chapter 2

Nichols Early Years:
Captured on the Rose

None who ever knew Captain Nichols
can doubt that the lion heart of the man
did not beat strong and resolute, under
the youthful frame of the boy ...

With the crew of the *Rose* he was sent
to Guadeloupe, whence escaping from his
captors, finding refuge in the mountains,
and eventually obtaining passage to
return to New York.

Rev. George D. Wildes
"Memoir of Captain William
Nichols of Newburyport"
1864, p. 230

Growing Up in Newburyport

William Nichols was born in Newburyport, Massachusetts, on July 1, 1781 toward the end of the Revolutionary War, and just before the fifth celebration of our Declaration of Independence.

He grew up in downtown Newburyport during the post-Revolutionary period only two blocks away from Market Square and the docks (Bayley & Jones, 1906, p. 369). Shipbuilding and foreign trade were then flourishing as the main mercantile activities. Market Square was teeming with business and trade activity in town that filled the harbor with sailing vessels traveling to Europe, the Caribbean, and China.

Market Square was constantly abuzz with noise and commotion from the shipbuilding and the constant rattling of carts on the cobblestone streets. Warehouses that were crowded next to each other down by the wharves teemed with merchandise ready to be shipped out. At every turn there was bustle, industry, and activity (Emery, 1879, p. 226). Newburyport was a prosperous seaport during this time (Chase, ca. 1920, p. 1). William's experiences along the waterfront during his boyhood sparked an enduring fascination with the sea.

While the Newburyport Harbor was a safe one, it had a narrow and limited access, because the river remained obstructed by a sandbar at the entrance. The mouth of the river is difficult and sometimes treacherous to navigate, as it has a great deal of loose, shifting sand and a narrow channel with dangerous shoals on either side. The bar extends across the mouth of the river and its greatest depth at high tide is only fourteen feet, barely enough to accommodate large vessels (Cushing, 1826, p.32). "Going over the bar" often became a challenge for shipmasters.

Most travel in Newburyport was by river. The Merrimack River became the 'Main Street' of Newburyport during this time. It was easier to travel on water that through mud-ridden roads. Hundreds of vessels, large and small, crowded the harbor on a daily basis.

Communication was slow in reaching Newburyport in the 18th and early 19th centuries. The most up-to-date news came from incoming vessels that arrived in Newburyport from Europe and other seaports. Travel across the sea was also quite slow, as it took almost three weeks to cross the Atlantic.

Young William became part of this world as he had the run of the wharves, making Market Square his playground amidst the high-energy bustling in downtown Newburyport. He mingled with boat builders, tradesmen, sailors, and sea masters in the dynamic setting of the square. He watched the construction of ships down by the wharves, smelled the aroma of tar and oakum fiber mingled with East Indian spices, and he listened to the tales of foreign voyages told by some rough seamen returning from their voyages (Chase, ca. 1920, p. 3).

Captain William Nichols, Senior
Father of Captain William Nichols, Jr.
Custom House Maritime Museum

He was eager to learn about the ships being built in his backyard. He saw the hulls and frames of ships being constructed, and he learned the basics of seamanship and navigation. He was fascinated by all of the activity along the waterfront and was constantly asking questions. He seemed destined to go to sea.

Young William's sea life began early. While growing up, he had the opportunity to travel on merchant ships to such faraway places as Cuba, China, and the East Indies. This was not unusual at the time. A young lad in Newburyport typically went to sea when barely in his teens, with the expectation that he would toughen himself early to the rigors of the sea (Coffey, 1975, p. 137). Many boys in Newburyport by the age of ten or eleven worked as "powder monkeys" on board ships, fetching gunpowder from the powder magazine in the ship's hold. This provided them the chance to often visit foreign ports. A young boy who secured such a position would probably see China before he would travel the twenty miles to nearby Salem (Chase, ca. 1920, p. 6).

Nichols started as a shipmaster's apprentice as he made several voyages as to the West Indies (Wildes, 1864, p. 230) where he learned the careful maneuvering of the sails and the ship and how to handle the rigging. It seemed natural that William would be drawn to the sea at an early age.

Captain William Nichols, Senior

His parents, Captain William Nichols Sr. and Mary Batchelder, were married in 1778 at the First Religious Society Church located in Market Square in downtown Newburyport (Newburyport Vital Records). There are no records presently available about the history of William's parents prior to their marriage. At the time of his birth, William's father was thirty years old, and his mother had just turned twenty-four. His sister, Polly, was two and a half years older than William, and his brother, Samuel, two and a half years younger.

His father had volunteered as a commissioned privateer during the Revolutionary War. At age twenty-five in May 1776, he was elected as a charter member of the Marine Society of Newburyport, a prestigious organization of shipmasters that started four years earlier in 1772, exclusively for men who had been commanders of vessels (Bayley & Jones, 1906, p. 328).

Captain Nichols Sr. was also a member of the Newburyport Marine Fire Society, which was an organization of shipmasters banded together for mutual protection. In accordance with regulation, each member kept two leather buckets hanging "in a convenient place" at their homes, and members agreed to assist in case of a fire to a member of the society. The two leather buckets of Captain Nichols Sr. have survived until the present day. They are shown in an image in this book and are now in the possession of the author.

Leather Fire Buckets of Captain William Nichols, Senior
Custom House Maritime Museum
Gift of Dr. G. William Freeman

On November 5, 1778, William Nichols Sr. petitioned the State of Massachusetts Bay to be commissioned as the commander of the privateer ship *Monmouth* (*Massachusetts Soldiers and Sailors,* 1903, p. 435). Nichols was the principal owner of the vessel. Equipped with twenty guns and a crew of 120 men, the *Monmouth* captured four British ships in 1778.

At the beginning of the Revolutionary War in 1776, Captain Nichols Sr. was in command of the privateer *Independence,* a six-gun schooner with a crew of twenty-five at the start of the Revolutionary War, and he captured six British vessels during his voyages. Two years later in 1778, he became part owner of the *Independence* and remained as captain of that vessel (Currier I, 1906, p. 638). His father-in-law, Captain Samuel Batchelder, was also the owner of some of Nichols' ships (Allen, 1927, p. 71).

Nichols was also in command of the *Monmouth* during the infamous Penobscot Expedition in August 1779 (Bayley & Jones, 1906, p. 328). During that expedition, the American fleet of forty ships with two thousand sailors and soldiers was pinned within Penobscot Bay by the British fleet. Captain Nichols was compelled, along with the other ship commanders, to retreat up the bay as a fleet of British ships approached. They were then ordered to scuttle and burn their ships to prevent them from falling into the hands of the British. All of the American vessels were self-destroyed, and more than five hundred sailors and soldiers were killed or missing in the battle. It was the greatest naval disaster for the United States prior to Pearl Harbor (Penobscot Expedition, www.uswars.net, 2004).

The panic-stricken crews and troops and their leaders rushed to the shore and into the forest. These survivors, including Nichols and his crew, made an overland journey of two hundred miles on foot through uncharted wilderness with minimal food and armament back to Newburyport and Boston (Bayley & Jones, 1906, p. 328).

Following the Revolutionary War, the elder Captain Nichols continued doing business as a merchant on Ferry Wharf in Newburyport (Wildes, 1864, p. 229). He resided with his wife and three children on Middle Street, two blocks from downtown Market Square. However, tragedy struck when Captain Nichols suddenly died at age thirty-three in April 1794, leaving his wife and three young children.

Death of Father

William Jr. was only three years old when his father died. His mother, Mary, was twenty-seven, his sister, Polly, was five and a half, and his brother, Samuel, was just six months old. His mother never remarried, and the children grew up without a father. He grew up feeling very different from the other children who had fathers, often feeling alone and remaining independent and apart from others. Angered by his father's death, he became rather oppositional. He developed a need for control and became a serious and determined young man.

Though his father could not be there for him, his legacy served young William well following his untimely death. His father was a man with a rich sailing history, as both a merchant mariner and a privateer, a well-respected shipmaster, and a charter member of the Newburyport Marine Society.

The records of the Marine Society of Newburyport show that the society provided a regular stipend for his family after his death. Article 4 of the society's "Standing Laws" indicates that, "Each new member of the Society shall pay into the box (of funds) for the use of the Society at the time of his entry 28 shillings and eight pence monthly" (Bayley & Jones, 1906, p. 7).

This fund was established for charitable purposes for the unfortunate members of the society. One purpose of the society was to provide support for families of ship captains who died or who had been lost at sea, as stated in Article 8 of their Standing Laws: "That in case any member of this Society being a married man shall be totally lost or die on shore, the Society shall relieve the widow, child, or children of such member if the society thinks them a proper object according as the box (of funds) can afford" (Bayley & Jones, 1906, p. 7). Because Captain Nichols, Senior, was a member in good standing, his widow, Mary, received ongoing financial support from the Marine Society for a number of years.

In addition to monetary support, his father's heritage afforded young William the advantage of being tutored by members of the society, as he was learning the ropes as a seaman. Many of the Marine Society members who had been fellow shipmasters and close friends with Captain Nichols Sr. looked out for young William and kept him under their wing. These shipmasters became mentors and father-substitute men for William, as he was introduced early to the seamanship and navigational skills needed to successfully sail a ship. While he had mentors in his life, he began to feel that he wanted to become more independent and make decisions for himself. He wanted to build a legacy for the father he never knew.

The Pierce Family

Next door to the Nichols' family home on Middle Street was the family of an experienced sea captain, Captain Nicholas Pierce. Captain Pierce was ten years younger than William's father. He was an adolescent at the time of the Revolutionary War, but he had seen action on some privateer ships during that war. After the untimely death of William's father, Captain Pierce took a special interest in young William, became a father figure for him, and taught him the necessary nautical skills of how to navigate and maneuver a ship.

Captain Pierce's wife, Martha, suddenly died in childbirth in 1798 at age thirty-one; the child was stillborn. It was devastating to the Pierce family. Captain Pierce was thirty-seven years old at the time of his wife's death, and he had to then be responsible for raising six children ranging in age from three to fourteen, with Lydia as the eldest child. Lydia was fourteen and a half years old when her mother died; she was immediately thrust into a maternal role with her four brothers and sister.

William's mother, Mary, helped Captain Pierce and Lydia with the many housekeeping chores and childcare that Martha had done before her death. Later on, William would marry Lydia, his next-door neighbor.

Turmoil in Europe

During the latter part of the eighteenth century, Europe was in turmoil. These were anxious times. News from Europe was always impatiently awaited when ships came into Newburyport Harbor. Voyage out to the high seas became a treacherous business (Emery, 1879, p. 249).

NOTE: See Appendix A: Parts I, II, and III

The French Revolution started in 1789, and Louis XVI was deposed and executed in 1793 (Schlesinger, 1983, p. 162). William was twelve years old at the time. Newburyport initially felt positive toward France from their friendship during the Revolutionary War. Americans felt as though the United States owed a debt to the French for the help that they had provided fifteen years earlier during our Revolutionary War. There was lingering animosity toward the British from that War, and the people in Newburyport did not want to again engage in warfare with England (Labaree, 1962, p. 181). The American navy was already engaged in war with the Barbary Coast pirates along the coasts of Africa.

America wanted to avoid becoming embroiled in the European conflict, and chose to remain neutral in international affairs. In 1793, President Washington issued his proclamation of United States neutrality because of the harassment of America's merchant vessels during the war between France and England.

Despite this proclamation, both the British and French continued to interfere with American trade and harass merchant vessels. They were kidnapping our sailors, actions that became devastating to merchant marine trade (Schlesinger, 1983, p. 163). There was apprehension whenever a trading ship left Newburyport Harbor that it might be seized and the sailors impressed into the British naval service.

America had conflicts with both France and England. While the Jay Treaty signed with Britain in 1794 was favorable in resolving some residual issues between America and Britain from the Revolutionary War, it angered the French. In addition, the British thought that the neutral shipping of the United States was a "fraud" and that it was a cover for supplying Napoleon with food and war materials (Jenkins

& Taylor, 2012, p. 2). Politically, America was caught in the middle between the two warring countries.

News of the rampant impressment of American sailors into service in the British Royal Navy angered Americans and fostered the growth of an anti-British attitude throughout the United States. There was also a sharp rise in anti-French sentiment following the XYZ scandal in 1797 that resulted in the Quasi-War with France (Schlesinger, 1983, p. 170). France ordered the capture of ships from all neutral nations and increased the harassment of American merchant vessels. The British continued to board American ships to impress sailors and started seizing their cargo as well (Jenkins & Taylor, 2012, p. 3). American ships were being attacked by both the British and French navies.

In Newburyport, a sharp division of partisan politics emerged that significantly affected families and neighbors in town. The Democratic-Republicans initially favored the French, while the Federalists supported the British in order to maintain the merchant trade that Newburyport had developed with Great Britain (Schlesinger, 1983, p. 181).

Early Experiences: Captured on the *Rose*

Young William was keenly aware of the madness that was happening in the world and the turmoil that was occurring in the country and in Newburyport. He was well aware of the danger of possible impressment if he traveled out to the high seas, but these dangers were not a deterrent for him.

His participation in naval warfare began during his boyhood (Wildes, 1864, p. 230) (Bayley & Jones, 1906, p. 369). At age seventeen in 1798, he was aboard the *Fox* when it was captured. The *Fox* was a sixty-six-foot-long merchant ship that had been built six years earlier in nearby Amesbury. He was able to escape and return unhurt to Newburyport, avoiding impressment.

NOTE: See Appendix B: Impressment

Impressment was the forcible seizure of able-bodied men into military service that was sanctioned by a nation. The practice violated the individual rights of a sailor (Jenkins & Taylor, 2012, p. 13). Impressment was primarily a British Royal Navy practice to maintain their significant manpower demands during the Napoleonic Wars. Press gangs were authorized by the British government to force sailors to serve on British naval vessels. Press gangs would seize men from unarmed merchant vessels, and "they could disappear for years, if not forever" (Zimmerman, 1925, p. 19). The British arrogance of seizing sailors from American vessels led to the War of 1812 (Jenkins & Taylor, 2012, p. 13).

The following year in August 1799, at age eighteen, William was on board the merchant cargo ship, the *Rose,* when a dramatic incident occurred. Captain Chase was in command of a crew of twenty on the *Rose* during a homebound cruise to Newburyport from Surinam on the northeast coast of South America. The crew was expected to protect the ship's cargo, reported to be $100,000 in value, (Wildes, 1864, p. 230) with eight old cannons.

The *Rose* was encountered by the French privateer *L'Egypte Conquise,* meaning "The Total Conquest of Egypt." The French vessel, with fourteen nine-pound guns and four six-pounders, had superior firepower, rendering the modest armament of the *Rose* mostly useless in comparison (Chase, ca. 1920, p. 3).

Captain Chase made the unwise decision to throw the *Rose* into battle. The severe fight lasted for two and a half hours, leaving several of his crew killed or wounded. The crew of the French privateer boarded the *Rose* (Wildes, 1864, p. 230). Chase went below deck, but his first mate, Benjamin Dennison, refused to surrender and continued the battle. Dennison refused to yield, fighting until he was "literally cut to pieces." Several more of the crew were killed and wounded in the ensuing fighting on deck.

While young Nichols was able to escape injury during the battle, he was left shocked at the intensity of the battle (Bayley & Jones, 1906, p. 369).

News of the battle and the defeat of the *Rose* spread past Newburyport. It was chronicled in an article published on September 17, 1799 in the *Salem Gazette* in Salem, Massachusetts by Captain Moses Brown, Commander of the frigate USS *Merrimack*. In the article was a letter Captain Brown wrote to William Bartlett, owner of the *Rose,* documenting the capture:

> Captain Chase of the ship *"Rose"*, owned by Mr. Wm. Bartlett, of Newburyport was taken the beginning of the present month (August) by the privateer *"L'Egypt Conquise"*, and after a brave defence of one hour and a half was obliged to submit to superior force. I suppose you will have heard the fate of your ship *"Rose"*, ere you receive this, but perhaps not the particulars. The enclosed list of killed, wounded, etc. is handed me at this place by a Mr. Starks, as an authentic account.
>
> Captain Chase behaved with the greatest bravery and conduct, but, at last was overpowered and boarded. It is supposed that Captain Chase had 25 men and that only 6 remain unhurt. The ship and cargo was probably the most valuable ever bound to this port from the West Indies.
>
> *Salem Gazette*, Sept.17, 1799

William was one of the six survivors that Captain Brown had referred to in his letter. The incident was traumatizing for Nichols, because he had witnessed for the first time, the death of someone being sliced apart and killed by a cutlass. However, he was able to retain his composure, as if befitting a sailor much more experienced, when he was taken prisoner. An additional article in the *New Hampshire Gazette* on November 5, 1799 further documented the capture of the *Rose:*

> Tuesday evening arrived in town, Capt. Chase, late master of ship *"Rose"* of this port, who was captured ... by the French privateer schooner, *"Le Conquise L' Egypt,"* mounting 14 guns and 120 men, after an action of two hours and a half, in which Captain Chase lost his mate and two men killed and 14 wounded, and the Frenchmen had 25 killed and 21 wounded.
>
> *New Hampshire Gazette*, Nov. 6, 1799

Captain Chase lost the *Rose* and some of his men, but considerable injury was inflicted on the crew of the *L'Egypte.*

It is of note that two months after the well-fitted out and larger French privateer *L'Egypte Conquise* who captured the *Rose*, was engaged in a battle with the USS *Pickering*, a smaller fourteen-gun schooner with seventy men, on October 18, 1799. This was the outset of the Quasi-War with France. After a fierce battle of nine hours, the *L'Egypte Conquise* finally surrendered to the *Pickering* ("Pickering," www.history.navy.mil, 1959).

Nichols Escapes

After the battle, Captain Chase and the remaining crew were taken to Guadalupe, a group of islands in the Caribbean Sea. William and some of the crew managed to escape to St. Thomas, another island in the Caribbean just east of Puerto Rico. Wildes explained,

> "Escaping from his captors, Nichols found refuge in
> the mountains of the islands. He eventually obtained
> passage on a Swedish brig and returned to New York
> by way of Hispaniola" (Wildes, 1864, p. 230).

While on board that Swedish vessel in the West Indies, young Nichols witnessed the young Commodore Isaac Hull, age twenty-six, cutting out and capturing a French eighteen-gun ship. Nichols would meet Captain Hull twelve years later when Nichols was in command of the *Decatur* in a startling incident at the beginning of the War of 1812 (Chase, 1864, p. 3).

The experience was Nichols introduction to the turmoil happening in the world outside of Newburyport, increasing his awareness of the danger that existed when sailing across the high seas. Thanks to the enemy, Nichols had become a man during this voyage on the *Rose* with his capture and escape. The oceans had become battlefields.

Nichols was resilient enough to escape and find his way back to the United States. He demonstrated his intelligence and an emerging spirit of determination necessary to steel himself in the face of adversity as a successful sea captain. This formative experience at sea gave rise to his ardent and fearless nature, which he later demonstrated as a commander of naval vessels.

Wildes commented on Nichols' incident with the *Rose*,

> "Foremost in all deeds of daring in every Emergency in
> his life, in this, as in all other of his naval experiences,
> he strangely escaped injury"
>
> Wildes, 1864, p. 230

Chapter 3

Shipmaster of the Sally Ann

I remained in Paris until the twelfth day of
May 1809, using every exertion to obtain the
release of the Sally Ann, but finding no prospect
of her being restored to us, nor of her being given
to the Dutch Government, and feeling confident
that she would be condemned, I returned
to Amsterdam …

While the *Sally Ann* was in the possession of
the captors at Amsterdam, she was stripped of all
her running rigging, her standing rigging, with
her sails and cables cut and carried off, and her
boats were lost. I frequently went on board, but
was ordered away and told not to carry away
anything belonging to her.

> Captain William Nichols,
> in a deposition recorded
> at Salem, MA
> (Currier II, 1909, p. 248)

During the early 1800s, William Nichols and his brother, Samuel, were building their mercantile business of foreign trade in Market Square. Prior to the War of 1812, he and his brother were merchant mariners on Ferry Wharf in Newburyport. They continued in the footsteps of their father, who was also a merchant trader on Ferry Wharf, both before and after the Revolutionary War.

This was also the time when Captain Nichols, Jr. began a friendship with Benjamin Hale, Sr., manager of the Eastern Stage Company. They became business associates, as Hale would negotiate with Nichols about the import and export of goods from foreign trade, which would then be transported on land by Hale's stagecoaches.

In September 1805, William, age twenty-four, married Lydia Pierce, age twenty-one. They had been next door neighbors when they were growing up on Middle Street in Newburyport. They were married in the new church of the First Religious Society on Pleasant Street. The new church replaced the original First Religious Society's church in the middle of Market Square, where William's parents were married in 1778.

The original church had been located amid the ongoing bustle and congestion in the center and was the location for many town meetings. However, the church had fallen into disrepair and had to be dismantled. The new church was constructed uphill from Market Square, and was dedicated in 1801.

William and Lydia's first child, a daughter, Martha, was born in March 1807 (Newburyport Vital Records). Both William and Lydia had experienced significant family tragedies earlier in their lives; he had lost his father when he was three years old, and Lydia had lost her mother when she was fourteen years old. Developing a safe and secure family life was important to the two of them.

Wars in France, Great Britain, and Africa

During this period, Americans were becoming concerned and anxious about what was happening in the world and how it was going to affect them. The country was a struggling, new nation attempting to remain independent and free of conflicts with other countries, but matters were escalating in Europe and Africa both on land and on the high seas that would eventually draw the United States into the turmoil.

By 1800, Napoleon was in power as the ruler of France, and he engaged in war with most of Europe (Schlesinger, 1983, p. 180). In a secret treaty, Spain ceded the Louisiana Territory to France, an agreement that the United States did not know about until seven months later. Americans were fearful that Napoleon was laying the foundation for a French colonial empire in North America (Schlesinger, 1983, p. 184). Newly elected President Jefferson was concerned about the possible danger of an aggressive, neighboring power that would close the Mississippi River to American commerce.

Concern about being drawn into an international conflict surged when Tripoli declared war against the United States in 1801 (Schlesinger, 1983, p. 175). For many years, the Barbary Coast pirates had been raiding American merchant ships and seizing sailors for ransom or slavery.

NOTE: See Appendix A: Part II

The United States lacked a substantial navy to defend itself and had been paying an annual ransom and tribute of one million dollars to the Barbary Coast States for years. War was declared against the United States by the Barbary States when President Jefferson refused to continue making these payments. The Tripolitan War continued for four years, during which congress was able to establish a navy capable of blockading Tripoli's ports.

Captain Decatur Burns the USS *Philadelphia*

An incident on February 16, 1804 in Tripoli Harbor uplifted the spirits of Americans. In October 1803, the frigate USS *Philadelphia* under the command of Captain William Bainbridge had run aground on a reef in the harbor. The Tripoli pirates captured the ship, and Captain Bainbridge and 307 crew members were held for ransom. The ship was left anchored in the harbor and was used as a gun battery by the pirates. The U.S. Commodore Edward Preble was unsure about what to do with the *Philadelphia*, debating whether to recapture or destroy the ship.

Under the cover of night on that February night, Lieutenant Stephen Decatur with seventy-five volunteers and marines stole into the harbor on the ketch, *Intrepid*, a smaller ship that was made to look like a local trading vessel flying British colors (Biedler, 2012, www. redecatur.com).The men were disguised in Arab clothes and remained below deck, as Decatur shouted to the Tripoli guards in Arabic that they had lost their anchor. Decatur and his men were able to deceive the frigate guards, board the *Philadelphia* and overpower the sailors, as they made a daring attack to recapture the *Philadelphia*.

The ship was then set afire with explosives, rendering it useless to the enemy. The guns of the *Philadelphia* began discharging from the heat and flames, with some firing into the town. The ship crashed into rocks at the harbor entrance, and the men escaped in the *Intrepid* without losing a single life ("Burning of Frigate *Philadelphia* 16 February 1804").

Stephen Decatur became an immediate war hero in America and was promoted to the rank of captain at the age of twenty-five, the youngest man to ever hold that rank in the US Navy. British Lord Admiral Horatio Nelson, known as a man of action and courage, called this "the most bold and daring act of the age" (ibid.).

William Nichols was 23 years old at the time of Decatur's raid in 1804. Nichols had a great deal of admiration for Decatur's courageous daring. Eight years later, Nichols would name his privateer ship the Decatur in honor of Captain Stephen Decatur.

The captain and crew of the *Philadelphia* were eventually released to the United States a year later when a peace treaty was signed on

June 4, 1805. The United States paid a one-time ransom of $60,000 for the crew and Tripoli granted the American Navy the right to sail unmolested in the Mediterranean Sea. The war ended inconclusively (Schlesinger, 1983, p. 179).

Britain and France were both continuing to seize neutral American merchant ships. The so-called press gangs of the British Royal Navy were still impressing sailors who were alleged deserters from the British Navy. Britain declared war on France in 1803, and both countries were blockading neutral ships from entering enemy harbors (Schlesinger, 1983, p. 179). American merchant ships trying to maintain their neutrality were caught in the middle. Trading vessels from the United States had to constantly be vigilant for possible capture by either British or French ships.

On October 21, 1805, the British fleet won a decisive naval victory in the Battle of Trafalgar over Napoleon's combined French and Spanish fleet. This gave Great Britain dominance of the seas. Napoleon was then able to conduct only land battles against Britain, and he abandoned the idea of a North American empire. However, the lack of a formidable opponent for the British also meant increased seizure and impressment of American ships by the British Royal Navy ("Napoleon," *Oxford Dictionary*, 2010).

William Nichols was aware of what was happening in the nation and the world. He listened intently to the news of the world from the sailors on incoming vessels and exercised caution when sailing out of Newburyport Harbor. It was risky business, as the British were blockading ports along the Atlantic coast of the United States to prevent American merchant ships from leaving port.

There was also considerable political conflict and ongoing friction among the citizens of Newburyport during this time. There was a great deal of bitterness and scorn between the Federalists and the Democratic-Republicans (Emery, 1879, p. 240). The political division in town escalated when President Jefferson purchased the Louisiana

Territory from France in 1803. The Federalist Party began to express secession sentiments from the Union and started to develop plans for a Northern Confederacy of the New England States, New York, and New Jersey (Schlesinger, 1983, p. 188).

Brink of War with England

Great Britain and the United States came to the brink of war in June 1807, following the volatile HMS *Leopold*-USS *Chesapeake* incident (Schlesinger, 1983, p. 185). The fifty-two-gun British *Leopold* stopped the thirty-nine-gun *Chesapeake* just outside the three-mile limit off Norfolk, Virginia. The British commander demanded surrender of four seamen that the British Royal Navy alleged were deserters.

The American commander, James Barron, refused to capitulate, and the British opened fire, killing three, wounding eighteen, and forcibly removing the four alleged deserters. Americans became outraged at this incident, as it was perceived to be an insult to American honor. This event created an uproar in America and reinforced the strong antipathy that was developing toward the British.

The Embargo Act

In response to the Leopold-Chesapeake incident, President Jefferson issued a proclamation in 1807 for all British ships to vacate the waters of the United States. He asked Congress for an embargo that would restrict all trade and commerce with foreign nations. The embargo was to be imposed against Britain and France in response to the continued violations of United States neutrality and seizure of American merchant vessels. Americans were also expressing strong isolationist sentiments. They didn't want any part in Europe's centuries-old tradition of perpetual warfare, and they wanted to appear as neutral as possible in order to maintain America's freedom of action and choice. Coles explained, "President Jefferson resorted to economic pressure and launched one of the boldest experiments in the history of American foreign policy" (Coles, 1965, p. 8).

President Jefferson anticipated that this drastic measure of "peaceful coercion" using the Embargo Act would bring economic hardship to the enemy nations and force them to respect the neutrality of the United States. He hoped that the embargo would stop the seizure of American commercial ships and halt the impressment of sailors. Jefferson thought that by cutting off trade with both the English and the French by means of economic strangulation, he could coerce these two countries into negotiating some sort of peace between them (Coles, 1965, p. 5). Jefferson assumed that commercial warfare, rather than military action, would appease his domestic critics.

While the Federalist faction in Congress was opposed to the embargo, the measure passed the Senate twenty-two to six and the House of Representatives eighty-two to forty-four. The Embargo Act became law on December 22, 1807, forbidding any ship of the United States to sail in or out of American harbors to any foreign port (Schlesinger, 1983, p. 186).

However, both Britain and France viewed the plunder of United States shipping as being necessary for their own financial survival (Coles, 1965, p. 5). Great Britain reigned supreme on the sea, and France had conquered most of the land in Europe. Both countries needed considerable financial support and manpower to maintain their forces. There was a sweeping system of harbor blockades and counter blockades that Britain and France imposed on each other (Jenkins & Taylor, 2012, p. 2).

The embargo order, however, devastated foreign trade and seaport economies like Newburyport, throwing them into a financial depression. A great deal of anti-sentiment was generated by the citizens directly against the United States government. Coles said that the Embargo Act essentially functioned as a self-blockade; as he stated, "This noble experiment with such high hopes accomplished nothing, but it succeeded in turning American people against one another" (Coles, 1965, p. 10).

All segments of the United States were affected by the embargo, though the consequences were most severe in New England. It had a devastating effect on the United States economy, resulting in a near financial collapse of the country. Trade plummeted 80 percent in the first year after its enactment, and ten thousand ships were left idling in seaports (Jenkins & Taylor, 2012, p. 5). However, as with virtually every piece of legislation directed at curtailing commerce of any sort, a black market rose up in place of the regulated market. There were a number of clandestine voyages that left American seaports during the Embargo Act, as smuggling of goods became commonplace.

The public's strong opposition to the embargo undermined any sense of national unity. Bitter protests, especially by the Federalists, occurred in many New England trading centers (Coles, 1965, p. 10). This naval restriction had unwittingly drawn the United States into Napoleon's continental warfare.

The Embargo Act backfired and failed, hurting Americans more than the enemy nations. The act inflicted devastating burdens on the American people. Ships were left rotting at the wharves, and farmers could not sell their produce on the international market. Many coastal towns were scenes of desolation and economic depression (Coles, 1965, p. 9).

While it was expected that the British would suffer the most, their merchant marine actually made considerable profit. Britain was quite pleased that American trade competition had been removed by the action of their own government (Schlesinger, 1983, p. 186). The British took over the lucrative trade routes that had been relinquished by the United States merchantmen. As a result, demand for English goods rose in South America, offsetting losses from the absence of trade with the United States.

In France, the Embargo Act actually aided them in their war with Britain by denying British foodstuffs and supplies that had been coming from the United States. This was something that France had been unable to do herself, but it became an inadvertent outcome of the embargo.

The Embargo Act in Newburyport

The prosperity of Newburyport depended on foreign trade, and the town became economically vulnerable because of the embargo. Emery states, "The Embargo Act wholly disarranged the business of Newburyport and brought much suffering" (Emery, 1879, p. 240). Shops were closed, people were out of work, and no ships were being constructed. The Embargo Act created great hostility in Newburyport for the majority of people.

In her 1854 book, *History of Newburyport,* E. Vale Smith wrote of the betrayal that the citizens felt at the hand of the federal government: "There was an utter stagnation of business in Newburyport. Whatever its good intentions, the federal government had taken a scalpel in hand and slit the throat of mercantile New England" (p. 181).

In December 1808, the one-year anniversary of the Embargo Act was observed in Newburyport by the tolling of bells and firing of guns, signals of extreme distress. Flags were hung at half-mast, and a procession of sailors marched the streets with muffled drums and a cart drawn by horses with a flag bearing the words "Death To Commerce" (Smith, 1854, p. 181).

Embargo Act Repealed

The effects of the trade restriction and resulting economic depression had significantly affected commercial trade in Newburyport. Clandestine shipments and smuggling became widespread in town. The Embargo Act made a significant impact on the mercantile business in Newburyport.

Unrelenting, widespread opposition to the Embargo Act led Jefferson to repeal it fifteen months later on March 1, 1809, just before his presidency ended. The Federalists were regaining political strength, as the embargo had vastly increased support for the Federalist Party in New England.

The day that the Embargo Act was repealed, Congress replaced it with the Non-Intercourse Act. This opened trade with all other countries except Britain and France. The president was also given power to suspend the trade restriction if either of these countries would stop the seizure of United States merchant ships. This was a power that Jefferson's successor, James Madison, never invoked despite continuing hostilities against American ships.

After the Embargo Act was repealed, hostilities against American ships and impressment seizures by both the British and French navies continued and increased. Napoleon issued his Milan and Bayonne decrees, ordering not only the seizure of American vessels by the French that had been searched by the British but also the capture of American ships entering French harbors (Schlesinger, 1983, p. 184). Britain responded to those French orders by proclaiming that all United States vessels trading with non-British ports were subject to capture. The United States was again caught in the middle, because the neutrality of maritime commerce could not be carried on without violating the restrictions of at least one of the two antagonists (Coles, 1965, p. 6). Before the War of 1812, British and French vessels seized more than fifteen hundred American ships between 1803 and 1812.

Nichols Sails on the *Sally Ann*

In November 1807, just prior to the Embargo Act, Captain Nichols, age twenty-six, sailed out of Newburyport Harbor as the shipmaster of the merchant brig *Sally Ann* with a full cargo on a trading voyage to Amsterdam. While he was able to successfully run the British blockade surrounding Newburyport Harbor, he was later captured by the *Diana*, a British letter of marque. It was fortunate that he and his crew were not impressed into British naval service. In a deposition recorded at the Salem Registry of Deeds in Salem, Massachusetts, Nichols wrote:

> I, William Nichols of Newburyport in the County of Essex Commonwealth of Massachusetts, mariner, testify and depose, That in the month of November A D, One thousand eight hundred and seven I sailed from Beverly in the brig *Sally Ann* belonging to Abner Wood of said Newburyport and myself, as master of said brig, on a voyage to Amsterdam.
>
> On the fourteenth day of December … I was captured by the *Diana*, British Letter of Marque, and the brig carried into Bristol, England: I with the rest of the people, except the mate, was taken out of said brig on board the *Diana*, in which we arrived at Bristol on the twenty eighth day of said December, which was three days after the arrival of the *Sally Ann* at the same place.
>
> *Essex County Probate Index*, 1987
> in Currier I, 1906, p. 247

Nichols reported that three days after his arrival in Bristol, he was released, and the *Sally Ann* was returned to him without a trial.

However, he found that the cabin stores were entirely gone, including a barrel of sugar, seventy pounds of coffee, forty gallons of wine, and other articles. Additionally, some of the water casks had been scuttled, two barrels of the ship's provisions were missing, and some of the rigging was cut and destroyed. However, Captain Nichols was silent and remained resolute about the losses and destruction. He and his crew continued on to Amsterdam with their cargo that had been left intact by the British.

Nine days after leaving Bristol, they arrived at Texel Island off the coast of the Netherlands. As they were taking a pilot on board to assist them in bringing the ship into port, they were again captured, this time by a French privateer. Captain Nichols and two of his officers were taken on board the French vessel, and a prize crew from the French vessel was put on board the *Sally Ann*. Both ships then proceeded to New Dieppe on the northern coast of France (Currier I, 1906, p. 248).

A few days after they docked, Nichols and his crew were allowed to put part of the remaining cargo from America onto a barge that was sent to Amsterdam. The cargo that had been loaded in Newburyport consisted of sugar, coffee, ginger, potash, pearlash, and logwood from America. After a long delay on the French coast, Nichols was then allowed to take the rest of *Sally Ann's* cargo to Amsterdam where the entire cargo from the *Sally Ann* was deposited into the government stores of the Netherlands without any payment being made.

However, Dutch Admiral Van Kinsbergen, the highest-ranking commander in the Dutch Navy, then laid claim to both the *Sally Ann* and its cargo. Captain Nichols became outraged, laying claim to them himself. He used a lawyer for assistance but without success (Currier I, 1906, p. 248).

Nichols Attempts to Have *Sally Ann* Released

Nichols worked independently to have his ship returned and to receive payment for his cargo. He unsuccessfully petitioned King Louis Bonaparte of the Netherlands to intervene; King Louis had recently been appointed king of Holland by his brother Napoleon.

Nichols' attorney informed him that papers for the *Sally Ann* had been sent to Paris. In a further attempt to have his ship released and receive some compensation for the cargo, he decided to leave Amsterdam for Paris in the spring of 1808. He traveled four days to Paris where he immediately engaged another attorney to represent him. The attorney then presented a statement of Nichols' entire voyage to the Office of the Council of Prizes (Currier I, 1906, p. 248). But it was to no avail.

Nichols remained in Paris for more than a year in his effort to have the *Sally Ann* released and to receive compensation for his cargo. Finally, on May 12, 1809, frustrated and angry by the lack of response to his requests, he decided to return to Amsterdam, hoping to work out some type of compromise with the Dutch authorities. As he reported later in his deposition, he was "using every exertion to obtain the release of the *Sally Ann*, but finding no prospect of her being restored to us, nor of her being given to the Dutch Government." Ultimately, he conceded the fate of his ship: "feeling confident that she would be condemned, I returned to Amsterdam" (Essex Country Probate, 1987 in Currier I, 1906, p. 248).

Undeterred by the loss of his ship, Captain Nichols continued in his effort to regain at least some part of his property. As direct contact with the authorities had proven futile, he decided to use a back channel, employing a merchant to discreetly ask the captain of the French privateer and present owner of the ship what he proposed to do with the brig and cargo. At first, it was proposed that the vessel and cargo be sold, and Captain Nichols would receive one-eighth of the proceeds. It was later proposed that the ship and cargo be sold at auction and that Nichols would be allowed to receive one-third of the net proceeds. Upon the advice of the merchants involved, Nichols agreed to the latter arrangement.

While the *Sally Ann* was in possession of the captors in Amsterdam, Nichols was able to go on board his ship but was told to not take anything belonging to her. He found that all of the ship's running rigging, standing rigging, sails, and cables had been carried off the vessel. The ship's smaller boats had also been removed (Currier I, 1906, p. 248).

He returned to America in 1810, feeling frustrated and dismayed at having been unable to get his ship returned. However, he took some comfort in knowing that he had received some measure of compensation for the vessel and cargo. The series of incidents that occurred with the *Sally Ann* was part of the ongoing turmoil between the British and French. While he failed in his effort to have his ship returned, his fierce determination demonstrated the emerging perseverance that was developing that would make him a successful sea captain in the upcoming war.

Nichols Returns Home

While Nichols was in the Netherlands and France attempting to have his ship, the *Sally Ann,* returned to him, he knew about the embargo that was taking place in America. He had been spared the disastrous effects of the Embargo Act, but when Captain Nichols was finally able to return to Newburyport in 1810, he came home to a highly charged, politically divided town. He saw fractious discord throughout the community because of the embargo - neighbor against neighbor, and family members against one another.

While some people were in favor of the trade restrictions to end impressment of American sailors and the seizure of merchant ships, others felt strongly that their livelihood was being devastated from the embargo. Significant problems were created for merchants in Newburyport by the embargo, as they were desperately attempting to maintain their mercantile trade businesses in town. This extended to the merchant business that Captain Nichols and his brother, Samuel, were operating on Ferry Wharf. There was hope that newly elected President Madison would help the country move out of its economic depression.

Nichols had been away from home for more than two years. His daughter, Martha, who was only seven months old when he left on his voyage, was now three years old and did not know her father. Nichols now had the opportunity to become more of a father to her.

His long absence had been difficult for his young wife, Lydia. However, the simple pleasures of family life could not assuage his love of adventure and the sea. He would be at home for only a short time before embarking on another voyage at sea.

Chapter 4

The *Alert:* Captured and Retaken

Captain Nichols in command of the brig *Alert* sailed
for Bordeaux, France in 1811. He was captured, but
regained possession of his ship. A week later he was
captured again, placed in confinement in England, but
he escaped and returned to Boston.

John J. Currier
History of Newburyport II,
1909, p. 249

America Moving Toward War

Following the end of the Embargo Act in 1807, negotiations
collapsed between the United States and England in an effort to
end the hostilities in April 1809. The British Minister to the United
States, David Montague Erskine, sent a message to the US Secretary
of State Robert Smith. To the great relief of the American public,
he informed Washington that the British Orders of Council of
1807 against American ships would be revoked and that British
impressment would end. Subsequently, President Madison issued
a proclamation reinstating trade with Great Britain (Schlesinger,
1983, p. 189). However, Erskine had gone beyond his authority to
make such a statement, and England rejected the agreement. The
proposal never went into effect. American joy turned to rage against
the British. Erskine was then recalled by the British foreign secretary
because of this incident (Malone & Rauch, 1964, p. 123).

Then, on May 16, 1811, the Little Belt naval battle occurred, bringing the United States and England to the brink of war. The American forty-four-gun USS *President* frigate and the much smaller British sloop HMS *Little Belt* engaged in a battle off the coast of North Carolina.

Believing the *Little Belt* to be the British frigate *Guerriere*, American Commander John Rogers of the USS *President* pursued the ship. There was some dispute about who fired the first shot, but both ships opened fire and engaged in battle. After fifteen minutes, the barrage stopped, as the American ship had an overwhelming advantage. The USS *President* sustained only one injury, while the HMS *Little Belt* had nine deaths with twenty-three injured, and the British ship was left badly damaged in the battle (Schlesinger, 1983, p. 192).

The two nations argued about this incident for months. It was reminiscent of the Chesapeake-Leopold incident that happened four year earlier and that also had brought the two countries to the brink of war. The British HMS *Leopold* had seized the USS *Chesapeake* and impressed four seamen, which created considerable uproar among Americans. In a reversal of fortunes, the British were outraged about the *Little Belt* incident, and it began to prepare the minds of people in America of an impending war with England (Smith, 1854, p. 191).

Captain Benjamin Pierce of Newburyport

During the early 1800s in Newburyport, the Federalists represented a large majority of citizens, but the minority of Democrat-Republicans continued to maintain a strong voice in town. The Second Presbyterian church on Harris Street became the nucleus of the Democrat-Republicans, and Captain Benjamin Pierce was a member. Captain Pierce was one of the most prominent and influential merchants in Newburyport. Despite the small size of the

Town and the many links between its citizens, no connection has been found between Captain Pierce and the Pierce family who were next-door neighbors to the Nichols family.

Pierce had a number of ships built for him, and he owned some of the ships that Captain Nichols mastered, including the privateer *Decatur* that Nichols commanded during the War of 1812. Later, Captain Pierce wrote a very supportive letter when Captain Nichols was imprisoned in Great Britain.

Nichols was at sea again as a merchant trader on the *Alert* in early 1811. Captain Pierce owned the brig *Alert* that was built in Amesbury in 1806. It needed a crew of eight and had no heavy artillery cannons mounted on the ship. Pierce asked Captain Nichols to be the master of the merchant brig. The *Alert* was commissioned for a passport by President Jefferson. Soon after his return to Newburyport from Europe, Nichols was once again at sea.

Great Fire of Newburyport

Captain Nichols was on a voyage to France with the *Alert* and was not in Newburyport during the town's Great Fire on May 31, 1811 (Emery, 1879, p. 261). The fire destroyed 250 buildings, left ninety families homeless, and burned through sixteen acres of the most crowded and wealthiest part of town ("The Great Fire of Newburyport," 2001, www.everything2.com). The firestorm ravaged the entire core of downtown Newburyport, including Market Square, along the wharves, Water Street, Center Street, and the lower section of State Street (Hendricks, 2011). The conflagration rapidly spread in all and directions and was soon out of control. Firefighters who arrived from various towns were unable to keep the fire from spreading. High winds jumped the blazes from one street to another. Buildings around the fire were blown up or torn down to help control the flames ("The Great Fire of Newburyport," 2001, www.everything2.com).

Sarah Emery witnessed the event and described the tragedy in her book. She explained that people "watched and moaned in helpless anguish bordering on despair … it was a fearful night … all night long the flames swelled and surged with a roar like a distant sea" (Emery, 1879, p. 262). The Elder John Peak, minister of the First Baptist Church in Newburyport, also observed the fire from the rooftop of a neighbor's house, where he had "a fair view of the whole field of fire":

> Here I saw the roof of our meetinghouse tumbling in, leaving the brick walls principally standing. But what an awful sight! Bright flames ascending to a great height; explosions of powder, spirits, etc; vast columns of cinders and flames ascending in quick succession to the clouds; a dense smoke ascending from the burning of tar, pitch, etc. formed think clouds which spread over the town in awful majesty. The roaring of the flames accompanied with wind; the sound of trumpets and voices of the firemen; the crash of buildings; the cry of the sufferers for help to secure their goods, and the increasing progress of the conflagration altogether was the most appalling scene I ever witnessed. The destructive element continued its desolating ravages … comprising a large portion of the most ancient, wealthy, and commercial part of town. Thirteen wharves with their stores, and about ninety dwelling-houses were consumed. The whole number of buildings destroyed was two hundred and forty. The estimated loss about one million dollars.
>
> *Memoir of Elder John Peak*, 1832, p. 11

Downtown shops, homes, and businesses were decimated in the fire's wake. In one night, most of the town's wealth was destroyed. At the time, Newburyport was the fifth wealthiest city in Massachusetts, and it was lost forever in nine hours (Hendricks, 2011). It was the second severe economic blow to strike Newburyport within a decade. The first had been the devastating Embargo Act of 1807 four years earlier that prohibited trade with foreign ports and became a significant detriment to merchants ("The Great Fire of Newburyport," www.brickandtree.wordpress.com).

All told, the loss from the Newburyport fire reduced the town's wealth by half. Offices and shops of the most prominent citizens were destroyed. Many wealthy men suddenly found themselves poor, and without a merchant class equipped to start their businesses again, Newburyport was left dangerously close to bankruptcy ("The Great Fire of Newburyport," 2001, www.everything2.com).

The Board of Selectmen in Newburyport authorized a reward of one thousand dollars for discovery of the "incendiary" that set the fire. They also appointed a committee to "ferret out the miscreant," but both measures failed, and the person remained undiscovered (Smith, 1854, p. 101).

Citizens could do little to regain what they had lost. While no lives were lost in the fire, the prestige and aristocratic splendor of the town were gone forever. Suddenly, many prominent businessmen and merchants lost their positions of power and authority in Newburyport. To this day, no other event has ever changed the city as much as the Great Fire of 1811 ("The Great Fire of Newburyport," 2001, www. everthing2.com).

The rebuilding process followed a unified urban plan in which it was mandated that all new construction be made of stone and brick. Newburyport was transformed into the beautifully Federalist architectural style of downtown that still exists today. It is now one of the most picturesque towns in all of New England ("The Great Fire of Newburyport," www.brickandtree.wordpress.com).

Nichols On a Voyage During Great Fire

Captain Nichols was on a trading voyage to Bordeaux at the time of the Great Fire. While the business offices that he had with his brother, Samuel, on Ferry Wharf were destroyed, his home on Middle Street narrowly escaped the flames.

In addition, the new Unitarian church on Pleasant Street where he and Lydia were married in 1805 was not claimed by the fire. This helped the family retain a sense of normalcy and routine in the midst of the turmoil (Hendricks, 2011).

During the fire, Nichols' wife, Lydia, and their child, Martha, were terrified at the approaching firestorm. They were forced to flee as the flames advanced in the direction of their home. They narrowly escaped disaster. She was also pregnant at the time, and she gave birth to a son three months after the fire.

The Pierce family, next door to the Nichols home, lost their home in the fire, but the Nichols home remained standing ("Account of the Great Fire," Gilman, 1811). While their house was spared from the fire, Lydia had to care for herself and her young daughter through the trauma.

Alert Captured and Retaken

Still smarting from the injustice he experienced in France and the Netherlands with the *Sally Ann*, Captain Nichols was now mastering the *Alert*. The ship was headed for Bordeaux in 1811, loaded with a full cargo of brandy, wine, and silks. On his passage into the Bordeaux port, he was able to successfully run the British blockade that controlled French coastal harbors. After unloading his cargo from Newburyport, he refilled his vessel with French cargo. He was able to, again, successfully run the blockade when he set off back to America.

Nichols was always apprehensive about running the British blockade for fear of capture, but he always had good sailing ships. He was persistent and determined, and he remained confident that he could always out-sail the British ships. He did remain anxious, not only of possible capture by the British but also about the possible kidnapping and impressment of his crew into the British Royal Navy. He remained concerned until he had successfully run the gauntlet and was on the open sea.

His fears were realized, and unfortunately his ship was captured on the open sea on July 6, 1811, by the British frigate HMS *Semiramis*. He had no guns on board and was unable to defend himself against capture. The British seized most of his men and took them to England. Only Nichols, his mate, and three boys remained on the *Alert*. The *Semiramis* placed a prize crew of nine men on board the *Alert*, and the ship was ordered to Plymouth, England (*Lloyd's Register 1811–1814*, 1969). One of the young boys on board the *Alert* was Benjamin Pierce, son of the ship's owner, Captain Benjamin Pierce (Wildes, 1864, p. 281).

Despite the desperate odds against him, Nichols did not want to surrender his vessel without an effort to save her. He developed a plan to recapture the ship. His crew then consisted of only three young boys and his mate, but he found that his mate was quite timid and could not be relied upon. Fortunately, he would have some firepower to back him up. Before being captured by the *Semiramis*, Nichols had loaded and concealed some pistols ("Memorabilia," *Newburyport Herald*, August 1, 1855).

During the evening, Nichols noticed that the British officer who was the prize-master in charge was asleep below deck. Nichols casually went on deck to note the condition of things. On watch were a quartermaster and four men with some pistols lying nearby. After talking about the weather, Nichols slowly moved forward to the forecastle and saw three more sailors. He quietly fastened the forecastle door and then returned below as if nothing had happened ("Memorabilia," *Newburyport Herald*, August 1, 1855).

At midnight, Nichols awoke his mate and said, "Follow me." They climbed up to the deck, seized the pistols that Nichols had previously concealed, and surprised the watchman on duty. Nichols held his pistol to the quartermaster at the helm, saying, "One word, and I will blow you through!" The helmsman submitted, and the other four seamen, who were without arms, were forced by Nichols to retreat to the stern boat. As the mate precariously held a pistol with unsteady hands, the men were each ordered to come out one by one as Nichols tied them up with their hands behind them ("Memorabilia," *Newburyport Herald*, August 1, 1855).

Leaving the deck to his mate, Nichols then went below and threw the British lieutenant from his hammock before he was well awake. Nichols told him, "Every man of your crew is dead ... you must die or submit."

Begging for his life, the terrified officer surrendered and was tied up. Then, Nichols had young Benjamin Pierce call one of the men in the forecastle, saying that the quartermaster wanted to see him. As he came out, Nichols clinched him, threw him down to the deck, and tied him up. Nichols did the same with a second man, and he then went down after the third man below deck and subdued him ("Memorabilia," *Newburyport Herald,* August 1, 1855).

Nichols almost singlehandedly had captured nine men! He was able to execute the successful recapture of his ship because the members of the British prize crew were lax in their supervision of Nichols, his mate, and the three boys. Nichols had maintained a quiet and amicable manner, setting the crew at ease, which made it easier for him to overcome them. Captain Nichols later described the affair simply: "Myself and mate rose on the Englishmen, lashed five on deck and three below" (Wildes, 1864, p. 281).

This incident occurred prior to the War of 1812 and required aggressive defense on the part of Nichols to regain his ship. The prize crew never expected this young captain to be brave enough to singlehandedly attempt to recapture his own ship (Wildes, 1864, p. 281). This incident gave notice to the British of his ability to be shrewd and calculating in his manner.

After seizing control of his vessel, Nichols demonstrated his moral character when deciding what to do with his prisoners. He did not want the responsibility of taking care of nine prisoners from the *Seminaris*. He could have shot them or thrown them overboard, but instead in order to reduce the number of prisoners, he chose to set some of them adrift in a long boat. He put the officer and four of the prize crewmembers in a boat with the means to reach the coast. The *Alert* was only a few miles from land, and it was summertime, when the seas were calm. Nichols rigged the smaller boat with sails and oars and stocked it with food, water, and wine, all of the crew's clothes, a compass, and a quadrant ("Memorabilia," *Newburyport Herald*, August 1, 1855).

Nichols asked the lieutenant if he wanted to go, and he replied, "Yes! ... anywhere to get clear of this craft." When one of the prize crew in the boat asked the British officer if he thought they would ever reach land, he said, "I hope not ... I am damned in my reputation, and I don't care about living." Nichols was later charged with murder of the seamen he set adrift. However, they did live. They all reached the coast of France where they were taken and imprisoned by the French soldiers, as France was then at war with England ("Memorabilia," *Newburyport Herald*, August 1, 1855).

Alert Captured Again

Nichols then continued on his homeward voyage for a few days, but luck was against him. Five days after resuming his journey, he was hailed by the British frigate HMS *Vestal*. Captain Maurice

Berkeley of the British ship, seeing only two men on the *Alert,* became suspicious and boarded her. Nichols told the captain that he had already been boarded by the HMS *Semiramis.* While that was true, he omitted the episode about the recapture of his ship.

Captain Berkeley, age twenty-three, had been promoted just six months earlier in December 1810 from the flag-lieutenant on the HMS *Barfluer* to be in command of the HMS *Vestal* (O'Byrne, 1849, p. 75). He was the nephew of Admiral George Cranfield Berkeley, who was in command of the HMS *Barfluer* at that time. Admiral Berkeley had given the original order to British sea captains to search for and recapture deserters on United States warships (Tucker, 2012, p. 58). Also, in 1807, Admiral Berkley was on his flagship, the HMS *Leopold,* when he ordered Captain Humphreys to fire the shot across the bow of the USS *Chesapeake* that resulted in the Chesapeake-Leopold Affair and ultimately led to the War of 1812 (Stewart, 1927, p. 27).

Captain Berkeley of the *Vestal,* seeing no other men on board the *Alert,* continued to be suspicious. He boarded the *Alert* and discovered the remaining prize crew from the *Semiramis* who were imprisoned below (Wildes, 1864, p. 281). Seeing no way to escape, Nichols related the entire story to Captain Berkeley. Because of his actions with the *Semiramis* prize crew on the *Alert,* Berkeley sent Nichols to Portsmouth, England, where he would be tried in court. The *Alert* was condemned and sold. *Lloyd's Register* recorded the following entry on Tuesday, July 21, 1811:

> The American Brig *Alert,* Nichols, from Bordeaux to Newburyport, was detained on the 6th of July by the *Semiramis* Frigate and put in charge of an officer and six men, but the *Alert* crew took possession of her. She has been since detained by the *Vestal* Frigate and sent into Portsmouth.
>
> *Lloyd's Register 1811–1814,* (1969)

Captain Nichols was to have another unfortunate encounter with Captain Berkeley a year and a half later in Barbados during the War of 1812.

Nichols Escapes to Liverpool

When Nichols arrived in England, he was confined to a prison-ship. When he was later taken ashore by four marine guards to stand trial, the office of the magistrate was not open, and Nichols suggested that the sergeant and his guards go to a nearby inn for some "refreshment." After several rounds of stiff rum punch, the marines were in an intoxicated state, which Nichols used to his advantage to quietly make a bold escape from the guards (Wildes, 1864, p. 281).

Not being familiar with the local area, Nichols began running randomly across gardens and leaping hedges, finally arriving at a road that led to London. He hailed a stage but was told by the driver that it was against the law to take an unknown person as a passenger on the road. However, Nichols offered the driver a half guinea and a promise that he would get off before they reached the city, and the driver was satisfied (Wildes, 1864, p. 281).

Nichols had been in London only a few days when he ran into the sergeant from whom he had escaped. The officer exclaimed, "Ah, Mr. Nichols … the very man I am after. Glad to see you." Nichols' nerve never faltered, as he replied with flashing eyes and a stern demeanor, "Glad to see you! But I'm the very man you can never take … here are three guineas you can have, but you'll not take me alive" (Wildes, 1864, p. 28).

The officer took the money, and Nichols immediately walked away. He then continued on his way to Liverpool. Once in Liverpool, Nichols was able to obtain passage on a ship back to America, leaving behind his reputation as a daring, young privateer captain. This reputation continued to grow and spread throughout Britain's naval forces. Most of Nichols captures and escapes happened before the start of the War of 1812, when he was a merchant mariner.

Nichols Sails on the *Dolphin*

When he arrived back home in November 1811, he saw for the first time what was left of the center of downtown Newburyport after the Great Fire a few months earlier. He was relieved to find that his family was safe and that his house was still standing, as the fire had come very close to his family home. This marked the second time that Nichols returned to his hometown in the wake of a disaster. The first had been the devastation in town from the Embargo Act that greeted him when he returned from his ordeal with the *Sally Ann* in Europe. Both events directly affected his mercantile trading business he had with his brother.

Nichols was overjoyed that his wife and children were safe from the fire and that their home was still secure. He was able to hold his newborn son for the first time. Lydia had given birth to William Wallace two months before and was relieved to have her husband home after a long absence of eight months.

Their daughter, Martha, was now four and a half years old and was able to feel that she had a father. Nichols was able to provide some needed comfort and support for his family, who had experienced the trauma of the fire and near loss of their home.

However, Nichols' time at home with his family at home was fleeting. After only spending a short time at home, Nichols sailed out of Newburyport on a new vessel, the brig *Dolphin,* in February 1812. He was headed to Bordeaux with a cargo of fish. He was again able to successfully run the blockade out of Newburyport, and he also ran the British blockade without incident when both entering and leaving the Bordeaux port. He was now on the open sea and heading home.

Again, his luck ran out. After being at sea for thirteen days, the *Dolphin* was captured by the British frigate HMS *Rosamond S.W.* in company with a sloop of war (Benjamin Pierce, 1813). *Lloyd's Register* (1969) recorded the following entry for Tuesday, February 11, 1812, "The *Dolphin*, Nichols, from Newburyport to Bordeaux, detained by the *Rosamond S.W.*, arrived at Portsmouth on Thursday" (*Lloyd's Register 1811–1814*, 1969).

It was because of his capture this time that Nichols discovered the extent of his fame. The captain of the frigate that captured the *Dolphin* asked Captain Nichols if he was the person who retook the *Alert*. Word had quickly spread about his recapture of the *Alert*. Captain Nichols replied in the affirmative, and the British captain exclaimed, "It was a brave act, and you should be treated as a brave man deserved" (Benjamin Pierce letter, 1813).

While the British captain was very much aware of the encounter Captain Nichols had with the *Alert*, he did not know about Nichols' escape from the British guards following the incident. Captain Nichols experienced the best of treatment by the sea captain and was not restrained upon his arrival in England. Even though his ship was sold in England, he remained at large until he was able to get passage back to the United States.

Benjamin Pierce Jr. was the son of Captain Benjamin Pierce, the owner of both the *Alert* and the *Dolphin*. Young Benjamin had witnessed the daring recapture of the *Alert* by Captain Nichols, and he spread word about the encounter when he was eventually released and returned to his home in Newburyport. News of the recapture also swept through the British Navy, and the reputation of Nichols as an intrepid captain spread throughout the British naval world.

Voyage Home with Aaron Burr

Frustrated and angry about his ordeals with the *Alert* and the *Dolphin,* Nichols then boarded the *Aurora*, an American ship from Newburyport, for his passage back to New York (Benjamin Pierce, 1813). Nichols arrived in May 1812, about six weeks prior to the declaration of war.

There was some intrigue during his trip across the Atlantic, as there was a passenger on the same ship by the name of Adolphus R. Arnot. The passenger was actually Aaron Burr, former vice president of the United States and former senator from New York who was traveling under an assumed name. Burr had been in Europe for three years and was returning incognito to the United States (Wildes, 1864, p. 281).

Aaron Burr wrote a private journal during his travels through Europe. The journal was edited by Matthew Davis and published in 1858. On March 26, 1812, Burr wrote in his journal, "Captain Potter of the ship *Aurora* agrees to take me for 30 guineas ... I accepted the proposal and am to embark under the name of Arnot ... Potter has the secret of my name, and I believe he will keep it secret" (Davis, 1858, p. 350).

Of his boarding the *Aurora* during the night, Burr wrote that, "All hands were aboard and asleep when I got on board. The captain and mate got up and also a Captain Nicholls, an American passenger, who is a passenger" (Davis, 1858, p. 367).

Burr later made an entry into his journal about the secret of his identity, recording that,

> "Captain Potter only, of all on board this ship, knows me ... I came on board under the name of Arnot and am so called. It will be very wonderful if this secret should be kept during the whole passage"
>
> Davis, 1858, p. 368

Presumably Captain Potter was the only person on board to whom Burr admitted his true identity, but Captain Nichols recognized him. It seems that Burr noticed this, and he wrote in his journal,

> "Suspect that Captain Nichols knows me"
>
> Davis, 1858, p. 368

Nichols, in turn, attracted Burr's attention. In his journal, Burr made a number of entries about Captain Nichols' broad knowledge of navigation, the sea, and the weather.

Later during the voyage, Burr remained unsure about Nichols, considering in his journal,

> "Shall I make a merit of necessity and put confidence in him, or take my chance?"
>
> Davis, 1858, p. 402

Burr became concerned,

> "Captain Nichols asked me today if I knew V. D. L., the painter. Now as Nichols was in Paris when I was there, ten to one he has seen me; certainly, he has seen my picture".
>
> Davis, 1858, p. 402

"V. D. L." was the set of initials that John Vanderlyn used on his paintings. Vanderlyn became a protégé of US Senator Burr, and he sent Vanderlyn to Paris in 1796, where he studied for five years. Upon returning to the United States in 1801, Vanderlyn lived in Burr's home where he painted portraits of Burr and his daughter (Schleicher, 1937). Vanderlyn returned to Paris in 1803 and remained there for seven years, where he prospered as an artist ("Vanderlyn the Artist",2014, info@senatehousekingston.org).

It is not known how much Captain Nichols knew about Vanderlyn's relationship with Burr, but in all likelihood, he had seen Vanderlyn's portrait of Burr in Paris, as he had been in Paris for a year. By mentioning "V. D. L." to Burr, Nichols was confiding to him in a very subtle manner that he knew who Burr war. The question of what Nichols knew remained unresolved in Burr's journal. The voyage continued, and Burr's secret was safe with Nichols.

Aaron Burr's History

Aaron Burr, a lawyer and a senator and attorney general from New York, was the vice president from 1801 to 1805 under President Thomas Jefferson. Alexander Hamilton, a strong Federalist, was the first US secretary of treasury and he advocated a strong central government. Burr represented the old Republican Party that supported Thomas Jefferson. Their relationship was charged with political rivalry and personal animosity, and they clashed repeatedly in the political arena ("Duel at Dawn, 1804," 2000, www.eyewitnesstohistory.com).

They became bitter rivals in New York state politics, and they were at the center of double-crosses in the presidential election of 1800. When Thomas Jefferson and Aaron Burr tied in the Electoral College, Hamilton worked behind the scenes to have Burr successfully defeated, and Burr became vice president, instead ("Duel at Dawn 1804," 2000, www.eyewitnesstohistory.com).

Hamilton did not let the feud with Burr drop, and the final straw for Burr was a newspaper article that showed Hamilton trash-talking about Burr's character. Burr demanded an apology for fifteen years of insults, but Hamilton remained silent. Burr responded by challenging his antagonist to a duel that Hamilton felt compelled to accept ("Burr vs. Hamilton: Behind the Ultimate Political Feud," 2013, www.constitutioncenter.org).

On July 11, 1804, two shots rang out. Hamilton deliberately misfired, but Burr inflicted a mortal wound (Schlesinger, 1983, p. 180). Burr was indicted but not arrested for the illegal duel. Though hoping that a victory in the duel could revive his declining power and political career, Burr's victory actually helped end it, as the northern Federalists who had been very supportive then abandoned him. He then began to "weave a web of intrigue which confounded the administration and has never ceased to fascinate and baffle the historians" (Malone & Rauch, 1964, p. 109).

Vice President Burr was a brilliant but reckless man who was possibly making plans to invade Mexico or to have the western states secede from the union and establish a new empire. There was considerable outcry against Burr and his alleged traitorous activities. He was put on trial for treason in August 1807 and, though acquitted, fled to Europe in disguise to save himself from angry mobs that pursued him (Schlesinger, 1983, p. 174). For the next four years, Burr lived in disgraced exile in France. He traveled in Europe, trying to gain support for his plans to overthrow President Jefferson and unite France and England against the United States. But he was snubbed.

Nichols and Burr on the *Aurora*

In September 1811, Burr was on the *Vigilant*, heading for America, when the ship was captured by a British frigate, and he was taken to Yarmouth. He remained there until March 12, 1812, when he sailed for America on the *Aurora*. This ship fortuitously was the same vessel on which Captain Nichols was a passenger. Burr returned penniless to New York, and for the rest of his life, he was stigmatized as the murderer of Hamilton and a traitor to his country. He remained in the United States until his death at age eighty in 1836 (Schlesinger, 1983, p. 175).

The *Aurora* was a cartel ship for passengers commissioned to sail under a flag of truce. During the passage to Boston, the *Aurora* was boarded twice by British frigates to examine papers. There was considerable anxiety on the part of both Burr and Nichols, and they were quite tense during these boardings. They each had matters that they wanted to remain hidden.

Burr was a disgraced ex-patriot traveling under an assumed name, and his return to the United States was perilous. Nichols was fearful that he might be discovered as a fugitive, given his recent escape from the British authorities. However, no problems arose with either of them from the boardings. Both Nichols and Burr were unsure about what the other one knew, or did not know, about their affairs.

During the voyage, Burr often observed Captains Potter and Nichols talking about an impending war with Great Britain, and they both expected to find war by the time they arrived in port in May 1812. They were seriously alarmed that war would be declared before they arrived home, exposing them to the risk of capture (Davis, 1858, p. 368). They were nearly right, as war between the United States and Great Britain was declared the next month on June 19, 1812 (Schlesinger, 1983, p. 194).

As the *Aurora* neared the American coastline, the two captains noticed they had not seen any outward-bound ships and only one inward-bound vessel. They both agreed that there were always fifteen to fifty vessels passing by that location.

Burr reported: "Our captains concluded that there must be a very rigorous embargo in the United States" (Davis, 1858, p. 400). The captains were correct in their conclusions, as the United States Congress had declared a ninety-day embargo that started on April 4 (Schlesinger, 1983, p. 193). The *Aurora* later sailed into port in May 1812 during the middle of that embargo. This time Nicholas had been away from home for more than four months.

Brig *Alert* of Newburyport
Captain William Nichols, Jr. Master
Reproduced from the Sailing Ships of New England 1607-1907

Chapter 5

The *Decatur* Enters the War

The Town is disgraced with but two
privateers, one of which is the *Decatur*
–fitted out by Democrats – with Captain
Nichols, but they are not likely ever to
"set the river on fire".
> Editor Ephraim Allen
> *Newburyport Herald*, August 11, 1812

Arrived, privateer brig *Decatur* from a very
successful cruise. She captured 11 prizes with
54 prisoners including two masters and two mates.
> *"Herald* Ship News"
> *Newburyport Herald*, September 25, 1812

The *Decatur* came proudly up the river, with
fluttering flags from truck to rail – the English
Union upside down – her Captain saluted the
town, while cheering hundreds lined the banks.
> Sidney M. Chase
> "Captain William Nichols
> and the Privateer *Decatur"*
> ca. 1920, p. 10

William Nichols had anticipated that war was imminent. Not
only had he been experiencing continued harassment and capture of
some ships that he had mastered in the past few years, but he also

had knowledge of the events that were leading up to the war from his contact with other sea captains and sailors at various ports.

When Nichols returned to Newburyport from England in May 1812, he found that people in town were alarmed about the prospect of war. The impending war was not popular in Newburyport, as well as in other parts of New England (Hurd, 1888, p. 1763). Many felt that it was a fight without a cause. As the war started, Newburyport had a regiment ready to go into battle, but it did not enter the war. "The nation was at war, but Newburyport remained at peace" (Labaree, 1962, p. 187).

This was also a time when Nichols friend, Benjamin Hale, was expanding his stagecoach business, the Eastern Stage Company, which he owned and managed. It became the largest stagecoach line in New England. He also purchased the infamous Wolfe Tavern in Newburyport. The War of 1812 did not adversely affect the success of the Hale stagecoach business.

Madison Declares War

On June 19, 1812, the recently reelected fourth president of the United States, James Madison, officially declared that the United States was at war with Great Britain. War had been threatening for a decade (Coles, 1965, p. 74). Earlier in the month, the House of Representatives voted in support of the war seventy-nine to forty-nine, and the US Senate voted nineteen to thirteen in favor, ignoring the opposition of all of the Federalists in Congress (Schlesinger, 1983, p. 194).

The War of 1812 was the first declared war of the United States under the new constitution. President Madison declared war against Great Britain because of the continued impressment of American seamen, their interference with the United States neutral commerce trade, and the blockade of American ports.

NOTE: See Appendix B: Impressment

After long years of the British Royal Navy stopping neutral United States merchantmen and impressing real or alleged British deserters from their vessels, Americans became infuriated (Schlesinger, 1983, p.182). Great Britain had ignored America's sovereignty and neutrality, as they took the best men from merchant ships to build crews for their navy vessels. the British had been attacking the nation's merchant commerce for many years with no redress (Coggleshall, 1856, p. vii).

Negotiation was exhausted, and the United States was compelled to resort to war as a last alternative. Prior to the war, Britain and France together had seized nearly fifteen hundred American merchant vessels between 1803 and 1812. The motto for the war became, "Free Trade and Sailors' Rights," which was often put on the flags of some of the American ships (Schlesinger, 1983, p. 194). The War of 1812 continued for two and a half years from June 1812 to December 1814.

Most people in the country supported the war, especially in the south and the west, where the "war hawks" had pressured Congress for a declaration of war.

However, there was strong opposition to the war in New England because of its deep trading ties with Great Britain (Jenkins & Taylor, 2012, p. 2). The United States had attempted to remain a neutral nation in the war between France and England for that reason. Opponents to the war referred to it as "Mr. Madison's War."

Since the Revolutionary War, America had been developing an increasing amount of foreign trade. In 1805, the United States maritime trading fleet ranked second to Great Britain, with nearly ten thousand American ships carrying goods around the world (Jenkins & Taylor, 2012, p. 2). The interference and harassment of American commerce, together with America's own Embargo Act, had significantly impacted maritime trade. This had also seriously affected the mercantile trade business that Captain Nichols had with his brother, Samuel, also a merchant mariner, on the Newburyport waterfront.

In Newburyport, the war was exceedingly unpopular and created a great deal of anxiety with the town's citizens and merchants because the economy depended on continued trade with the British (Emery, 1879, p. 274). Commerce had been entirely stopped because of the ninety-day embargo that was reenacted just prior to the war, causing prices to rise exorbitantly. While there was a great deal of shipbuilding of mercantile ships taking place in Newburyport, the fitting out of privateers was strongly opposed among the townspeople.

Governor Caleb Strong of Massachusetts, a Federalist, declared a public, statewide fast to protest the war (Schlesinger, 1983, p. 194), and he refused to send out the state militia to defend the country (Emery, 1879, p. 275). Historically, the militia in each state was used to supplement regular army military forces. However, "Americans' traditional fear of a standing army resulted in the young republic depending heavily upon militia, rather than regulars ... the Constitution divided authority over the militia between state and federal governments" (Gabriel, review of Skeen, 1999).

When the federal government tried to mobilize the militia for the War of 1812, Federalist governors who opposed the war resisted the mobilization effort and maintained state control over the militia. They claimed that the "current situation did not meet the constitutional provisions necessary to mobilize their forces" (Gabriel, review of Skeen, 1999). At the start of the War of 1812, "the Army consisted of only 6744 men and officers. The militia of the states was called into federal service and 489,173 militiamen responded" ("State Organized Militia –war of 1812." 2011. www.globalsecurity.org/military/agency/army/militia-1812).

Federalists were opposed to the war because of the threat to trade profits and fear of possible British invasion again. However, there were some ardent supporters of the war, including Captain Benjamin

Pierce, a strong influential Democrat-Republican and prominent ship owner in Newburyport (Emery, 1879, p. 276). Proponents of military action felt, as the president did, that continued interference with commercial trade and impressment of seamen by the British could no longer be tolerated.

It was paradoxical that just prior to the declaration of war by the United States, Great Britain had proclaimed suspension of the British orders that were affecting American shipping and impressment of sailors. This decision was motivated by the worsening economic depression in England brought on by lack of trading between the United States and Britain as a result of the Non-Intercourse Act. This was a belated triumph for the economic coercion that followed the Embargo Act. There had also been considerable concern in Great Britain about the effect that Napoleon's continental war was having upon England (Coles, 1965, p. 74).

The British were moving toward conciliation and did not want war. They were unaware of the United States declaration of war when they officially suspended the orders in council of interference with American shipping and impressment of sailors (Coles, 1965, p. 71). Conversely, the United States had been unaware of this major concession made by Great Britain when the US Congress voted in favor of the war. Communication and travel across the Atlantic Ocean was very slow, and the delays added to the madness of the world (Schlesinger, 1983, p. 194). It was an unfortunate occurrence and set of events.

Great Britain initially viewed the war with the United States as an affair of secondary and inferior important, as they had to deal with more global and pressing battles in the Napoleonic War (*War of 1812*, DVD, 2011).

America Unprepared for War

At the time of the declaration of war, the United States was completely unprepared for battle. Our navy consisted of only three frigates and eight smaller vessels (Young www.FPY1229@aol.com). The British Royal Navy at that time had 1048 vessels, which included 254 ships-of-line, 247 frigates, 183 brigs and many armed yachts and fire ships; it was the largest and strongest naval fleet in the world. "It seemed a foolish notion to think that the United States could take on the British at sea…a weak nation had grabbed the lion by its tail" (Coles, 1965, p. 71).

America could not hope to overcome Britain's supremacy as the undisputed master of the seas (Coles, 1965, p. 106). However, American Navy officers were well trained, experienced, and highly efficient as sea captains. It was to their advantage that they were often seeking out offensive opportunities in naval battles (Coles, 1965, p. 74).

The US Congress then called upon private ships to compensate for its small navy. There were no privateer ships in existence when President Madison declared war in June 1812 (Garitee, 1977, p. 255). By arming existing merchant ships and outfitting them for battle, America rapidly developed a fleet of privateer vessels. There was an overnight flurry of activity in our seaports, and within two months after war was declared, 150 privateers had put to sea. It became relatively easy to transform a merchant vessel into an armed ship. America relied heavily on privately owned warships to compensate for its small navy.

NOTE: See Appendix C: Privateering

The United States also lacked a strong army. America's land forces had only a few thousand troops and an ill-prepared militia along the western frontier. Most soldiers had never seen combat. The army had not yet developed effective military organization or discipline in its forces (Jenkins & Taylor, 2012, p. 25). Because of its military inadequacies compared to the other players on the stage, at the outset, the British viewed the United States declaration of war a "sideshow" (Malone & Rauch, 1964, p. 29).

United States Expands War

Knowing that Great Britain ruled the seas, the United States turned north to Canada. There was a growing expansionist movement in America, and many people, especially the so-called war hawks in the west, dedicated and ardent expansionists, wanted to seize land belonging to the Native Americans and the land that is Canada and absorb it into the United States (*The War of 1812*, Canadian Public TV, 2011). The Native American tribes believed that the land from Canada to the Gulf Coast and everything west of the Mississippi River belonged to them. Their leader, Tecumseh, a Shawnee warrior, had a vision of a great tribe of Indians from the Great Lakes to the Gulf of Mexico and wanted to stop the American expansion. The Indian tribes in the west became allied with the British, who supplied the Indians with war materials (ibid.).

Acquiescing to the expansionist ideology, President Madison ordered an invasion of Canada, thinking that they would welcome the United States as their liberator. President Jefferson had earlier said that annexing Canada was "a mere matter of marching there." However, it was a misplaced judgment to think that the Canadians and the British would not resist (*The War of 1812*, Central Canadian Public TV, 2011). The Canadian invasion did not go well; American forces were repelled during three major battles to the north.

In the south, New Orleans, sitting astride the mouth of the Mississippi River, was a strategic location that the British wanted access to; controlling the river would mean controlling trade to the north. The overall result was that the United States, by declaring the War of 1812, immediately created a broad, wide-ranging war against the British on different fronts, with slow communication that necessitated travel over thousands of miles. There were naval encounters on the Atlantic and land battles in Canada on the western front, and along the Gulf coast at the Mississippi River.

People in Newburyport were in conflict about the war. While news of American victories at sea was viewed positively by the town as protecting their trading interests, they denounced the "practice of privateering as unprincipled" (Labaree, 1962, p. 187). Upon the declaration of war, the town appointed a committee and declared that its people would march only under the orders of the governor in defiance of the president's authority; "We will not stir an inch beyond our soil" (Hurd, 1888, p. 1763).

The editor of the *Newburyport Herald*, Ephraim W. Allen, a strong Federalist, discredited the few privateers that sailed from the Merrimack River and had little sympathy for lost crews (Labaree, 1962, p. 188). When the privateer *Manhattan* returned to port without any prizes in early August, Allen disdainfully reported: "The privateer *Manhattan* returned to port Saturday, without prizes. We congratulate the owners that she has saved herself!" ("*Herald* Ship News," *Newburyport Herald,* August 4, 1812).

Decatur Enters War

In 1812, ship owner Captain Benjamin Pierce was having a ship constructed for him at Salisbury Point, just across the Merrimack River from Newburyport. It was to be a fast-sailing ship meant to run the British blockade. Pierce had owned the *Alert* and *Dolphin* merchant ships that Captain Nichols mastered. Both vessels had been captured and sold in England. Pierce and Nichols named the new brig the *Decatur*, in honor of Captain Stephen Decatur, the hero of the daring attack in Tripoli Harbor in 1804. Pierce stated,

> "Captain Nichols was selected as a suitable character to take command as he proceeded on a cruise against the British"
>
> Benjamin Pierce, 1813

Nichols was given a letter of marque by the federal government, which authorized him to become a commissioned privateer captain. This was his first command of a naval warship.

NOTE: See Appendix C: Privateering

A privateer ship was a privately owned, armed vessel commissioned by a government to attack enemy ships. These ships carried no cargo and were devoted exclusively to wartime encounters ("Privateering," *Columbia Encyclopedia*, 1950, p. 1601).

A letter of marque was a license of reprisal upon an enemy during wartime and authorized privateer captains to arm vessels and take property of merchant ships of the enemy (Macintyre, 1975, p. 3). A letter of marque commission that was issued by a government differentiated a privateer ship from the nation's warships and from pirate crafts.

For the first time in all of his voyages, Nichols now had the freedom to be on the offensive instead of having to always yield and reluctantly surrender his ships without any protest. (The only exception had been when he singlehandedly recaptured his ship, the *Alert*, the previous year.)

By accepting Pierce's offer and agreeing to this expedition, Nichols was going against the prevailing sentiments in Massachusetts, as many were people resistant to the war effort. It was noted in the *Newburyport Herald* that,

> "The *Decatur* was followed by more curses than prayers for its safe return".
>
> "Memorabilia," *Newburyport Herald*,
> August 8, 1855

The captain and crew had to conquer the prejudices of their families and neighbors in order to serve their country. Endeavors were made by many residents to prevent enlistments on the *Decatur*, and some crewmembers were arrested and treated like criminals. Nichols was hindered in every possible way from fitting out his vessel.

A display of patriotic fervor was Nichols response to the treatment he and his crew received from the town when attempting to prepare for the *Decatur's* cruise. On the day that the *Decatur* sailed, a full rank of more than one hundred blue-coated sailors marched along High Street in Newburyport to the "rattle of drums and shrill of fifes" (Chase, ca. 1920, p. 6). They arrived at the home of Captain Benjamin Pierce, the *Decatur's* owner.

Pierce and his wife appeared in their doorway, and she tied a wide, blue ribbon on every sailor's hat. The sailors gave her three strong cheers, and then the crew marched back down State Street to the wharf, singing "Yankee Doodle."

The anchors were soon hauled, and with cannons booming and many Newburyporters cheering, the *Decatur* sailed out of Newburyport Harbor (Chase, ca. 1920, p. 6). The *Decatur* was armed with fourteen guns and provisions for a crew of 150 men. She cleared the Custom House in Newburyport for her first cruise on August 4, 1812 (Wildes, 1864, p. 232).

The following week, Editor Allen could not resist declaring,

"This town is disgraced with but two privateers, one of which is the Decatur – fitted out by Democrats – with Captain William Nichols, but they are not likely ever 'to set the river on fire'."
"*Herald* Ship News," *Newburyport Herald*
August 11, 1812

Nichols had become part of the effort to defend the country and its vast seacoast of unprotected cities and towns along the Atlantic. He also sought some vindication on the high seas for the earlier losses of the *Alert* and the *Dolphin* (Hurd, 1888, p. 1763).

From Newburyport, the *Decatur* stopped at Salem to complete her crew. Arthur Knapp from Newburyport, age fourteen, had known that the brig was due at Salem (Chase, ca. 1920, p. 6). His father had refused to let him join the crew, but Arthur slipped away and walked twenty-two miles to Salem. Nichols allowed him to join the crew of the *Decatur* when the ship sailed from Salem.

Nichols would soon invalidate Allen's lackluster predictions; the events of Nichols' first *Decatur* voyage were indeed significant. His encounters captured the imagination of all Newburyporters. Of this time, Wildes would later write in his memoir dedicated to Captain Nichols: "the *Decatur* under the command of Captain Nichols, proved a terror to English commerce under the guns of ships guarding the English coasts … ranging over the ocean, the *Decatur* was known and feared wherever an English flag was spread to the breeze" (Wildes, 1864, p. 232).

After completing his crew in Salem, Nichols sailed along the coast and captured nothing for the first two weeks, which did not indicate an auspicious start. Then, on August 18, as he was sailing east off the coast of Nova Scotia, the *Decatur* was chased by a British ship, which was made out to be the frigate HMS *Guerriere* (Chase, ca. 1920, p. 6).

Captain Nichols later reported that,

"One morning as the fog scaled, I saw a British frigate just under my lee, who hailed me with, 'Brig ahoy! What ship is that?'"

Nichols responded with a ruse to avoid a battle:

"The *Liverpool* packet from Halifax, bound to Liverpool. Any commands? ... What ship is that?"

The reply came,

"His Britannic Majesty's frigate *Guerriere,* Captain Dacres, on a cruise. Report my position to the Lords of the Admiralty."

"Aye, aye, sir," Nichols responded.

Nichols continued in his report;

"As soon as possible I put on sail. I suppose he now suspected who I was and who had captured so many English merchantmen; for I was not over two miles away, before he fired over my bow for me to heave to; but we were soon out of reach of his guns"

Newburyport Herald, March 13, 1877

A strong wind was blowing that day, and the *Decatur* lost some of her sails and the jib beam. However, because of her fine sailing qualities, the *Decatur* was able to out-sail the slower frigate. In less than three hours, the crew had repaired all the sails, "a feat that was seldom equaled" ("Memorabilia," *Newburyport Herald*, August 2, 1855), The *Decatur* "preserved her distance" until after dark when Nichols was finally able to elude the larger vessel (Wildes, 1864,

p. 232). It was fortunate that this event occurred just prior to the *Decatur's* next encounter.

Decatur's Mistaken Twist of Fate

Later the same night, the lookout on the *Decatur* was startled when he saw a large ship looming close to the stern. Full sail was ordered immediately, but the situation looked grave. Thinking that it was the *Guerriere* catching up with him, without delay Nichols searched for the best way to outrun the frigate. Desperate to put some distance between them, he ordered twelve of the *Decatur's* fourteen cannons to be thrown overboard to gain speed and elude the larger frigate, leaving them with only two brass, four-pounder cannons. For more than two hours, the frigate crept closer as Nichols and his crew were frantically wetting the sails for more speed (Chase, ca. 1920, p. 7).

The *Decatur* was driving ahead with "every stretch of canvas drawing" (Chase, ca. 1920, p. 7). Suddenly, there was a crash as the foretopmast came plunging down, carrying sails and rigging to the deck. No one was injured, but the ship slowed considerably and the frigate was then able to draw up beside the *Decatur.*

Nichols wrote of this moment:

> "I now gave myself up and was thinking of concealing our valuables, as the hail came from the frigate, 'What ship is that?'"

Nichols again attempted to use another ploy as he stepped up on the quarterdeck and replied,

> "The Brig *Decatur* that is bound from London to Halifax … What ship is that?"
>
> Chase, ca. 1920, p. 7

Dr. G. William Freeman

There was a tense silence as Nichols and his crew awaited an answer. Then came the delayed and unexpected reply,

"The United Sates Frigate *Constitution*!"

A great sigh of relief swept through the crew. It had not been the *Guerriere*! Three cheers were given for the *Constitution* (Chase, ca. 1920, p. 7).

While the *Decatur* had been able to elude the original pursuer, she had been unable to out-sail the *Constitution*, even with the mistaken sacrifice of having thrown most of her guns overboard. Had the foretopmast not broken away and fallen to the deck, the *Decatur* may have escaped, and the events that followed would not have occurred.

Commodore Isaac Hull, age thirty-nine, of the *Constitution* was sailing south from Cape Race, Newfoundland, at the time of his encounter with the *Decatur*. Nichols recalled witnessing Captain Hull cutting out and capturing a French eighteen-gun privateer ship at port 12 years earlier. Nichols had observed the capture by Captain Hull in a West Indies harbor while on board a Swedish vessel, as he was beginning his return trip to America after escaping from the capture when on the *Rose* (Wildes, 1864, p. 230).

Nichols went on board the *Constitution,* and Commodore Hull inquired of Nichols, "Have you seen the English frigate *Guerriere? I am in pursuit of her.*" Hull said that it had been reported that the *Guerriere* was reported to have been cruising in the area. Nichols explained to Hull about the chase the day before with the *Guerriere.*

Nichols provided Hull with the latitude, longitude, and the course of the British frigate (Coggleshall, 1861, p. 23). Having seen the *Guerriere,* Nichols also informed Hull how to best maneuver the *Constitution* for its best advantage when attacking the British vessel ("Cabbages & Kings," *Newburyport Daily News,* June 13, 1963).

Commodore Hull's Journal

Commodore Hull kept a journal in which he recounted all of the *USS Constitution's* activities from the beginning of his cruise until the eve of his engagement with the *Guerriere*. Hull's Journal that was directed to the US Navy secretary states

> Saw nothing till the night of the 18th; at half-past nine, P.M., discovered a sail very near, it being dark; made sail and gave chase, and could see that she was a brig. At eleven brought her to, sent a boat to board her, and found her to be the American privateer **Decatur ...** with a crew of one hundred and eight men, and fourteen guns, twelve of which she had thrown overboard while we were in chase of her. The Captain came on board, and informed us that he saw the day before, a ship-of-war standing to the south-ward, and that he could not be far from us. At twelve A.M. made sail to the southward, intending if possible, to fall in with her.
>
> from Journal of Captain Isaac Hull
> in Dudley & Crawford, 1985, p. 232

Hull immediately resolved to give chase in pursuit of the British frigate. Before leaving, Hull replenished Nichols with a new topmast and a quantity of muskets, cutlasses, and handcuffs (Harris, 1977, p. 32).

Hull also offered to replace the *Decatur's* battery of guns, but that would have taken more precious time. Nichols graciously declined the offer, wanting to provide Hull with the opportunity to forge ahead and pursue the *Guerriere* with all haste (Chase, ca. 1920, p. 7). Captain Hull then headed south and caught up with the *Guerriere* the next day.

Dr. G. William Freeman

USS Constitution vs. HMS Guerriere

Nichols' information had proved worthwhile, as the rest of the story is firmly embedded in American history. The next day, August 19, the *Constitution* fell in with the *Guerriere* six hundred miles east of Boston. The *Constitution* defeated the *Guerriere* in a fierce, two-hour naval battle (Chase, ca. 1920, p. 7). The *Constitution's* cannon shots repeatedly pierced the hull of the British frigate, hurling chunks of lethal splinters and sending grape shot ripping through her sails and rigging. The *Guerriere's* mizzenmast crashed over the side, causing her to slow down and turn into the wind under an intense hail of musketry from the *Constitution.*

It was during this battle that crewmembers of the *Guerriere* witnessed, to their astonishment, British cannonballs harmlessly bouncing off the *Constitution's* hull and falling into the sea. They cried out in amazement, "Her sides are made of iron!" thus bestowing her renowned nickname of "Old Ironsides" (Harris, 1977, p. 33).

Captain George Coggleshall was a commissioned privateer captain during the War of 1812 who was captured by the British in the *Leo.* He escaped from a courtroom, and following an infamous voyage on a Portuguese ship for fifty-eight days, he finally arrived back in New York Harbor. He later became an author of a number of naval history books. He stated in his 1856 book, *History of American Privateers,* that "in the annals of naval warfare, the battle between the *Constitution* and the *Guerriere* stands as perhaps the most brilliant as between ships" (Coggleshall, 1856, p. 232).

Had it not been for the information that Captain Nichols afforded Commodore Hull of the location of the *Guerriere,* the battle might never have been fought, and the *Guerriere* never defeated. If Nichols had not had the opportunity to point Commodore Hull in the right direction with an approximate distance, the gallant encounter between the *Constitution* and the *Guerriere* would not have occurred.

During Nichols' brief exchange with Hull out at sea, they arranged for the *Decatur* to follow the *Constitution* into battle. Nichols and his crew would act as a boarding party if Hull fell in with the British frigate within a certain time. However, this arrangement did not transpire because the *Constitution*, a faster vessel, went out ahead and engaged with the *Guerriere* before the *Decatur* could arrive. Nichols and his crew heard the cannonading in the distance and knew that the *Constitution* had been victorious. The *Guerriere* was later scuttled because she had sustained too much damage to save her (Wildes, 1864, p. 232).

The British couldn't believe the loss of the *Guerriere*. Both Americans and the British had become generally accustomed to thinking of the English Navy as invincible. The defeat of the *Guerriere* sent a resounding message to the British that the American Navy could be successful in a direct naval battle (Coggleshall, 1861, p. 24). This dramatic victory boosted American morale at an early stage of the War of 1812 and raised the spirits of the whole nation (Chase, ca. 1920, p. 7).

The incident with Captain Nichols of the *Decatur* and Commodore Hull of the *USS Constitution* was recalled in verse by Rowan Stevens, son of the late Rear-Admiral Thomas Stevens, who wrote:

> And on through the summer seas we bore,
>   Until off stern Cape Clear
> Our ship fell in with a sloop-o'-war,
>   A Yankee privateer.
> We hailed for news, and the sloop hove to,
>   And off her skipper came,
> And boarded us in a leaky yawl
>   With his wrathful cheek aflame.
> For "Down to the south'ard he'd been chased
>   By a powerful ship

That was just too slow for his flying heels,
    And just too big to whip.
We sent him back with a cheerful heart,
    And down to the south we swept,
And a sharp lookout o'er the vacant sea
    A low and aloft we kept.

in Maclay, 1899, p. 310

Nichols Quells Mutiny

Following the incident with the *Constitution*, Nichols continued on with his cruise instead of heading back to Newburyport. While this was his first command of a naval warship, he had experienced considerable adversity in prior engagements on the high seas. He had confidence in his decision to continue the voyage, trusting that the *Decatur* would be capable of defending herself in an encounter. While circumstances became quite difficult for him, Nichols was not timid, and he did not back away from the challenge. It was not in his nature to acquiesce in a difficult situation.

As a captain, he had to be unflinching. Like many men who live to brave the dangers at sea, he chose not to plan according to what could possibly go wrong but instead on what would probably go right. Sailing without most of his guns to defend him didn't deter his ambitions; he still intended to take other ships, as he had a crew of 150 men. To intimidate other ships into submission, he planned to arrange a pretense by making some old logs look like cannons (Bailey & Jones, 1906, p. 370).

His crew, however, did not share his confidence that the deception would succeed. They felt that it was a reckless gamble. Because the *Decatur* had only two guns, if the ruse was found out, any potential foe would not react favorably to being duped, and the *Decatur* would have little firepower left to defend itself. It was not surprising that the men were showing their discontent ("Memorabilia," *Newburyport Herald*, August 2, 1855).

On August 22, four days after the incident with the *USS Constitution,* the crew attempted a mutiny feeling that Nichols was rendering the *Decatur* defenseless, (Bailey & Jones, 1906, p. 370). The editors of the *Newburyport Herald,* who wrote four lengthy articles about Nichols in their "Memorabilia" section in August 1855, reported the incident,

> "This was a moment when the fate of that voyage and
> the reputation of that captain was to be determined."

When the boatswain called the crew to shorten sail, no one from below moved. When called to duty by the first lieutenant on deck, the crew again remained below. The officer then had to inform the captain that mutiny existed. Wildes described the incident as it had been told to him,

> "Nichols came out of the cabin with his brows
> lowering above his flashing eyes, his lips tightening
> over his teeth, and his hands upon his pistols and the
> knife in his belt. He presented himself with pluck and
> an iron will as he appeared before his mutinous crew".
> Wildes, 1864, p. 233

Ship's Clock and Barometer Set of Captain William Nichols
Custom House Maritime Museum
Gift of Dr. G. William Freeman

Ships' Half Hour Glass of Captain William Nichols
Custom House Maritime Museum
Gift of Dr. G. William Freeman

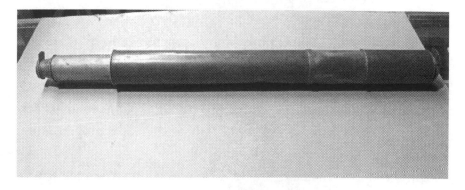

Captain William Nichols Telescope
Custom House Maritime Museum
Gift of Donald Hale Baumgartner

Nichols once more ordered the boatswain to call the men to duty. When there was no reply, he "strode over to the main hatch to the deck below with a firm and measured step" (Wildes, 1864, p. 233).

"What does this mean?" Nichols demanded.

The crew replied, "No more duty. The guns are overboard. We can take no more prizes".

Nichols retorted strongly to his men, "You shall be masters of this brig, or I will!"

Nichols turned to his officers and said,

"A mutiny can never succeed on board a man-of-war where the officers are true to their commander"
                                                    Wildes, 1864, p. 233

Nichols then grabbed a billet of wood and jumped alone down through the main hatch into the mutineers. He felled the ringleader to the floor with a blow to the head with the club. The officers followed, and after a few blows, the short conflict ended, and order was restored (Wildes, 1864, p. 233)

The courage Captain Nichols demonstrated by quelling the mutinous disposition of his crew won the men over to him. He had to demonstrate significant skills as a leader at that moment when they doubted him the most. His boldness inspired his men and built enthusiasm among his crew. The cruise would have undeniably been unsuccessful if he had not shown his character of daring courage during the attempted mutiny (Wildes, 1864, p. 233).

He demonstrated that he was confident and tough, and they came to trust that he could be an excellent captain in battle. He built a loyal crew that would follow him anywhere. This became apparent when he later asked the crew if they wished later to fight a battle with an oncoming larger British ship, the *Commerce*. They trusted that he would not misread the situation and that he was devoted to the care of his men. The crew knew that Nichols would use good judgment and strategy in naval battles that the *Decatur* would encounter ("Memorabilia," *Newburyport Herald*, August 2, 1855).

It is essential that a ship's captain maintain absolute control and reign supreme in order to ensure the success and safety of his ship and its crew. This requires excellent leadership, navigational skills, seamanship, and good survival skills. A captain has to employ all of his personal resources in becoming a successful commander (*Great Ships: The Frigates*, DVD, 1996). In quelling the mutiny, Nichols demonstrated that he surely had the needed qualities to be a privateer captain of the *Decatur*.

Thus far, the first cruise of the *Decatur* had been unsuccessful at securing any prizes, but the fortune of the ship would soon turn. On the very same day, August 22, that his crew had become despondent and mutinous, luck changed for Nichols and the *Decatur*.

Chapter 6

Battle of *Decatur* vs. *HMS Commerce*

The extraordinary success of Captain
Nichols is ascribed to a peculiar and original
mode of naval tactics which he used; the first
rule was, when engaged with a ship, to order
some trusty men, good marksmen, to "keep the
helm of the enemy clear".

E. Vale Smith
History of Newburyport, 1854, p. 195

In the *Decatur,* Captain Nichols made
two cruises, and he is entitled to all that
we have claimed for him as one of the
very first heroes of the War.

"Memorabilia #8,"
Newburyport Herald, August 2, 1855

Fortune changed for Nichols and the *Decatur.* Having just
repressed an attempted mutiny by his crew and having taken no
prizes in almost three weeks at sea, luck had been turning badly for
Nichols. He had been chased by the frigate HMS *Guerriere* and was
mistakenly chased by the USS *Constitution* when he decided to throw
most of his guns overboard.

Decatur Captures British Prizes

Later on the same day as the mutiny, a barque was sighted. It was
the *Duke of Savoy* bound for Canada. Nichols gave chase, and his

armed crew swarmed onto the boat. As he had only two guns left, Nichols had some logs made over to appear as cannons, and the bluff worked. The barque's colors came down, and she became the first prize for the *Decatur*. There was no cargo, but her four cannons were shifted to the *Decatur* with a large supply of arms. A prize crew took her safely back to Newburyport (Wildes, 1864, p. 233).

The next day, August 23, Nichols took the *Thomas* laden with only ballast in her hold and two guns, which Nichols put on the *Decatur*. He sent the *Thomas* back to Newburyport with another prize crew. Later the same day, Nichols captured the brig *Pomona* that was bound for St. Lawrence from Aberdeen. She was also in ballast with no cargo, but two more guns were added to the *Decatur's* armaments. Nichols now had a total of ten guns in his arsenal. He took thirty men prisoner, and he ordered a prize crew to take the *Pomona* to Halifax along with the prisoners (Chase, ca. 1920, p. 8).

Two days later on August 25, the brig *Elizabeth* was captured, and it had a cargo of salt and coal. A fourth prize crew took her to Newburyport. The remaining crewmembers of the *Decatur* were now becoming enthused and motivated, as they had taken four prizes in four days. Nichols was feeling more confident and at ease, as he had been able to replace most of the cannons on the *Decatur*.

Prizes now came quite rapidly. The next day, August 26, was very busy, as three brigs were captured. Nichols first took the brig *Devonshire* with a cargo of fish and oil. He decided to send the cargo to France with a prize crew, and it was later reported that she arrived safely in Quimper where the fresh fish were sold. The brig *Concord* was then captured and sent to Halifax as a cartel flying a truce flag with twenty prisoners. Later the same day, Nichols took the brig *Hope*, which was also in ballast. He took the crew onto the *Decatur*, and he then scuttled the *Hope* by burning her at sea (Chase, ca. 1920, p. 8).

By this time, Captain Nichols was beginning to feel much better after his initial discouragements on the voyage, as he had made seven captures in only five days. A few days later on August 30, he drew in the large transport barque *William and Charlotte*. This ship had five hundred tons of Canadian oak timber for the British government that included four yellow pine masts and twenty-eight bowsprits for the British Royal Navy. She also had four guns, which were welcome on the *Decatur*. Nichols sent her back to Boston with a prize crew, where she was sold (Wildes, 1864, p. 233).

Two days later, Nichols headed out to mid-ocean looking for more of the "Atlantic lottery." Nichols had the good fortune to fall in with and capture the *Diana* headed to the West Indies from London. She had a cargo of rum, sugar, and coffee valued at $400,000 - a significant amount in those days! The *Diana* also had ten guns that were not used in the encounter, and Nichols added the guns to his armament. He now had a total of twenty-four guns, including the two that he had not thrown overboard a few days earlier. He ordered the *Diana* to Newburyport, but the British recaptured the ship after the *Decatur* left (Wildes, 1864, p. 233).

On the same day, he met the St. Thomas fleet of twenty vessels that was under convoy with the British frigate *HMS Amaranthus*. In full view of the convoy, Nichols cut out the brig *Fame* with a cargo of sugar and rum. He also ordered the *Fame* to Newburyport with a prize crew. Both the *Fame* and the *Diana* were recaptured on September 13 by the British frigate HMS *Polyphemus* and sent to England (Wildes, 1864, p. 233).

In ten days, Nichols and his crew had captured ten prizes. Everyone was feeling quite exhilarated, and Nichols had been able to replenish his arsenal. During the cruise, Nichols had sailed the *Decatur* within a few leagues of the English Channel (Smith, 1854, p. 194). He had dared the enemy into combat in their own waters, having sailed within sight of their seaports.

However, Nichols had become shorthanded because of all the prize crews that had been assigned to the captured ships. Each vessel required nine to eleven seamen to take a ship back to port, and he had ordered nine prize crews to make the return trip to Newburyport. From the original crew of 150 men, only twenty-seven remained to sail the *Decatur*, man the guns, and be in charge of the prisoners.

Decatur Battles the *Commerce*

On September 6, 1812 as the *Decatur* was making a return voyage to Newburyport, she fell in with the British ship *Commerce* on the banks of Newfoundland (Wildes, 1864, p. 233). In one last battle before arriving in port, Nichols was called upon to meet one of the most severe trials of his skill and courage as a privateer captain (Chase, ca. 1920, p. 9).

There was a thick fog that suddenly lifted, and Nichols saw a large English ship close aboard, which hoisted a British flag. The ship immediately fired a shot over the bow of the *Decatur*. Nichols' plight was critical, and he knew the odds were against him because his vessel "was so feebly manned" (Wildes, 1864, p. 233).

Knowing that he had little more than two-dozen crew, Nichols called his men together at the stern of the boat. He asked them whether or not the *Decatur* should fight this ship. His crew answered with three cheers, which showed their loyalty and allegiance to Nichols. They trusted he would know what to do in battle. He immediately chased after the *Commerce* as the crew prepared the brig for action. Nichols used a ploy and raised an English color ("Memorabilia," *Newburyport Herald,* August 8, 1855).

The handling of a sailing ship in a battle situation became very complicated and required excellent navigational skills (Coles, 1965, p. 78). Very intricate and delicate maneuvering of a ship was needed to win a battle at sea. Ships had a few cannons in both the bow and stern, sometimes with pivots, but the main batteries of guns were on the port and starboard sides. Cannons could fire just over a mile. Only officers could speak during a battle, as they gave the orders. Also, the deck was covered with sand to avoid slipping, and young boys were "powder monkeys" that supplied the guns with ammunition.

The object in a battle was to maneuver the ship so that the full weight of either battery of guns could be brought to bear without the enemy being able to reply with a broadside. The ideal positions were to rake the enemy ship fore and aft. The wind also played an important role in every commander's decision. While no ship can sail directly into the wind, a ship wanted to have the "advantage of the wind" (Coles, 1965, p. 78).

Initially it could not be determined if the ship that the *Decatur* had encountered was a merchant vessel or a British Navy ship. It was a larger ship with fourteen guns, and the *Decatur* had a much smaller crew (Wildes, 1864, p. 233). Hoping that the other ship would view his vessel as an English one, Nichols hailed the other ship, saying that he would send his long boat on board. In that boat, he sent two officers and five men from the *Decatur,* leaving only twenty men on board the *Decatur* ("Memorabilia," *Newburyport Herald*, August 8, 1855).

It was later discovered that the ship was the *Commerce* with Commander Watts as the master, and it had fifty-seven men and thirty passengers. The vessel had a large cargo of rum, sugar, cotton, and coffee and was bound from the West Indies to Glasgow, Scotland.

Immediately upon reaching the larger ship, the *Commerce* discovered that the boat crew from the *Decatur* were Americans. The two officers from the *Decatur* went up over the side of the *Commerce* and were immediately seized and thrust below the hatches.

The long boat with five crewmen pushed away from the *Commerce,* and the British ship made an attempt to sink the long boat by firing a cannon. However, Nichols forged ahead to sail between the long boat and the *Commerce.* The *Decatur* received the broadside that was intended for the long boat. The *Commerce* then made sail to avoid a battle with the *Decatur* ("Memorabilia," *Newburyport Herald*, August 8, 1855).

Nichols pursued the *Commerce*, and in a few minutes the two vessels were again in close proximity to each other. The situation was perilous for Nichols. The *Decatur* had a much smaller crew and was battling a larger ship with heavier guns, and the British crew were well equipped with small arms. Broadsides from the *Commerce* were crippling the sails and rigging of the *Decatur*, as the foretopsail had lost twenty square feet of sail. Some other sails were rendered useless. Nichols knew that some desperate measures had to be taken, or he would have to surrender ("Memorabilia," *Newburyport Herald*, August 8, 1855).

During the battle that ensued, the second officer of the *Decatur*, Moses Knight, became furious, threw his cap on the deck, and swore with a solemn oath that, "I would neither eat bread nor drink water till I get these men on board" (Chase, ca. 1920, p. 9). Knight had the crew drag a gun forward, and he rammed bolts and scrap iron into the muzzle. He dropped to one knee, sighting carefully, and fired. When the smoke cleared, the mizzenmast was dragging alongside the *Commerce*, a splintered wreck.

Captain Nichols, as commander of the *Decatur*, was "as inflexible in spirit as he was always in appearance" (Wildes, 1864, p. 234). He had to not only manage his vessel but also work his guns. He was seen to be moving rapidly between the helm and a small cannon. While he was doing this, the British Captain Watts took deliberate aim at Nichols and repeatedly fired at him with his musket fourteen times. Watts finally threw the musket down on the deck, swearing, "The Yankee was never born to be shot" (Wildes, 1864, p. 234).

Nichols was determined to board the enemy's ship, and he ordered the helmsman to put the *Decatur* under the lee quarter of the large ship. Having only twenty men on board, he told ten of his crew to watch the prisoners on board the *Decatur,* as he had five prisoners who were British officers that were confined in his cabin.

Five members of his crew were still in the long boat at some distance from the *Decatur*, and two of his officers had been captured on the *Commerce*. With only ten men, Nichols made a desperate attempt to take the enemy's vessel. He gave the commands, "Fire!" and "Boarders away!" as though he had a hundred men to respond to the orders. Then came his call that changed the nature of the battle ("Memorabilia," *Newburyport Herald*, August 8, 1855).

"Keep the Helm Clear"

Calling out as though his force was a large one, Nichols shouted, "Marines, cut away that fellow at the wheel."

"I've got him," replied a tall seaman with a rusty gun, who was the only marine that Nichols had on board. The man at the helm of the *Commerce* fell.

Commander Watts yelled, "Put another man at the wheel."

Nichols again shouted, "Keep the helm clear," and the response came, "Aye-aye, sir! There he goes," as the second man fell.

A third time, the fatal order was given, and a third crewmember fell at the helm.

Then a fourth crewmember and the captain himself attempted to manage the wheel by lying on the deck. Nichols then ordered a final broadside, which thundered along the waters as it reached the *Commerce*. As the smoke cleared, the enemy ship's after-spars were disabled, the wheel was blown away, and the English captain was desperately wounded (Wildes, 1864, p. 234).

With the helmsmen being successively picked off, men of the *Commerce* crew became fearful to take up the fatal position. The vessel became unmanageable and it more readily fell prey to the shrewd and brave captain (Smith, 1854, p. 195).

> "The extraordinary success of Captain Nichols can be ascribed to the peculiar and original mode of naval tactics which he adopted. The first rule when engaged with a ship was to order some good marksmen to 'keep the helm of the enemy clear'."
>
> Smith, 1854, p. 195

Captain Watts waved a flag and fell to the deck. The *Commerce* crewmembers retreated below deck without striking their colors. Nichols hailed the enemy's ship three times without an answer, and he threatened to sink the *Commerce* if the flag was not struck. Finally, the *Commerce* sent the two captured officers from the *Decatur* on deck to strike the colors (Wildes, 1864, p. 234).

This fierce battle lasted an hour. The five men out on the long boat were returned to the *Decatur*, and repairs on the rigging were done. The *Decatur* did not lose a man during the battle, but three sailors were killed on the *Commerce* with two wounded. Dr. John Brickett, age thirty-eight, a surgeon from Newburyport, was on board the *Decatur*. He was sent over to the *Commerce* where he remained through the night to attend to Commander Watts, but the captain died during the night (Currier II, 1909, p. 303).

The prisoners being taken on board the *Decatur* were immediately put into irons as they came over the side and sent below deck. This was to avoid having them learn the weakness in numbers of the *Decatur's* crew and possibly create a revolt ("Memorabilia," *Newburyport Herald*, August 8, 1855).

Nichols had so few men that he was unable to send a prize crew to sail the *Commerce* back to port with the *Decatur*, and he was planning to scuttle her. However, nine seamen from the *Commerce* who were Swedes and Portuguese offered to enlist with Nichols, on condition of a share of the prize money. They sailed the *Commerce* and followed Nichols and the *Decatur* back to port.

Decatur Arrives in Newburyport

The *Decatur*, with its valuable cargo, arrived safely in Newburyport on September 23, 1812, along with the *Commerce,* where its rich cargo was sold. He had returned without the loss of one man, except for the three prize crews that were recaptured by the British. From a cruise of seven weeks, Nichols captured twelve prizes and returned with fifty-four prisoners, including two shipmasters and two mates ("*Herald* Ship News" *Newburyport Herald*, September 25, 1812).

As the *Decatur* came proudly up the Merrimack River into Newburyport Harbor, she had flags and streamers on her rigging, and the English union was being flown upside down. The *Decatur* was followed through the harbor by the *Commerce*, the brig *Elizabeth*, the *Duke of Savoy*, and a French schooner.

Even though most people in Newburyport were Federalists who did not support the war, there was a crowd of hundreds waiting at the landing. Captain Nichols saluted the town as the cheering throng of people lined the banks when he came up to the wharf. Knowledge of his many captures had preceded his arrival in Newburyport from the prize ships he had ordered back to Newburyport (Emery, 1879, p. 276).

He immediately became Newburyport's hero and two hundred years later continues to have the same reputation in Newburyport. Even Editor Allen of the *Newburyport Herald,* a strong Federalist, was unwilling to deprecate Nichols' accomplishments (Labaree, 1964, p. 188). Allen announced in a lengthy article about the triumphant return of the *Decatur* to Newburyport,

> "Arrived, privateer brig *Decatur*, Nichols, from a very successful cruise, having captured the following vessels,
> Aug.22 captured the barque *Duke of Savoy*, (arrived here);

*23*d, captured brig *Thomas,* from Aberdeen, for the St.
  Lawrence, in ballast, mounting 2 guns, etc. sent
  her as a cartel to Halifax, with 30 men;

25ᵗʰ, captured brig *Elizabeth* (arrived here) with salt
  and coals;

26ᵗʰ, captured brig *Devonshire*, laden with fish and oil,
  put on board Mr. Wingate Pilsbury and a crew,
  and ordered her for France, on captors account;

Same day, captured brig *Concord,* put on board 20
  prisoners and ordered her for Halifax, as a cartel;

Same day, captured brig *Hope*, in ballast, and
  burnt her;

30ᵗʰ, captured brig *Wm. & Charlotte*, from Quebec
  for Portsmouth, Eng. with 500 tons of oak timber,
  deals, etc. on Brit. gov't account, ordered her for this
  port – she mounted four 6-pounders, armed, etc.

Sept.1, long.50 w. fell in with the *St. Thomas* homeward
  bound fleet, of 19 sail under convoy of an 18-gun
  brig, and captured the ship *Diana*, with a cargo
  of rum, sugar and coffee, mounting ten 9 and 12
  pounders, etc. ordered her for this port;

also, Brig *Fame*, loaded with sugar and rum, mounting
  2 four pounders, etc. bound for Dublin – ordered
  her for this port;

Sept.6, fell in with ship *Commerce,* Watts, from
  Demarara for Glasgow, with a full cargo of rum,
  sugar, cotton, coffee, etc. mounting 14 nine and
  six pounders, armed with small arms, etc. boarded
  her under English colors and commenced an action
  which lasted 25 minutes when she struck ..."

("*Herald* Ship News," *Newburyport Herald*, Sept.
  25, 1812).

Maclay reported that Captain Coggleshall later remarked in his 1856 book,

> "The *Decatur* was a fine brig carrying fourteen guns and one hundred and sixty men, under Captain Nichols, of Newburyport, and was one of the most successful privateers from the Eastern ports".
>
> (Maclay, 1899, p. 309).

Captain Nichols had become a "Holy Terror" to the English commerce, often capturing vessels under the very guns of squadrons guarding the English coast. The courage and audacity of this young daredevil skipper procured him fame, as he became very familiar to the British Royal Navy.

> "Nichols became both the terror and the admiration of the British Navy"
>
> Chase, ca. 1920, p. 10

Chapter 7

Decatur Captured by the British

Captain Nichols had become a terror
to the enemy, and lest he should again escape,
they confined him to a wooden cage on deck
five feet by seven feet where they kept him
for 34 days like a lion, allowing not a person to
converse with him during the whole time.

Bayley & Jones
History of Marine Society of Newburyport,
1906, p. 371

The only reason assigned for the unusual
and cruel treatment of Captain Nichols, was
one which was most honorable to him – his
having retaken the *Alert* and his subsequent
activity during the War.

E. Vale Smith
History of Newburyport,
1854, p. 196

Death of Captain Nicholas Pierce

At home, when he left on the *Decatur* at the end of November 1812, he saw his father-in-law, Captain Nicholas Pierce, for the last time. Shortly after the *Decatur* left Newburyport on her second cruise, Captain Pierce, a merchant and mariner, died suddenly on December 20, 1812 (*Newburyport Herald*, December 22, 1812). Captain Pierce had become a father figure for young Nichols when he was growing up. Pierce was fifty years old when he died. He was living on Lime Street, where he moved after his house was destroyed in the Great Fire of Newburyport the previous year. His wife, Martha, had died fourteen years earlier in childbirth.

Pierce's eldest child, Lydia, had become the wife of Captain Nichols. She was twenty-nine years old at the time of her father's death. She had been fourteen years old when she lost her mother and was thrust into a parental role in the Pierce family, with five younger siblings.

Captain Nichols was not present to console his wife during her time of mourning from the loss of her father, as he was on a cruise, and was then captured and imprisoned for one and a half years.

Captain Pierce was known for having been in command of the schooner *Thankful* during the Revolutionary War in 1799 when it was captured by a French privateer. The ship was carried to Cayenne in French Guiana on the coast of South America, but Pierce returned safely back to Newburyport (Bayley & Jones, p. 342). Pierce was also the captain of a number of ships from Newburyport, including the brig *Beaver* (1786), brig *Mahitable* (1790), schooner *Rambler* (1796), brig *Dove* (1800), schooner *Amazon* (1802), and the schooner *Manhattan* (1802) (Historical Collection, Custom House Maritime Museum).

Captain Pierce was elected into the prestigious Newburyport Marine Society on November 28, 1793 (Bayley & Jones, p. 69). In addition, Pierce's father, Captain Nicholas Pierce Sr., was also a sea captain and was in command of the ship *Liberty* during the Revolutionary War.

Napoleon Wreaking Havoc in Europe

At the beginning of the War of 1812, Napoleon was continuing to march across the countries of Europe. However, the start of the

War of 1812 was the beginning of the end for Napoleon. The decisive Battle of Trafalgar in 1805 had prevented Napoleon from invading Britain, and he had to resort to land victories.

In June 1812, he now had many of the European countries aligned with him, and Napoleon raised a massive army of 500,000 troops. Ignoring the advice of his closest advisors, Napoleon ordered his enormous army into Russia. He prophesized that the war would be over in twenty days, but he spent three months making his way across Russia to the west. As the Russians retreated, they used a "scorched earth" tactic by burning all the crops and villages behind them, making them unusable by Napoleon's troops. The French soldiers were unable to sustain themselves on their own supplies. This tactic created starvation for thousands of French soldiers. After two months of the invasion, 150,000 soldiers were out of action ("Napoleon's Disastrous Invasion." 2012. www.history.com).

On September 7, 1812, Napoleon engaged in the Battle of Borodino. It became the bloodiest single-day action of the Napoleonic Wars. While Napoleon was victorious as the Russians finally retreated, there was a heavy cost of thousands of his men, including fifty officers ("Napoleon's Disastrous Invasion." 2012. www.history.com). A week later, on September 14, 1812, he marched into a deserted Moscow. A total of 275,000 people had fled the city! That night, a huge fire was started in Moscow, allegedly by Russian patriots, and in three days, two-thirds of the city was destroyed (ibid.).

Napoleon was then forced to lead his starving army out of Russia. Weather conditions became unbearable as they retreated. It was a disastrous defeat as the army suffered continual harassment from the merciless Russian Army. At one point, Napoleon burned a bridge leaving 10,000 of his army stragglers on the other side. With only 100,000 troops remaining, the army finally escaped Russia on December 24, 1912 ("Napoleon's Disastrous Invasion of Russia."

2012. www.history.com). This led to the eventual demise of Napoleon in Europe.

The invasion into Russia resulted in an 80 percent loss of his men, as 400,000 of his soldiers died. Within six months, Napoleon's army had become almost completely wiped out from freezing temperatures, food shortages, disease, desertion, and continuing Russian attacks. This became a significant turning point in the Napoleonic Wars, as the French Army was dramatically weakened ("Napoleon's Disastrous Invasion." 2012. www.history.com). The invasion of 500,000 men into Russia, the evacuation and burning of Moscow, and the loss of 400,000 men from Napoleon's French Army during their retreat from Russia became a catastrophic failure.

Napoleon's actions were creating considerable relief for Great Britain, who had been apprehensive about an invasion of England by the French. This was part of the turmoil and madness that was going on in the world at that time.

It is of note, contrary to popular belief, that the famous *1812 Overture* had no connection to the War of 1812 between the United States and Britain. Instead, it was written by Russian composer Tchaikovsky in 1880 to commemorate Russia's successful defense of its country against Napoleon's invading French Army in 1812. The invasion was a disastrous defeat for Napoleon's troops.

For the past forty years, the *1812 Overture* has been performed during countless United States Independence Day celebrations. This has been due largely to an exhilarating performance by the Boston Pops Orchestra in 1974 conducted by Arthur Fielder who used fireworks, cannons, and steeple-bell chimes in his presentation (Green. www.classicalmusic.about.com).

America Not Faring Well in War of 1812

At sea there had been some victories for America with the USS *Constitution* destroying the HMS *Guerriere* in August 1812, and the frigate USS *United States* defeating the British frigate HMS *Macedonian* on October 25. Later the British HMS *Java* was captured by the USS *Constitution* during a three-hour battle on December 29. The sloop USS *Wasp* captured the twenty-two-gun HMS *Frolic* on October 15, but then the seventy-four-gun British ship-of-the-line HMS *Poictiers* appeared on the scene and overwhelmed the *Wasp* (*Great Ships: The Frigates,* DVD, 1996. www.history.com).

However, the war was not going well to the north and west, as the United States was unprepared to protect its borders. The offensive actions of the United States failed in every effort to capture Canada. All attempts to invade Canada failed quite spectacularly (*The War of 1812*, 2011, Central Canadian Public TV).

There had been a strong desire by the war hawks for the United States to expand its boundaries beyond the Appalachian Mountains and along the American-Canadian border. Canada was in British hands and was one of the reasons for America going to war with Great Britain (*The War of 1812*, 2011, Central Canadian Public TV).

On July 17, 1812, a combined British and Native American force captured the Fort Mackinac Island from the United States. The fort is located at the northern tip of Michigan where Lakes Huron and Michigan meet. The fort was America's most remote outpost at the edge of Canada, and was of great strategic importance. The British needed Indian support to defend Upper Canada from an American attack. As long as the United States had control of Mackinac Island, they could prevent that British support (ibid.). "The narrow waterway was also the gateway to the lucrative northeast fur trade" (Rickard, 2007. www.historyofwar.org).

Lieutenant Porter Hanks, commander of Fort Mackinac, did not know that America had declared war against the British until he was attacked on July 17. News of the war had reached British Captain Charles Roberts, commander of nearby Fort St. Joseph, and using a combination of British and Indian forces, he captured Fort Mackinac from the United States. The Americans were taken by surprise, and the garrison troops were badly outnumbered. American Lieutenant Hanks surrendered the fort to the British without a fight. "Hanks and his men became some of the first official prisoners in a war they didn't even know had started" (Rickard, 2007. www.historyofwar.org).

President Madison had ordered Brigadier-General William Hull to invade Canada. After successfully crossing the Detroit River on July 12, General Hull was notified about the American defeat at Fort Mackinac on August 8, and he retreated back to Detroit. After the British capture of Fort Mackinac, General Hull ordered an evacuation of Fort Dearborn in what is now Chicago because Fort Dearborn was now in great danger. Deciding that Fort Dearborn was at risk, Hull ordered Captain Nathan Heald, garrison commander, to abandon the fort to the safety of Fort Wayne (Fort Dearborn Massacre, 2000. prairieghosts.com/dearborn.htm).

Heald delayed in carrying out Hull's orders but eventually led a group of about a hundred soldiers, militiamen, women, and children from the fort. However, on August 15, the column was attacked by five hundred Indians. The battle lasted for only fifteen minutes, as it was a total victory for the Indians. More than half of the American party was butchered, and the survivors were taken as prisoners. The Indians burned Fort Dearborn itself to the ground, and the massacre victims were left where they had fallen (Fort Dearborn Massacre, 2000. prairieghosts.com/dearborn.htm).

The next day, General Hull, "under pressure from a British attack, surrendered Detroit and his entire force" (Rickard, 2007). Hull felt that he could not hold out against a force of thousands of British troops, and he surrendered without a fight. The British had won control over the Michigan and Detroit territories. And the American public "was outraged by the brutality of the Fort Dearborn massacre and cried for revenge" (Fort Dearborn Massacre, www. prairieghosts.com/dearborn.html). These defeats became a startling and humiliating series of events for Americans. Hull was later court-martialed and sentenced to death, but his sentence was commuted by President Madison to dismissal from the army.

In addition, there were continuing problems with the Native Americans to the west. The Natives were strongly opposed to the United States expansion into their territory. The British were supplying firearms to the Native Americans along the western frontier. In November 1811, the Battle of Tippecanoe occurred between the United States and the Native American warriors. The American troops were led by General William Harrison, later to become President Harrison, and he ordered the burning of Prophetstown after the Natives had abandoned the town.

The Natives soon rebuilt their town, and frontier violence increased after the battle. After the defeats of the Americans from attempts to invade Canada, Native Americans continued to attack American settlements and military outposts along the western frontier (*The War of 1812*, 2011, Central Canadian Public TV).

Decatur Captured by *HMS Surprise*

In Newburyport, after remaining at home for two months, Captain Nichols was eager to set out on another voyage. He fitted out the *Decatur* again, reassembled his crew, and left Newburyport for a second voyage on November 24, 1812 (Currier I, 1906, p. 651). Nichols continued with his pursuit of British ships.

Things were quiet at first, but in December, just before Christmas, he captured the brig *Devonshire* (*Newburyport Herald*, December 25,

1812). He put a prize crew on board and sent her to France. A short while later, he took another vessel and also sent her to France. Both vessels had cargos of fish that were sold when they arrived in France (Currier I, 1906, p. 651).

Shortly thereafter, on January 9, 1813, he cut out the *Neptune,* a twelve-gun vessel from a large British convoy that was headed from London to Rio de Janeiro (Smith, 1854, p. 196). It was a desperate conflict, but the *Neptune* was compelled to surrender (Bayley & Jones, 1906, p. 249). Nichols sent a prize crew with her to Portland, Maine. Nichols sent a letter dated at sea with the prize-master reporting that the *Neptune* was a valuable ship with a full cargo of dry goods, brandy, wine, and jewelry. A pilot from Newburyport was summoned to Portland, and he brought the *Neptune* safely back to Newburyport (*Newburyport Herald*, February 19, 1813).

In the course of his second cruise with the *Decatur,* Nichols captured three prizes. He placed prize crews on those vessels and sent two to France and one to the United States. As a result, he had a greatly reduced crew on board the *Decatur* (*Newburyport Herald*, March 13, 1886).

However, on January 17, 1813, the *Decatur* was overtaken off the coast of Cape Verde near Africa by the British frigate *HMS Surprise* of thirty-eight guns (Wildes, 1864, p. 235). The *Decatur* was not in condition for sailing.

> "The *Decatur* had been to sea for some time and she
> was not in good sailing order"
> > "Memorabilia," *Newburyport Herald,*
> > > August 9, 1855

The ship and smaller crew were unprepared to sail and could not escape the enemy. Otherwise, Nichols would have avoided capture in his faster-sailing vessel.

Captain Sir Thomas Cochrane, age twenty-four, commanded the *HMS Surprise* (Wildes, 1864, p. 235). He was the son of Admiral Alexander Cochrane, who also fought in the War of 1812. In August 1814, Admiral Cochrane later landed the British troops that burned Washington, and he directed the bombardment of Fort McHenry in Baltimore.

The *HMS Surprise*, a newly constructed ship, sailed from England in December 1812 with young Captain Thomas Cochrane as the commander. The *Decatur* was the first prize that was taken by the *Surprise*.

A desperate struggle ensued between the *Decatur* and the *Surprise*. It was a gallant fight by the *Decatur*, but it was a hopeless one. The *Surprise* was a much larger and more heavily armed ship (Smith, 1854, p. 195). The frigate opened fire, and there was a lengthy and intense battle between the *Decatur* and the *Surprise*. After a few broadsides from the *Surprise*, Nichols' vessel became shattered, and there was "nothing left of the quarterdeck." Many men had been killed and wounded, and most of Nichols' men were disabled (Currier, 1909, p. 249). Nichols was compelled to yield to the superiority of his antagonist.

Nichols finally had to haul down his flag only when all of his men had been killed or wounded (*Newburyport Herald*, March 13, 1886). "There was not a man about him who was not wounded, nor a whole plank on that part of the deck where he stood" (Wildes, 1864, p. 235). A letter from First Lieutenant Nathaniel Swazy, of the *Decatur*, describes the battle:

> I, Nathaniel Swazy, Lieutenant of the brig *Decatur*, being influenced by pure motives of truth, come forward to favor the candid public with a true statement ... On the 16th of January 1813, the brig *Decatur*, commanded by Capt. Nichols, was captured

by his Majesty's frigate *Surprise* commanded by Thomas Cochran in lat. 13.44 N., long 49, W. After the *Surprise* had hailed four times, being distinctly and correctly answered every time, she fired a broadside and five rounds of musket balls from fifty-seven marines, into the *Decatur*, which killed one man and wounded seven.

First Lieutenant Nathaniel Swazy
Newburyport Herald,
September 23, 1905

Nichols on Board the *Surprise*

Nichols hailed that he had surrendered, but the *Surprise* still fired another broadside at pistol range into the *Decatur*. This made Nichols furious (Wildes, 1864, p. 235). When the angered Nichols arrived on board the *Surprise,* Commander Cochrane met him and said,

"I'll take your sword, sir."

"Not by a damned sight," Nichols blazed, "unless you take it through your body."

He quickly drew his sword, and the captain and crew of the *Surprise* immediately tensed up, anticipating a battle with Nichols, but he swiftly threw the sword into the sea with disgust (Chase, ca. 1920, p. 10).

Lloyd's Register reported on Tuesday, March 9, 1813,

> "The *Decatur,* American Privateer is taken by the frigate *Surprise*, and carried to Antigua."

On March 19, 1813, The *Newburyport Herald* also reported the capture:

"The privateer, *Decatur,* Nichols, of this port, was taken on her cruise from Cape de Verde, where she had watered, by the British frigate *Surprise*, commanded by Sir Thomas Cochrane, a new vessel on her first passage, and the *Decatur* her first prize."

In a letter from one of the officers of the privateer *Decatur*, written to his brother in Boston and dated "Bridgetown, Barbados, February 15, 1813," he described the capture:

"This is to inform you that I am a prisoner of war. We were taken on the 17th of Jan. by the *Surprise* frigate, commanded by Sir Thomas Cochrane. She fired 40 small arms into us, and seventeen 18-pound shot: killed one man and took off the leg of Mr. Foote, and wounded several. We had taken three prizes, two of which we sent to France and one home".

Newburyport Herald March 19, 1813

Nichols in Barbados

The *Decatur* was then taken to Barbados and arrived there nine days later. On the way to Barbados, the officers and crew of the *Decatur* had to sleep on top of the deck of the *HMS Surprise* in freezing weather, and they were given only short rations. When they arrived in port, they were taken to a damp dungeon beneath the town jail and held by a brutal guard (Chase, 1864, p. 10).

However, Commander Cochrane of the *Surprise* admitted Nichols to parole in Barbados out of respect for his bravery during the battle at sea (Wildes, 1864, p. 285). Nichols was able to walk the streets of

Barbados, and was often pointed out on the street by others (Chase, ca. 1920, p. 10).

There were a number of other American vessels in Barbados that had been captured, and the *Decatur's* name and that of Captain Nichols were on the lips of his admiring countrymen. He was frequently spoken of in Barbados (Wildes, 1864, p. 236), especially about the story of Nichols recapture of the *Alert* before the war and his escape from the British authorities in England. His story had spread throughout the British fleet,

> "His daring deeds during the war on the *Decatur* were told from vessel to vessel until the British dreaded the very thought of the *Decatur* … Nichols' name had become the scourge of the seas for the British Navy".
> "Memorabilia," *Newburyport Herald*,
> August 9, 1855.

Nichols had become both the 'terror and admiration' of the British Royal Navy. Wildes reported:

> "Seamen of that period, well remember how the name and deeds of Captain Nichols rendered him as a living terror at the time".
> Wildes, 1864, p. 285

Nichols Imprisoned in Cage on Deck

All of his captures and escapes before his capture on the *Decatur* occurred before the War of 1812 when he was a merchant mariner. The War had continued for six months when Nichols was captured on the *Decatur*, and his imprisonment continued for the next 18 months.

An unfortunate turn of luck occurred for Nichols in Barbados. Shortly after his capture, things changed dramatically for Captain Nichols when the *HMS Vestal* arrived in Barbados with young Captain Maurice Berkeley, still as the master. A year and a half earlier, before the war in July 1811, Captain Berkeley captured the *Alert* following the incident with the *HMS Semiramis,* where Nichols had retaken his own vessel.

Nichols had been captured by the *Semiramis,* but Nichols and his mate had overcome nine British prize crewmembers of the *Semiramis* to recapture his own ship. Nichols set most of the captured crew off in a long boat to reach the coast of France, where they were captured and imprisoned by the French.

A few days later, the *Alert* was taken again by Captain Berkeley in the *HMS Vestal.* Nichols attempted to deceive the British commander, but it didn't work.

Since that time, Berkeley had remained angry at Nichols, not only for recapturing the *Alert* but also from Nichols' attempt to outwit him. Berkeley was even more resentful about Nichols having escaped after he was sent to England and confined in Portsmouth. A proclamation for the apprehension and arrest of Nichols had been issued because of his escape from the Marine guards in England.

When he arrived in Barbados, Berkley received information that Nichols was on parole, and he immediately ordered Nichols to be arrested. While Captain Cochrane had allowed Nichols to be on parole in Barbados because of his bravery during the recent battle between the *Decatur* and the *Surprise,* Captain Berkeley used his influence to have Nichols arrested and placed in close custody.

Berkeley took this opportunity to become vindictive and get even with Nichols. He was seeking revenge with Nichols because he was,

> "The privateersman who had the presumption to
> recapture a prize of His Britannic Majesty's frigate".
>
> > Maclay, 1899, p. 311

Nichols was also being accused of murder of the British sailors from the incident on the Alert where he "set his prisoners adrift in a long boat". Much later, it was discovered that the British sailors had actually survived. They had been captured by French soldiers in the long boat Nichols had provided them, and they were then imprisoned by the French

Knowing Nichols ability to escape, Berkeley had a cage constructed on the deck of a prison-ship anchored in the harbor. It was built on top of the quarterdeck and was five feet wide and seven feet long. Nichols was confined there for thirty-four days in the winter and was not allowed to communicate with anyone except his guard. He had to not only endure the blazing Caribbean sun, but also suffer the elements of the weather. He was kept under constant guard day and night, and he was left isolated and alone. "It was demeaning and humiliating to be locked away from any human contact" (Wildes, 1864, p. 235).

He received this cruel punishment because of the revenge of young Berkeley. He justified the cruel treatment because of Nichols history of escapes. He wanted to severely punish Nichols and was fearful that Nichols would try to escape again (*Newburyport Daily News,* December 17, 1948). The lengthy imprisonment of Nichols in England was the direct result of Berkeley's vengeance.

Chase provided the report from the *Essex Register* of Salem that made this comment about the treatment of Captain Nichols:

> "Thus, are Americans treated by British savages.
> And while Captain Nichols is thus barbarously
> treated, English prisoners are here used as tenderly
> as brethren. Surely this calls aloud for retaliation.

Hostages, (naval commanders, if possible) ought to be detained in closed confinement, to answer for whatever may befall Captain Nichols. Painful as retaliation, it is a duty"

Chase, ca. 1920, p. 11

Nichols Transferred to Prison in England

While he was confined in the cage, Nichols was visited by an older commander of a British seventy-four-gun ship. He asked Nichols why he was being confined so seriously. Nichols explained the circumstances about the *Alert* and the *Decatur* to the commander, and the English officer said to Nichols that he had committed no crime.

"On the contrary, such conduct should have given you the command of a frigate. Had you been in the English service, you would have been so rewarded".

"Memorabilia," Newburyport Herald,
August 9, 1855

Through the interest of this British commander, Nichols was removed to the frigate *HMS Tribune* on April 23, 1813, and sent to England. The only reasons for the unusual and cruel treatment of Captain Nichols were having retaken the *Alert,* his subsequent activity during the war, and the fear that he would escape again (Smith, 1854, p. 196).

The story of his confinement in the cage was retold many times on the streets of Barbados, but the cage was just the beginning of his traumatic experiences during his incarceration.

While Nichols was on his way to England, being held in chains and solitary confinement, his crew from the *Decatur* returned safely to Newburyport. In a notice on March 19, 1813, the *Newburyport Herald* announced that the crew had arrived back in the United States at Providence, Rhode Island, on the cartel ship *Perseverance* from Barbados. Their release was two months after the capture of the *Decatur*, but Captain Nichols would not be released for another year.

Chapter 8

Imprisonment on *Nassau* Prison-Ship

For bravery and daring he has had but few equals;
it was impossible to have a superior, for probably he
never knew such a sensation as fear in his life. It is
an absolute stranger to him.
"Memorabilia "*Newburyport Herald*,
August 1, 1855

"They could kill Bill, but they couldn't scare him."
Nichols' wife, Lydia, upon hearing of his cruel
treatment by the English.
Newburyport Daily News, June 23, 1905

It is said that he never knew what fear was.
Sidney M. Chase
"Captain William Nichols
and The Privateer *Decatur*"
ca. 1920, p. 14

When Nichols arrived in England, he was still regarded as a criminal. He had been held in chains and in solitary confinement during his voyage to England. He was then again chained and held in close confinement on the heavily armed *Nassau* prison-ship in Chatham harbor. The HMS *Nassau* had been constructed in 1740 in Chatham and had been converted into a prison hulk in 1767 (Phillips, 2007). When Nichols was imprisoned on the *Nassau*, the vessel was almost fifty years old and was decaying and rotting in the harbor.

Captain Nichols was being put on trial for murder, and the British "had a strong desire to hang this troublesome captive" (Hurd, 1888, p. 1736). No records are available of Nichols' experience at Chatham, and he was always reticent to talk about his imprisonment (Chase, ca. 1920, p. 11). While he remained silent about his incarceration, the conditions he experienced on the British prison-ship were quite harsh.

British Invasion of America

While in prison during 1813 and early 1814, Nichols had limited knowledge of what was happening with the war. He became aware of some events only when sailors arrived at the prison from having their ships captured by the British.

The British had been ravaging towns along the eastern coast of the United States. Rear Admiral George Cockburn commanded a fleet of British frigates with orders from Rear Admiral Sir Alexander Cochrane that stated:

> You are hereby directed to obliterate the ports and harbors in the most strict and rigorous manner according to the usages of war ... to capture and destroy trade and shipping off Baltimore and particularly in the Potomac, York, and James Rivers ... and to destroy and lay waste such towns as you may find assailable.
>
> Rear Admiral George Cockburn
>
> 2012. www.destinationsouthernmaryland.com

Given these strong orders, Cockburn then wreaked havoc in his invasion of small towns along the United States coastline from Delaware to North Carolina, "destroying property of the defenseless citizens with cruel and useless barbarity" (*War of 1812*, 2011, Central Canadian Public TV). Americans were horrified and became panic-stricken as their countryside was devastated. Many defenseless towns were raided, and the British expected victory with their orders to "destroy and lay waste." During that time, American troops were a thousand miles away, fighting land battles with the British-Canadian and Native-American forces. Matters were becoming desperate for the United States.

Prison Hulks

Throughout his imprisonment, Nichols was chained on the prison hulk *Nassau*. Abell describes prison hulks as "one of the most beautiful objects of man's handiwork that was deformed into a hideous monstrosity" (Abell, 1914, p. 37). The hulks lay like gigantic black coffins in the harbor. It was part of England's "diabolic policy to kill or incapacitate prisoners of war" by neglect and ill treatment (Abell, 1914, p. 43).

As prisons became overcrowded in England from the Napoleonic Wars, the British government started using old navy vessels as "floating prisons." Prison hulks were vessels that had become unseaworthy, and they were salvaged as prisons ("Prison Hulks," 2010). "The British Parliament authorized the use of prison-ships for a two-year period in 1776, and they continued to house prisoners for 82 years!" ("Nineteenth Century Justice," 2006). Some of the most notorious hulks were moored at Chatham ("Incredible Hulks." 2012. www.urbanghostsmedica.com).

Insufficient food and clothing and long, weary hours of enforced idleness and mental neglect made the British prison hulks "hell upon water" (Abell, p. 37). Those condemned to the hulks had lives of long, unbroken suffering. There was ongoing sickness and a high rate of mortality. "From 800 to1200 prisoners of war were heaped together on a prison-ship and became buried alive in those floating tombs" (Abell, 1914, p. 41).

A letter from an American prisoner on board a prison-ship to his mother in Philadelphia demonstrates the cruelty with which the British treated the Americans:

> Myself and a great many of my brave countrymen have been suffering every deprivation on board of this old prison ship for 12 months … The provisions are scanty and of the very worst kind. We have not a second shirt to our backs and those we have on mostly in tatters. We are used with as much barbarity as possible … We are hardly allowed to say our lives are our own.
>
> Samuel Davis
> "On Board of a Prison Ship,"
> March 10, 1814

Prison hulks held the worst offenders and were intended to be a "terror to evil-doers!" Conditions were extremely harsh, as prisoners were kept below deck in cramped conditions, and many were often sent to solitary confinement below the ship's waterline. Violence and cruel punishments by the British guards were condoned ("Prison Hulks," 2010). At night, prisoners were chained to their bunks to prevent them from escaping ("Nineteenth Century Justice." 2006. www.vcp.e2bn.org).

Prison-ships were "rife with death, disease, and despair" (Harris, 2012). Hygiene conditions were so poor that outbreaks of disease spread quickly. Typhoid and cholera were common, and there was a high death rate among the prisoners ("Nineteenth Century Justice." 2006. www.vcp.e2bn.org).

Conditions on prison hulks were far worse than "regular prisons." Doctors' reports indicated a significant difference between the poor health of prisoners on hulks and those incarcerated at regular prisons (Druett, 2010). Maritime historians estimate that 13,000 prisoners died on British hulks between 1803 and 1814 from neglect, starvation, and diseases (Harris, 2012).

These were the conditions that Nichols experienced on the *Nassau* prison-ship at Chatham, England. Nichols remained in chains during his confinement so that he would not escape. Given his history of escapes, the British were apprehensive that he would attempt another escape. It is a wonder that he survived his seventeen months of imprisonment. "Prison life became a matter of survival" (*War of 1812*, 2011, Central Canadian Public TV). In order to survive, Nichols had to be resilient, tough, and persevering.

Letter to Captain Nichols from Nathaniel Pierce

Nathaniel Pierce, son of Captain Nicholas Pierce, was William Nichols' younger brother-in-law. At age sixteen in 1811, prior to the War of 1812, Nathaniel was captured by the British and imprisoned on the HMS prison-ship *Roy William* in Portsmouth, England. He was suspected of being born in England and being a deserter from the British Royal Navy. He was being held for impressment into the British Royal Navy.

On February 19, 1812, Captain Nicholas Pierce wrote a letter to his son Nathaniel while he was imprisoned on the *Roy William.*

NOTE: See Letter in Appendix E

Knowing that the British authorities would screen the letter before giving it to Nathaniel, Captain Pierce made it clear that Nathaniel was a native of the United States. He made reference to Nathaniel's mother, his brothers and sisters, and his friends in his hometown of Newburyport. He used such phrases as "you are American born," "keeping you from coming home," "clarifying your nativity," and "returning to your own country of America" to indicate that Nathaniel was American-born and was not British. Nathaniel was eventually released and returned home to Newburyport.

On December 1, 1813, Nathaniel, then eighteen years old, wrote a letter to his brother-in-law, Captain Nichols, who was imprisoned on the *Nassau* prison-ship. Nathaniel knew what Nichols was experiencing, as he himself had been held a prisoner on a British prison-ship two years earlier.

NOTE: See Letter in Appendix F

It was a relief for Nichols to hear from Nathaniel's letter that his family and friends in Newburyport were well. His anxiety was also somewhat alleviated when he heard that the crew of the *Decatur* had returned safely to Newburyport. The letter was comforting to him, as he previously had no knowledge of what was happening at home in Newburyport.

However, he had a sharp pain of loss when he read Nathaniel's postscript on the back of his letter about the death of his father-in-law, Captain Nicholas Pierce. It saddened him to hear that Captain Pierce had died shortly after Nichols left Newburyport on the *Decatur* in November 1812. The Pierce family lived next door to the Nichols, and Captain Pierce had become a father figure for Nichols after his father died, when William was only three years old (Nathaniel Pierce, 1813).

Nathaniel also informed Nichols that efforts were being made to have him released from prison through the exchange of two British captains. It was then that Nichols became aware that the United States was holding two British shipmasters in close confinement as retaliation for the cruel treatment of Nichols. He could then feel some degree of hope for eventual release and vindication for the treatment he had suffered by the British.

Nathaniel Pierce's Journal at Dartmoor

Less than a year after his letter to Captain Nichols, Nathaniel himself, then age nineteen, was captured and taken to Dartmoor Prison in England. He was imprisoned toward the end of the war, but he remained in confinement for more than seven months until well after the war ended.

Nathaniel was captured in November 1814 and was not released until July 1815. The war had ended in December 1814. Captain Nichols was released in June 1814, and he was exchanged for two British sea captains prior to Nathaniel's capture and imprisonment. Upon hearing about his brother-in-law's capture and imprisonment, Captain Nichols became even more angry and resentful at the British and wanted to seek some revenge and retaliation for Nathaniel's capture, as well as for his own incarceration by the British.

During the time that Nathaniel was at Dartmoor, he wrote a daily journal that demonstrated how the British were treating American prisoners. His forty-eight-page handwritten journal is located in the War of 1812 Collection, Peabody Essex Museum, Salem, Massachusetts. His journal recounted his capture by the British:

> "We were captured by his Britannic Majesty's Ship *Bulwark* of 74 guns rate but mounting 88 in all. When I was taken onboard this ship, I found to my great surprise 137 unfortunate Americans... including two prize crews belonging to the Privateer *Harpy* of Portsmouth, N.H., master Captain William Nichols. Among them I found a number of my old acquaintances and shipmates"
>
> Nathaniel Pierce Journal, 1814, p. 1

Nathaniel was transferred from Halifax to England on the frigate *HMS Penelope*, then was transported under heavy guard to Dartmoor. At the prison, Nathaniel discovered two prize crews from Newburyport that were also in prison. The crews had been on British vessels that were captured by Captain Nichols, but were then recaptured by the British and taken as prisoners.

The descriptions in Pierce's journal provide some insight about what the conditions in prison were like for himself, Captain Nichols, and other seamen from Newburyport. His descriptions relate what he experienced while incarcerated in a British prison.

Pierce was held in Prison No. 7, which became his home away from home. He also discovered many fellow Newburyporters at Dartmoor. He provided a description of the conditions at Dartmoor as he explained in his journal,

> "This dreaded bastille held some 6000 prisoners, and there was a grim foreboding atmosphere that pervaded Dartmoor".
>
> Nathaniel Pierce Journal, 1814, p. 2

Shortly after Nathaniel's capture and imprisonment, the prisoners became aware that the Ghent Treaty of Peace had been signed. "On December 29 (1814) that good news of peace arrived. We received the joyful news of which makes great rejoicing amongst the prisoners" (Nathaniel Pierce Journal, 1814, p. 3).

Pierce and the other inmates expected immediate release, but that did not happen, as war lingered on after peace was declared. Their confinement continued into the new year with very unhealthy conditions. On February 11, 1815, Nathaniel wrote,

> "Never was there a place I believe so disagreeable and as unhealthy as this. Great numbers die daily

with the smallpox and other disorders; they average about five a day.

"But we are in hopes shortly to be landed on that Blessed Eden, the American shore, where we can enjoy our friends, health and liberty as we did once before"

Nathaniel Pierce Journal, 1815, p. 7

Notice of the ratification of the peace treaty by the United States arrived at Dartmoor on March 21, 1815. Prison authorities assured the prisoners that all of them would soon be released, but few believed it. Discouragement and discontent permeated the prison as the passing weeks produced only delays in discharging the captives. Impatience turned to resignation, and Pierce saw no likelihood of action for his release. Even though peace had been declared, the British were unwilling to immediately release the prisoners at Dartmoor.

On April 6, a riot occurred at Dartmoor, and many prisoners were either killed or wounded when the guards turned on them with gunfire. Life dragged on for Pierce as groups of only two or three hundred men were periodically released. He became discouraged when he learned that he must wait for the last draft.

Finally, when two thousand French prisoners arrived on July 2, notice also came that he would be released. His imprisonment had continued for six months after peace was declared. Nathaniel jotted down,

"At 12 noon it was cried around that 360 men would be called out tomorrow, and this draft takes me. There are now ... 2000 Frenchmen entering the gates, mostly soldiers. End pleasant and ends this journal for want of paper. Tomorrow I leave this cursed depot".

Nathaniel Pierce Journal, 1815, p. 4

Such was the experience of Nathaniel Pierce at Dartmoor. The conditions were not unlike those he had previously experienced during his imprisonment on a prison-ship. They were similar to what Captain Nichols had endured while on board the *Nassau* prison-ship. As bad as conditions were at Dartmoor Prison, they were worse on the prison-ship at the Chatham Dock where Nichols was incarcerated.

One can wonder whether the long delay in Nathaniel's release was related to the fact of Nathaniel being the brother-in-law of Captain Nichols, the Holy Terror. Was it retribution by the British for the two-for-one prisoner exchange that had taken place earlier with Captain Nichols, in June 1814? Or were the British still smarting from the significant damage that Nichols achieved in his naval encounters with British vessels?

Captain Nichols Imprisonment

Nichols was kept as a criminal and held in chains. He was accused of murder and sentenced to death. Nichols thought that he would soon be executed by hanging (Baily & Jones, p. 371). He expected to be transferred to the nearby Maidstone Prison, where most executions took place. Maidstone was constructed in 1811 and had become the normal place for executions in England ("Maidstone Prison." www. capitalpunishmentuk.org/maidstone.html).

After several months of imprisonment, Nichols and other prisoners were called together. They were expecting that the death sentence was going to be carried out. Nichols was asked,

> "If you were to be released, would you engage in the war again?"

Nichols defiantly responded, "Yes, as soon as I can get a vessel, and if I can do it in no other way, then I will enter the American service as a common seaman"
Newburyport Herald, Aug. 9, 1955

The *Newburyport Herald* issue of June 23, 1905, published an article reviewing the circumstances of Nichols' inhumane treatment titled,

"Captain Bill Nichols: Bold Newburyport Privateer Who Worried John Bull"

The article related how Nichols was cruelly treated by the British "because he had played sad havoc with British vessels … he was much sought after by the enemy, who finally captured him" (*Newburyport Herald,* June 23, 1905).

Nichols had endured a terrible imprisonment. He was subjected to ongoing cruel treatment and brutal torture in both Barbados and Chatham (*Newburyport Herald*, March 13, 1866). Initially, he was held in a cage constructed for him on the deck of a prison-ship in Barbados locked away from human contact. He was then transferred to England, where he remained on a prison-ship at Chatham and held in chains for the duration of his imprisonment. His incarceration was a severe and traumatic experience for him. What he experienced was more than anyone should have to bear, but he remained resolute and determined to survive his ordeal.

Battle Fatigue

Many men who have experienced combat or who have been prisoners of war have witnessed death and have been threatened with death themselves. These men who have been exposed to extreme trauma frequently develop symptoms of an acute stress reaction. They suffer what has been known as "shell shock" or "battle fatigue" ("Battle Fatigue," www.medicinenet.com). As a result, these men feel a sense of helplessness and ongoing stress long after their traumatic experiences.

They persistently re-experience the horror of the traumatic events, and they become disorganized, agitated, depressed, or aggressive in their behavior. Most men continue to have recollections of the horrendous, anxiety-producing events from their incarceration and wartime activities. Many men also develop a guilt complex for having survived when others have died (*Diagnostic and Statistical Manual of Mental Disorders,* 2013, p. 424).

These men make a deliberate effort to avoid any thoughts that might be associated with their trauma. They will persistently avoid triggers that may make them recall the events. There is also a numbing of responsiveness in their interactions with other people (*Diagnostic and Statistical Manual*, 2013, p. 424). The battles linger on for these men; they are still at war long after peace has been declared.

While many men become overwhelmed by the high level of anxiety, there are some that thrive and prevail over the symptoms of an extreme stress reaction. Captain Nichols chose not to recall his past trauma. He was an intelligent man who could not allow his emotions to cloud his judgment in naval encounters. While on the *Harpy*, he made an effort to shut out any recollections of his cruel treatment as a prisoner of war. He remained committed to perform his duties as a shipmaster by not becoming aware of his thoughts and feelings. Instead, Nichols was able to suppress his anger and anxiety into a determination to avenge his cruel treatment by the British. This emotional numbness became adaptive for him. After the war, he avoided any discussion that might remind him of the trauma he had experienced.

Nichols Released from Prison

Captain Nichols was finally released from prison on June 24, 1814, after seventeen months in captivity. He was not able to immediately obtain passage home, but he was eventually able to reach Boston on the cartel ship *Saratoga.* He finally returned home to his family and friends in Newburyport in September 1814.

A year before Nichols was discharged, the crew of the *Decatur* had been released and arrived safely back in the United States at Providence, Rhode Island, on the cartel ship *Providence* (Smith, 1854, p. 197). The *Decatur* itself was taken to England where the mast and rigging were removed, and his vessel was then used as a prison-ship (Wildes, 1864, p. 236).

After the war, while he shared his naval encounters with some close friends and relatives, he remained reluctant to divulge his experiences of torture and cruel punishment in prison. He suppressed it all and pushed it out of his mind. Nowhere in all of the writings about Captain Nichols is there a narrative of what he experienced while in the cage at Barbados or on the *Nassau* prison-ship, with the exception of the one incident when he was asked about engaging in the war again.

Talking about his imprisonment would have triggered unwanted recollections and emotional reactions to the incidents of his traumatic incarceration. He chose to avoid such memories, and he persisted with his silence. People really do not want to know about the horrors and crimes of imprisonment during a war, and many would not believe what they heard about prison life in Britain during the War of 1812.

Chapter 9

Prisoner Exchange: Nichols for Two Shipmasters

The *Decatur* was known and feared
wherever an English flag was spread to
the breeze ... For the evidence of, we have
only to cite the severe treatment to which
her bold Commander was subjected when
he fell into the hands of the enemy.

Wildes, 1864, p. 232

Nothing daunted Captain Nichols for all
the many months as an exile and prisoner.

E. Vale Smith
History of Newburyport, 1854, p. 196

War of Words: Mason vs. Barclay

As Captain Nichols was awaiting the scaffold, there was another battle occurring between the governments of the United States and Great Britain regarding the fate of Nichols. It was not a battle on the high seas; instead, it was a battle of words. Starting in June 1813, five months after Nichols had been captured and imprisoned, some sharp and terse correspondence transpired between the Esq. **US Commissary General of Prisoners John Mason,** and the **Britannic Majesty's Agent for Prisoners of War Colonel Thomas Barclay, Esq.**

Commissioner Mason was based in Washington DC, while Colonel Barclay was located in nearby New York City. Their communications with each other could take place in a relatively rapid manner because of the proximity of their offices on this continent. They did not have to wait for long, time-consuming journeys across the Atlantic for their correspondence. Their dialog regarding Captain Nichols extended for nearly a year until April 1814.

The correspondence between Mason and Barclay is recorded in the "Documents, Legislative and Executive of the Congress of the United States," *American State Papers,* Vol. III.

NOTE: See Correspondence Excerpts In Appendices G, H, I, J, K

While Nichols was being held on the *Nassau* prison-ship in Chatham, he was not aware of the charged correspondence between Mason and Barclay. Nichols was also initially unaware of the order from President Madison to hold two British shipmasters in retaliation for Nichols' cruel and inhumane treatment.

President Madison's Order

In June 1813, Commodore William Bainbridge of the United States Navy wrote a letter to the Honorable William Jones, Secretary of the United States Navy, in Washington regarding the "inhuman treatment Captain Nichols received from the British government at Barbados" (*American State Papers*, p. 648). Bainbridge was requesting that action be taken regarding Nichols' imprisonment. He also enclosed a deposition from Mr. James Foot, an officer on board the *Decatur* when it was captured.

NOTE: See Transcribed Letter from Bainbridge and Foot's Deposition in Appendix G.

In his affidavit, Foot described the capture of the *Decatur* and the inhumane circumstances regarding Captain Nichols. He related how Nichols was held in close confinement in a cage on the deck of a prison-ship in Barbados.

President Madison ordered that two captains of British ships who were prisoners of war in the United States be held in close confinement for the cruel treatment of Nichols. The letter from Commodore Bainbridge and Foot's affidavit had indeed reached the president from US Navy Secretary Jones.

On June 21, 1813, Commissioner General Mason wrote a letter to Mr. James Prince, the United States Marshall of Massachusetts, authorizing him, by command of the president, to hold two captains of British ships in close confinement.

NOTE: See U.S. Commissioner Mason's Transcribed Letter to U.S. Marshall Prince, Appendix H

The British government was informed by Mason that the officers' lives would be made to answer for the life of Nichols (Wildes, 1864, p. 235). This order was in retaliation for the way in which Captain Nichols was being treated by the British. (Commissioner Mason's letter is transcribed in Appendix H).

As Nichols was imprisoned on a Chatham prison hulk and was awaiting the scaffold, he was not initially aware of President Madison's decision to hold two British officers. He only knew that he had been wrongfully accused of murder and that he was waiting to be hanged. It was not until six months later in December 1813, when he received Nathaniel Pierce's letter, that he became aware of the president's order.

British Response to Madison's Order

Two weeks later on July 3, 1813, British Colonel Barclay replied to Mason and objected to the retaliatory order from President Madison. He was indignant as he explained that he had only been recently informed of the president's order as a retaliatory measure for the treatment of Captain Nichols. He seemed insulted that he had been made aware of the close confinement of Captains Barss and Woodworth only through a local New York newspaper. Barclay indicated that he was not aware of Nichols' confinement, and he provided his understanding of the particulars regarding the incidents with Captain Nichols.

Agent Barclay reviewed the *Alert* incident that occurred before the War of 1812, but some of his information was incorrect. He described the capture of the *Decatur*, but he totally omitted any reference to the episode of Nichols being held in a cage on deck for a month. Instead, Barclay referred back to Nichols' recapture of the *Alert,* as he explained, "Nichols was sent to England as a prisoner for trial, because he was under suspicion of his having murdered, or otherwise made away with the British seamen … After recapturing the *Alert,* Nichols compelled the British officer and the crew to go into a small boat of the *Alert* and turned them adrift at sea" (*American State Papers*, p. 647).

British Agent Barclay Threatens Counter Measures

Having not received an immediate reply from US Commissioner Mason, Colonel Barclay wrote another letter that bristled with anger. He made a point of reviewing some agreed-upon prisoner of war rules, preceded by his statement, "I beg leave to submit the following remarks, which, as they are founded on general principles, I flatter myself will meet your and the President's concurrence ... I have waited some time in the hope of receiving your answer ... I pray your early answer" (*American State Papers,* p. 647).

His letter reviewed the occurrences in Barbados with Nichols, but again, he omitted any reference to the cage in which Nichols had been confined. Barclay explained that the Captain of the *Vestal* was justified in having Nichols held in isolation because of the crimes he had committed before the war in 1811 as captain of the *Alert.*

He indicated that at the time, there was a proclamation for the apprehension and arrest of Nichols because of his escape when he was in England. British Agent Barclay then insisted in his letter that Captains Barss and Woodworth be released immediately. He also threatened that a counter measure might be adopted by Great Britain:

> "I trust retaliatory measures will not be used by the
> United States ... if they are, the inevitable consequence
> will be, that similar measures must be adopted on the
> part of His Majesty".
>
> British Col. Thomas Barclay,
American State Papers, p. 648

US Commissioner Mason's Angry Reply

Commissioner Mason responded in a sharp manner to Barclay, saying, "From the tenor of your letter ... it is proper to state that retaliatory orders do not originate with me; they come from a higher authority" (*American State Papers*, p. 648).

In his letter, Mason explained that two British captains were in close confinement to be held for the safety and the treatment of

Captain William Nichols. Mason then described his understanding of the events in Barbados:

> Captain William Nichols, who, while a prisoner of war on parole at Barbados during last spring, had been seized and inhumanely confined in a small hole on board a prison-ship, and barred from all communication for more than a month.
>
> He was then sent to England in close confinement. He was confined for no offence, other than that he was accused, by some of the British officers, of having recaptured an American vessel under his command, taken from him by a British armed vessel before the war.
>
> General John Mason, US Agent
> *American State Papers*, p. 648

US Commissioner Mason took strong issue with the veracity of the information that British Agent Barclay had explained about the incidents in Barbados: "You have taken a wide field in your recent letter, relative to the cases of Captains Nichols, Barss, and Woodworth … You have, however, given what you suppose, as you say, to be the circumstances of Captain Nichols case. I will remind you that you have more than once been mistaken on information obtained from irregular sources" (*American State Papers*, p. 648).

British Allege Sailors Refute Cage Incident

In subsequent correspondence, British Agent Barclay complained about the United States holding two British prisoners of war who had not been charged with committing any crime. However, he said that Nichols was being held because of a charge of murder. Barclay explained,

> "Captain Nichols, on regaining the possession of the *Alert*, put the prize-master and seamen in a small boat, and committed them to the mercy of the winds and waves. It is for this act, principally, he is sent to England to be tried"
>
> British Col. Thomas Barclay,
> *American State Papers*, p. 649

British Agent Barclay then introduced a totally new aspect to the Nichols case. He indicated that he had depositions from two sailors of the *Decatur* who were prisoners with Captain Nichols on board the prison-ship. These two men, George Thomas and John Williams, both alleged contradictory statements about the cage incident and Nichols' treatment in Barbados. Barclay related that the two men swear that, "Nichols was not inhumanely confined in a small hole on board the prison-ship. He had a state room in the ship with use of the cabin and quarter-deck" He explained that, "They never heard either Captain Nichols nor any other person complain of the treatment Captain Nichols received" (*American State Papers*, p. 649).

A month later in October 1813, US Commissioner Mason countered Barclay's allegations. He strongly defended Nichols by reminding Barclay of the previous affidavit by Lt. James Foot. He also enclosed with his letter a statement from Benjamin Pierce, owner of both the *Alert* and the *Decatur*, in order to rebut the statements that Barclay made about the Nichols' case. **(See Appendix I)** Mason stated emphatically:

> The commanders of British frigates HMS *Semiramis* and HMS *Vestal*, who made a prize of the *Alert*, brought no charge against him before the war. As

to the treatment of the English crew, from whom he bravely recovered his vessel, he did all that could have been expected in the unjustifiable situation. **He supplied the English crew abundantly in a good Boat, on a smooth sea, in sight of the French coast, on which they safely landed.**

General John Mason, US Agent
American State Papers, p. 650

NOTE: See Transcribed Letter from Benjamin Pierce in Appendix I

Toward the end of his letter to Agent Barclay, Commissioner Mason denounced the allegation of the two seamen who had denied the inhumane treatment of Nichols in Barbados: "All that Mr. Foot has stated was previously confirmed to me by declarations, made in person, by several officers of American vessels, who were on the spot, prisoners at the time in Barbados ... The affidavit of the two seamen, of which you have become possessed of, will be found to be proven incorrect" (*American State Papers*, p. 651). Mason concluded his letter by indicating that the United States would continue to hold Captains Barss and Woodworth.

James Foot, prize-master of the *Decatur,* reacted strongly when he heard of the statements made by the two seamen. He was outraged. These two men were trying to invalidate his deposition made in May 1813. He wrote a strong statement that was published in the *Newburyport Herald* on January 10, 1814, and also in the *Boston Patriot*, reaffirming his previous affidavit:

The deposition was made without the name of the magistrate before whom it was taken. The deposition did not bear the slight semblance of legality: it was not sworn to, nor was any magistrate present. Others have selected for their base purposes, two simple seamen from the crew of the *Decatur,* who have put their mark on a piece that has been published. They state that my means of information regarding Captain Nichols' situation was not so good as theirs ... It seems that some unprincipled persons have made tools of these fellows, at the expense of truth.

> Lt. James Foot, Prize-Master of *Decatur*
> *Newburyport Herald,* January 10, 1814

The *Newburyport Herald* article that reported Foot's response concluded with a statement by First Lieutenant Nathaniel Swazy of the *Decatur.* Swazy stated that "the two seamen were imprisoned on shore and never saw Captain Nichols nor the prison-ship" (*Newburyport Herald*, January 10, 1814). The statements by both Foot and Swazy were made in defense of Nichols while the captain remained imprisoned.

NOTE: See Entire Transcribed Statement by Swazy in Appendix J.

Reason for Nichols' Imprisonment Changes

Four months after British Agent Barclay had presented the issue of the two seamen refuting the cruel treatment of Nichols in Barbados, he wrote to Agent Mason again. This time, he suddenly changed the grounds for Nichols' imprisonment. It was a completely different and rather ludicrous reason for Nichols to be imprisoned. Barclay wrote:

> Captain Nichols is not detained now in prison for
> any particular offence alleged against him, but that

he is being held at Chatham a prisoner, **because the privateer which he commanded was not of a sufficient size to entitle him to parole ...** I request that Captain Woodworth be released on parole. He is a Quaker who was master of an unarmed merchant vessel ... and that Captain Barss, who was captured in a privateer of 14 guns, should also be paroled.

Col. Thomas Barclay, British Agent

American State Papers, p. 651

In his letter, British Agent Barclay did not again mention the alleged deposition of the two seamen who denied the cage incident with Nichols. Throughout his correspondence, **Barclay never acknowledged that the incident with the cage on the deck of the prison-ship had ever taken place**. He was now presenting this new basis for Nichols' imprisonment, which appeared quite ridiculous and transparent.

In disbelief, Commissioner Mason wrote a brief and terse response to Agent Barclay. He questioned why Nichols had been treated like a criminal at Barbados on the mere pretext that he did not command a privateer ship with as many as fourteen guns. There was no response to this inquiry. In his letter, Mason wrote:

I am informed that Captain Nichols, of the American privateer Decatur, is not detained now in prison for any particular offence alleged against him. This is, to be sure, taking a very different ground from that on which you so strenuously last July and August, insisted ...

As it is now declared that there is no intention of bringing him to trial. Orders have been given to retain

Captains Barass and Woodworth for special exchange against Captain Nichols.

General John Mason, US Agent

American State Papers, p. 651

Nichols Released from Prison

The remaining dialog about Nichols between US Commissioner General John Mason and the Britannic Majesty's Agent for Prisoners of War, Colonel Thomas Barclay consisted of notices about the proposed exchange of the two British officers for Captain Nichols. The British had no grounds for the lengthy imprisonment of Nichols. It was the result of the malicious vindictiveness of Captain Maurice Berkeley of the *Vestal*, who wanted to inflict punishment upon Nichols for his earlier actions on the *Alert*.

The prisoner exchange was made, and Captain Nichols was finally released from prison on June 24, 1814 after seventeen months in captivity from January 1813.

NOTE: See Transcription of Certificate of Release and Exchange in Appendix K

The original certificate is located with the Newburyport Maritime Society at the Custom House Maritime Museum in Newburyport.

The War of 1812 was not over when Nichols was released and continued for another year afterwards. At the end of the war, Americans held about 3,500 British prisoners, while the British had eight thousand American prisoners. As many as ten thousand Americans, mainly seamen, were held as prisoners in England during the war.

When Nichols was finally released from prison, he had been away from home for almost two years from the time when the Decatur left Newburyport Harbor in November 1812. Nichols had seen his young son only as an infant, and he was now almost three years old.

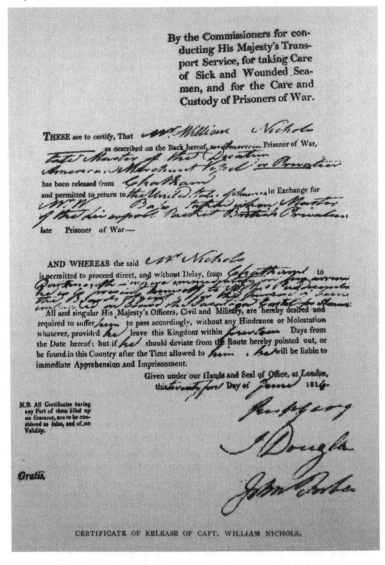

Certificate of Release and Prisoner Exchange
of Captain William Nichols
Newburyport Maritime Society
Gift of Eleanor Baumgartner Leninger

Chapter 10

Nichols Master of the *Harpy*

During the War, though many months
a prisoner and inactive, he captured 28 prizes
and 600 prisoners, making up a record which
cannot be excelled by any in the naval annals of
our own or any other nation.

D. Hamilton Hurd
History of Essex County, 1888, p. 1765

If success is any evidence of skill or
bravery, Captain Nichols could have few
equals among the privateer commanders
of that or any other period.

E. Vale Smith
History of Newburyport, 1854, p. 196

After a long absence of almost two years, Captain Nichols finally returned to Newburyport in September 1814. He was welcomed back by his wife and two children. He discovered the deepening crisis that was occurring with the war, both in Newburyport and in the country.

Nichols had not seen his family for almost two years when he left on the *Decatur* in November 1812 and was captured and imprisoned in England. His daughter, Martha, was now seven and a half years old, and his young son, William, had just turned three. It was the first time that his son was able to get to know his father, as he was an infant when they were together previously. It was an especially important time for Nichols to be with his son, as Nichols had lost his father when he was three years old. However, the family time together was not to be for very long.

Napoleon Defeated: British Attack America

Nichols always kept abreast of the war with Napoleon in Europe, because he knew that Napoleon's activities would have an impact on America. He was aware that the Coalition of European countries captured Paris in March 1814 and that Napoleon had abdicated and was exiled to Elba Island in April 1814.

While the British had been preoccupied with the war against Napoleon, they were now able to collect their newly available troops and ships to continue their war with the United States. Thousands of British troops now crossed the ocean to battle with America.

British troops were now invading America, and they were raiding towns along the eastern coast. The United States militia at Bladensburg was completely routed, and they were free to march into defenseless Washington on August 24. Also, British Admiral Cockburn's fleet was fast approaching Baltimore (Malone & Rauch, 1962, p. 136).

Nichols was eager to get back into the fight. Negotiations between Great Britain and the United States had started in Ghent, Belgium, in September 1814. There was hope that the war might soon be coming to an end.

British Invasion of Washington

With additional troops from Great Britain following the end of the Napoleonic Wars, British troops were laying waste to many of the coastal towns. British Major General Robert Ross captured Brandenburg on August 24, 1814 and then advanced toward Washington.

Anticipating an attack, the citizens of Washington abandoned their city. President Madison, the US Congress, and the government administration all retreated from the advancing British forces. On August 25, General Ross captured and occupied the defenseless United States capital. British troops set fire to the White House, the Capitol, and many other public buildings (Rear Admiral George Cockburn, 2010).

It was only a sudden, heavy thunderstorm the day after the burning, including a tornado, that forced General Ross's troops to retreat to their ships, which were badly damaged (Pitch, 1998. www.senate.gov/reference). The occupation lasted for only twenty-six hours, and the extremely heavy rain put out most of the fires (Malone & Rauch, 1962, p. 136).

The burning of Washington was in retaliation for the earlier American sacking of Toronto (Rear Admiral George Cockburn, 2010). The invasion and destruction of America's capital was a "lesson" to the Americans, because of the "disgraceful conduct of American troops in the wanton destruction along the north shores of Lake Erie in May 1814" (Malone & Rauch, 1962, p. 136). The burning of Washington was a humiliating defeat for Americans that made them outraged toward the British.

A Massachusetts legislative report written in February 1815 about the capture of Washington stated, "The people of the Commonwealth, especially those living on the seacoast of the state, were thrown into great alarm … in consequence of the capture of the city of Washington, the plunder of Alexandria, and the taking possession by the enemy of a part of the District of Maine … as a result, more militia were being called out in apprehension of the danger of an invasion" (*Newburyport Herald*, February 7, 1815).

Turn in the War

When Nichols returned from his imprisonment in England, he became aware of a possible turn in the war in favor of the United States. The military situation in America began to improve in 1813, while Nichols was away, as a result of Admiral Perry's remarkable victory on the Lake Erie. Perry was able to capture or destroy all of the British ships on Lake Erie. General Harrison was also eventually able to be victorious by taking Detroit. By the end of 1813, the United States controlled Lake Erie (Malone & Rauch, 1964, p. 133).

Nichols also knew of the decisive turn in the war to the north with Commodore Thomas Macdonough's victory over a British flotilla on Lake Champlain on September 11, 1814. (Hickman, 2014. www. military.about.com). The invasion force of 10,530 British men from Canada was stopped, as they were deprived of any naval support. 1,500 American troops under General Alexander Macomb forced the British to retreat back into Canada. The Americans now controlled the northern borders ("General Alexander Macomb." 2011. www. warof1812trail.com).

At Ghent the British and American negotiators were each demanding concessions from each other The British were demanding that Maine and Minnesota and a large part of the land around the Great Lakes be given to them. ("Treaty of Ghent." 2012. www. infoplease.com/enc).They were determined to end the expansion of the United States to the west (*The War of 1812*, 2011, Canadian Public TV). However, when the British learned of the American victory on Lake Champlain, the envoys decided to concede, and the British withdrew their demands (ibid. "Treaty of Ghent".)

Battle of Fort McHenry

Before Nichols sailed out on the *Harpy* on October 1, 1814, he had heard of the victory in defense of Fort McHenry in Baltimore on September 14. Following their invasion and burning of Washington, the British forces under Commodore Cochrane and General Ross sailed up Chesapeake Bay to attack and destroy Baltimore. That city had been the base for many American privateers that were seizing

British merchant ships, and the British wanted to take revenge on the Baltimore shipbuilders. Admiral Cochrane had a fleet of nineteen ships with five thousand troops (Hickman, 2014. www. militaryhistory.about.com).

Fort McHenry with a thousand men was under the command of Major George Armistead. On September 13, 1814, Admiral Cochrane ordered the fort to be bombarded, and the fort was continuously bombed for twenty-five hours with shells exploding every minute. It was an eventful night with heavy rain and high winds, the sky being lit with explosions, and with the mixing of sounds of thunder and the roar of bombs (Jenkins & Taylor, p. 191). The British fired between 1,500 and 1,800 cannonballs and 700 to 800 rockets at the fort but with little impact. There was a great deal of concern that the fort would be invaded by the British during the night (Hickman, 2014. www.militaryhistory.about.com).

By morning, the sky cleared, and considerable damage had been done to many of the bomb ships. As the sun began to rise, Major Armistead's forces were still at the fort. The United States had survived the battle and stopped the enemy's advance (Jenkins & Taylor, p. 191).

Major Armistead ordered the small storm flag to be replaced with a huge US flag that measured thirty feet by forty-two feet. Armistead had commissioned local seamstress Mary Pickersgill to make the large flag. The flag became clearly visible to all ships in the river. Commodore Cochrane, seeing the flag, was convinced that the harbor could not be breached. He ordered the bombing to stop, and the British soon retreated back down the river (Hickman, 2014. www. militaryhistory.about.com). Baltimore residents rejoiced. The victory restored America's confidence after the burning of Washington (Jenkins & Taylor, p. 191).

"Star-Spangled Banner" by Francis Scott Key

This battle is best remembered for inspiring Francis Scott Key to write the lyrics to the "Star-Spangled Banner." He was a Washington lawyer who had been sent by President Madison to negotiate the release of a prominent Washington doctor from the British.

He was aboard the British flagship two miles from shore. Upon returning to his boat where he was under British guard, he was forced to wait out the night through the duration of the bombardment. He witnessed the fiery event and scribbled a poem upon his return to the shore. When seeing the large flag still flying above Fort McHenry, he penned the lyrics to what became our national anthem. He described much of the battle in his lyrics (Pitch, 1998):

> "Oh say can you see, by the dawn's early light ..." Everyone could see the huge flag flying over the fort and realized that the United States had survived the bombardment and had stopped the enemy.

> "We hailed at the twilight's last gleaming ..." At nightfall, it was doubtful that the flag would still be flying in the morning.

> "Whose broad stripes and bright starts were so gallantly streaming ..." The large flag demonstrated to all, the nationalism that Americans had for their country.

> "And the rockets' red glare ..." The British, armor-plated rocket ship, *Erhaus* fired hundreds of rockets at the fort. They had great explosive force, and the red arc of their trajectory was very visible.

"The bombs bursting in air ..." There was a huge and lengthy bombardment of the fort from British ships throughout the night with cannons from the fort firing back at British ships.

"Gave proof that our flag was still there ..." It was such a relief for Americans to see that the flag was still flying over Fort McHenry in the morning, showing that the Americans had held their ground.

It was heartening for people to see the symbol of our country so starkly and flagrantly flying after a major victory in the war. The image of that flag resonated in the minds of Americans throughout the country and helped to preserve the nation's identity.

For two hundred years, Americans have sung the "Star-Spangled Banner" with great gusto at sporting events, military occasions, and whenever our flag is raised. Celebrations are often followed with fireworks that are designed to thrill and delight people.

However, it must be remembered that everyone enjoys those displays except those who have been in actual combat. The "Star-Spangled Banner" is a militaristic song and does not truly reflect the nature and character of our country. The "rockets red glare" and the "bombs bursting in air" take combat victims back to the shattering explosions and trails of fire that caused death and injury ... to a time they cannot forget. To them, war is not something to sing about or celebrate.

Nichols' First Cruise on the *Harpy*

As soon as he returned to Newburyport, Captain Nichols immediately began to look for another ship. Sensing the urgency of the war, he was eager to vindicate the suffering he had experienced at the hands of the British while imprisoned. He was prepared to again set sail against the British.

He was not feeling distressed by his imprisonment and mistreatment by the British for so many months. Instead, he compensated for his traumatic experiences and lingering anxiety by focusing his mind and energies on the next voyage to do battle with the British. He was determined to use all of his navigational and seamanship skills to capture British prizes.

He had a score to settle with them. He wanted to avenge the imprisonment he had experienced for a year and a half, and also for the wrongs he had endured from the British before the war. By remaining focused and determined to seek revenge against the British, he was able to maintain a high level of personality functioning as a sea captain. Smith commented on the strong character that enabled him to overcome the trauma of his incarceration, "Nothing daunted him by the fortune of war which had made him for so many months an exile and a prisoner (Smith, 1854, p. 196).

In Portsmouth, New Hampshire, he found the *Harpy*, out of Baltimore. It was a larger, faster, and better-armed brig than the famous *Decatur*. The *Harpy* had been constructed in Baltimore with fourteen guns and took one hundred men. The ship put into Portsmouth on August 10, 1814, for repairs and refitting of the hull and spars. Nichols was encouraged to be in command of her.

Nichols sailed out of the Piscataqua River in Portsmouth on October 1, 1814, in what was to be a successful cruise for the *Harpy* (Chase, ca. 1920, p. 11). The Baltimore-built brig *Harpy* was the fastest cruise ship of the privateering fleet from New England (Coffey, 1975, p. 150).

It was fortuitous that Nichols' vessel was called the *Harpy*. In Greek mythology, "Harpy" refers to a swift wind spirit that suddenly snatches people away (*Encyclopedia Britannica*, 2013). Similarly, that is what Nichols was about to do with the *Harpy* against the British ships.

Nichols was soon at sea, and he headed off toward Nova Scotia. He first came upon a fleet of British transports headed to Canada with supplies for the army. The convoy's British frigate that had been accompanying the transports was not in sight, as it had become disabled in a storm. However, the convoy continued on without the frigate's protection (Chase, ca. 1920, p. 12).

Using the tactics of naval warfare that he had used in previous encounters, Nichols first cut out and captured the six-gun transport ship *Amazon* on October 10 (Hurd, 1888, p. 1764). The *Amazon* was a well-armed vessel travelling from London to Halifax. The vessel was heavily loaded with a large cargo of beef, bread, pork, and flour needed for the British troops in Canada (Chase, ca. 1920, p. 12).

A few days later on October 15, Nichols chased another six-gun transport ship, the *Bridget* (Hurd, 1888, p. 1764). He rapidly caught the vessel, and with one smashing broadside, the *Bridget* brought down her flag. Nichols was elated when he discovered the cargo. She was bound for Quebec with provisions for the British Army that would never arrive. The cargo included 350 large casks of rum, fifty huge barrels of brandy, 360 pounds of beef and pork, two hundred bags of flour, and 180 barrels of bread (Chase, ca. 1920, p. 12).

The *Bridget* and the *Amazon* were carrying, respectively, ten and twenty additional cannons. There were many British Army troops aboard the two ships, and there were several British Army officers, including a major general. They were all taken as prisoners on the *Harpy*. Nichols "smiled grimly" as he placed prize crews on each of the two British vessels and had them follow him as he headed back to port (Chase, ca. 1920, p. 12).

The next day, October 16, he took another packet ship, a Scottish brig, also headed for Halifax. She had a valuable cargo of dry goods, cutlery, cut glass, beer, starch, and ropes for ships' rigging. She also followed the others, and Nichols headed for port.

During his return trip to Portsmouth, on October 19, he captured the schooner, *Britannia* of Liverpool, which was in ballast and had no cargo (Hurd, 1888, p. 1764). He burned the ship, because he could not spare the ten men he needed for a prize crew. He needed his crew to guard the many prisoners he had taken.

Nichols put into port at Portsmouth on October 26, after a very successful twenty-five-day cruise. The ships *Amazon* and *Bridget,* together with the Scottish brig, followed him into Portsmouth Harbor. He recovered his prize crews and started making plans for another cruise.

In three weeks, he had captured four British vessels and seized two other transport ships. He had taken sixty-five prisoners from the English transports that included some British Army officers and a major general. The provisions and troops never reached the British Army in Canada. Maclay reported, "The *Amazon* and *Bridget* belonged to a fleet that had sailed from Portsmouth, England. Both craft were laden with provisions for the British army. Among the prisoners were two majors and several other officers. It was estimated that the value of the prizes taken by the *Harpy* in this cruise was at least half a million dollars" (Maclay, 1899).

Captain Nichols had learned to fight with both power and fear in the enemy. Not only had he developed ocean power from the fast-sailing ships he was commanding but also, with his many naval victories, he was successful in creating fear in the British Navy. Captains of the British fleet became apprehensive whenever his vessel appeared on the horizon.

Nichols' Second Cruise on the *Harpy*

Feeling a sense of satisfaction and revenge from his first cruise with the *Harpy*, he knew he was making a dent in the British fleet. Nichols soon returned to the high seas, "stopping just long enough to draw a long breath of satisfaction" (Chase, ca. 1920, p. 12). This was to be the *Harpy's* banner cruise. Nichols left Portsmouth two weeks later on November 12 in what was to be his last, and quite remarkable, cruise on the *Harpy* in the war (Maclay, 1899, p. 460).

The *Harpy* was two days out when she was chased by the seventy-four-gun frigate HMS *Bulwark* off Cape Sables, Nova Scotia (*New York Times*, February 5, 1815). Nichols later wrote, "We hauled on wind and soon lost sight of her" (Chase, ca. 1920, p. 12). A number of other British brigs and frigates also chased the *Harpy*, including the sloop of war *Forward* off the Georges Bank. In addition, Nichols eluded several men-of-war on five successive days when he was sailing along the coast of Ireland. The *Harpy* continued to out-sail all of the British ships (*New York Times*, February 5, 1815). He always kept the *Harpy* ready for sailing, so that there would not be a repeat of the capture he experienced with the *Decatur* two years earlier.

Five days later on this cruise, Nichols first captured the British ship *Garland* on November 17 off the coast of Newfoundland (Hurd, 1888, p. 1764). The *Garland* was from St. Vincent Island in the Mediterranean and was heading for St. Johns, Newfoundland. It had a cargo of rum, sugar, and molasses. Nichols sent her to Salem with a prize crew, and she arrived safely (*New York Times*, February 5, 1815). The next prize was on November 29, ten days later. It was the British ship *Jane* from Miramachi, New Brunswick, heading from London to Antigua in the Canary Islands (Hurd, 1888, p. 1764). She had a full cargo of lumber, and Nichols burned her.

Following that, on December 13, he took the brig *William Neilson* off the Irish coast (Hurd, 1888, p. 1764). The brig left Quebec and was heading for Liverpool, but Nichols intercepted the ship. It had a cargo of timber with a number of passengers. After removing the cargo, Nichols placed the forty-seven prisoners he captured on board the *William Neilson* back on the vessel. He then gave her up as a cartel passenger ship and ordered her to Scotland (*New York Times*, February 5, 1815).

Next was the British schooner, *Nine Sisters*, on December 21 (Hurd, 1888, p. 1765). The vessel was bound for London from Lisbon with a full cargo of oranges. After unloading the cargo, he burned the ship (*New York Times*, February 5, 1815).

On December 31, he came across the British brig *Louisa*, heading to Greenock, Scotland, from Gibraltar ("Captain Nichols Naval Hero," *Newburyport Herald*, March 13, 1866). She had a cargo of wine, raisins, and figs. After removing some of the cargo, Nichols sent her to Baltimore with a prize crew.

The *William and Alfred* ship was next captured by Captain Nichols off the coast of Ireland on January 2, 1815 (Chase, ca. 1920, p. 13). He was ravaging British ships right under the nose of the British fleet along the coast of England. This vessel was heading for the West Indies with dry goods and plantation stores. Nichols wrote in his log about this encounter, "She struck after receiving three guns and a volley of musketry ... took out a number of bales, bottles, and puncheons of dry goods" (Chase, ca. 1920, p. 13). Nichols put a prize crew on board and was sending her back to the United States when he suddenly saw three ships "sailing to the windward."

He made them out to be a British frigate and two merchant vessels. He cleared his ship for action and "gave the frigate one gun." He continued to dodge the frigate and keep her attention for several hours as a ruse to distract the British ship. While the frigate was enticing the *Harpy* to engage with them, Nichols was actually attempting to get his recent prize ship, the *William and Alfred*, out of sight. He succeeded and later wrote in his log, "At midnight lost

sight of her, and next morning saw her standing to the southward …
she had not taken notice of the prize!" (Chase, ca. 1920).

On January 7, he captured another ship named *Jane* of Greenock
that was heading from London to Antigua with provisions. Nichols
stored as much of the cargo as was accessible on the *Harpy* and threw
a great part of her cargo overboard. He then paroled the forty-five
prisoners and gave the ship up as a cartel and ordered her to Ireland
(*New York Times*, February 5, 1815).

He also boarded the Portuguese brig *St. John the Baptists* that
was heading from Lisbon to St. Michaels in Newfoundland. The
captain of the Portuguese ship informed Nichols that the vessel was
a cartel dispatched to ascertain facts of some difficulties between
the British and Portuguese governments. Nichols allowed the ship
to continue her voyage. During the remainder of the *Harpy's* cruise,
Nichols boarded a number of other neutral vessels, and he allowed
them to continue on their journeys (*New York Times*, February 5,
1815).

However, returning home became difficult for the *Harpy*, as
she had to run a gauntlet of three British brigs and two frigates. He
continued to feel a strong sense of satisfaction when the *Harpy* was
always able to out-sail them, as Nichols proudly recorded in his log,
"The Harpy always left them with the greatest of ease" (Chase, ca.
1920, p. 13).

During his two cruises with the *Harpy*, Nichols was able to
"even the score with the British fleet," as he took prize after prize.
He demonstrated his fury and resentment at the British as he was
determined to seek vengeance for his lengthy imprisonment. His
reputation as a terror to the British first emerged early in the war with
his victories on the *Decatur*, and then continued with his successful
cruises on the *Harpy*.

The capture of the British ships was vindication for the suffering
he had endured by the British. His successful naval encounters

became a concern in England, as supplies were not reaching either England or the British troops in Canada. "The devastation of this dare-devil Yankee privateer had roused all of England" (Chase, ca. 1920, p. 13). Nichols had, indeed, become a Holy Terror to the British!

The *Harpy* arrived safely in Salem, Massachusetts, on February 5, 1815, having been at sea for eighty-five days. During this second voyage, Nichols captured eight more British ships, totaling fourteen for his two cruises. The *Harpy* had a valuable cargo of rich merchandise on board that was taken from the captured vessels, including:

> Nearly a thousand bales and boxes of goods, British manufactured goods, ladies rich dresses, broadcloths, cut glass, jewelry, plates, over 300 boxes and 55 baskets of fruit. Three barrels of gunpowder, cannonades, pistols, cutlasses, canvas, sails, signal flags, lamps, nautical instruments, and medicine. And upward of one hundred thousand pounds sterling in British treasury notes and bills of exchange.
>
> John Currier
> *History of Newburyport*,
> 1906, p. 662

Testimonials

With his encounters on both the *Decatur* and the *Harpy*, Nichols had created a personal legacy for his deceased father, whom he had never really known. His long-standing feelings of loss about his father's early death were mitigated by his successes over the British.

While known as the Holy Terror among the British naval vessels, the conduct of Captain Nichols with his prisoners was described as quite cordial and amiable by the captains of ships he captured. A tribute was written by the captain of the *William and Alfred* while on board the *Harpy*:

> Captain William Drysdale, late of the ship *William and Alfred*, captured January 2, 1815, by the brig *Harpy*, returns his grateful acknowledgment to William Nichols, Esq., commander of the said brig, and all his officers for their great civility, indulgent lenity, and humane usage while on board, and generously delivering up all his private property. And should, at any future time, Captain Nichols or any of his officers come to London, Captain Drysdale will be happy to see them at his house, Stephney Green, near London.
>
> Given under my hand, on board the *Harpy* at sea, this day, January 6, 1815
> Late captain of the Ship *William and Alfred,*
> William Drysdale
> in Coggleshall, 1861, p. 323,
> Maclay, 1899, p. 461, Currier I, 1906, p. 663

This testimonial of Nichols' gentlemanly manner on board the *Harpy* was endorsed by other shipmasters who were taken as prisoners:

> We, the undersigned, feeling congenial sentiments with Captain Drysdale, toward Captain Nichols, Lieutenant Place, and the officers on board the *Harpy*; And desirous that such humanity and goodness may be made public, as well in the United States as in England, declare that our treatment is worthy of every praise and econmium;

And that all our private property has been held sacred to us, and a cartel fitted for us as early as circumstances would permit.

Late Masters of Vessels taken by the *Harpy,*
Geo. Harrison, W. Newell, J. W. Hall, Andrew McCarthy,

in John Currier,
History of Newburyport
Vol. I, 1906, p. 663

NOTE: See Additional Testimonials
in Appendices G, I, J

While Captain Nichols could have been vengeful in his treatment of British prisoners because of his mistreatment while imprisoned, he remained gentlemanly in his manner with the prisoners he took. **He wanted to demonstrate how prisoners should be treated instead of lowering himself to the level of revenge and cruelty that the British authorities had shown**. While fierce in his naval battles against Great Britain, Nichols did not carry vindictiveness to a personal level. He remained compassionate with a strong sense of humanity in the treatment of his prisoners.

He demonstrated his underlying sense of fairness toward others not only with the *Decatur* and the *Harpy,* but also when he singlehandedly recaptured the *Alert* before the war. Knowing that he and his mate and three boys could not easily handle nine prisoners, he set five of them adrift in a long boat a few miles from shore. He decided to rig their smaller boat with sails, oars, a compass, and quadrant, and he supplied them with food, water, wine, and all their clothes. He provided the prize crew with the opportunity to survive - which they did, as they arrived safely on the French coastline. Some captains would simply have run them through or thrown them overboard.

Battle of New Orleans

After arriving in port with the *Harpy* at Salem, Massachusetts, on February 3, 1815, Nichols heard about the victory of General Jackson and the famous Battle of New Orleans. It was the final major battle of the War of 1812 that occurred the previous month on January 8, 1815.

The British fleet, rebuffed by the Baltimore troops at Fort McHenry, retreated south to the Bay of New Orleans. British General Sir Edward Pakenham marched 7,500 seasoned British veteran soldiers against an army of 4,500 sharpshooters and frontiersmen under the command of the American General Andrew Jackson. The American forces, in a spectacular land victory for the United States, soundly defeated the British. Both generals were unaware that peace had been declared by the Ghent Treaty in December 1814 (Schlesinger, 1983, p. 202).

While American casualties included only eight killed and thirteen wounded in the Battle of New Orleans, more than two thousand British soldiers were killed or wounded. The British failed in their frontal assault against Jackson's well-entrenched army, as British General Pakenham and two other generals were among the dead. The British retreated back to their ships and sailed home to their base in the West Indies (Malone & Rauch, 1964, p. 137).

The Battle of New Orleans made Andrew Jackson a national hero, and the encounter has been one of the most celebrated victories in American military history. It restored a badly battered national pride (Schlesinger, 1983, p. 202), as Americans had scored the greatest land victory of the war.

While making preparations for a third cruise with the *Harpy,* Nichols received news on February 11 that a treaty of peace had been signed in Ghent, Belgium, on December 24, 1814. **The war was over!**

While America had been on the brink of annihilation, it was the strong will of the people with their uncommon courage that prevailed. Americans were determined to defeat the British. In Newburyport, the announcement was received "with shouts of joy, roar of cannon, and ringing of bells" (Currier I, 1906, p. 665). Captain Nichols was able to then triumphantly return home from the war and reunite with his family.

Watercolor Painting of Brig *Harpy*
Custom House Maritime Museum
Gift of Eleanor Baumgartner Leninger

English Georgian Silver Tea Set
with Engraved Inscription
Custom House Maritime Museum
Gift of Eleanor Baumgartner Leninger

Chapter 11

Brink of Secession in Newburyport

Partisan politics divided the young country during
the 1790s and early 1800s.
> Cunliffe (in Schlesinger,
> 1962, p. 146)

At a meeting of the inhabitants of Newburyport
held January 16, 1815, a long and spirited letter
(of secession) to the Massachusetts General
Court was adopted ...

About two o'clock in the afternoon of February 13,1815,
news reached Newburyport that a treaty of peace
had been concluded ... the threatened disruption of the
Union was averted, and the incipient rebellion crushed
by the abrupt close of the War.
> John J. Currier
> *History of Newburyport*, 1906, p. 664–665

In Newburyport, news of the war's end was hailed
as if its Town meeting of January 16 had never been
held ... The end of the war forestalled a New
England separatist movement. Revolt was
prevented only by the war's end.
> Benjamin Labaree
> *Patriots and Partisans of Newburyport*, 1962, p. 199

The Treaty of Ghent ending the War of 1812 was signed on December 24, 1814. However, communication across the Atlantic was slow, and news did not reach America until February 11, 1815.

Captain Nichols lived in a politically torn community. Newburyport was a significantly divided town, as there were many who were strongly opposed to the war, while there were also many who were opposed to the British. The Federalists had developed a strong following in Newburyport in the early 1800s because of concerns about the foreign trade. Nichols remained in the minority as a Democrat-Republican. The secessionist movement was a continuous and controversial issue, and Nichols was dismayed by the conflicts of neighbor against neighbor and families against one another.

Newburyport Federalists Opposed to Privateers

There was a political undercurrent both before and during the war that was divisive in the nation, and especially in New England. In Newburyport during the 1800s, the Federalist Party dominated Newburyport politics. In 1807, of the twenty-five wealthiest citizens in Newburyport, at least ten were Federalists, while only two were Democrat-Republicans (Labaree, 1962, p. 140). Labaree stated, "There was a split in partisan politics that ran through every facet of Newburyport … even though Newburyport was prosperous, the divisive scar of partisan politics separated the town into two irreconcilable camps, slashing through business association groups, and even families" (Labaree, 1962, p. 139)

In 1804, Newburyport remained the only seaport firmly in the hands of the Federalists. They maintained a better than two-to-one margin in favor of Governor Caleb Strong, a conservative Federalist (Labaree, 1962, p. 130). The Federalists did not like Jeffersonian politics, and New Englanders were generally vehemently opposed to the War of 1812 (ibid., 141).

In Newburyport, "The *Decatur* was followed by more curses than prayers for its safe return" ("Memorabilia," *Newburyport Herald*, August 8, 1855). The captain and crew had to conquer the prejudices of their families and neighbors in order to serve their country. Endeavors were made to prevent enlistments on the *Decatur*, and some crewmembers were arrested and treated like criminals.

The spirit of Massachusetts was to resist the war effort. Federalist ideas were so strong in Newburyport that the fitting out of privateers, such as the *Decatur* with Captain Nichols, was strongly opposed (Smith, 1854, p. 194). Local Federalists denounced the practice of privateering as being unprincipled (Labaree, 1962, p. 187).

Nichols and his crew had to overcome the resistance and prejudices of the town. There had been attempts to prevent enlistments on the *Decatur*, and the crewmembers were treated as criminals. However, Currier, in his *History of Newburyport*, wrote that "although the war was unpopular in Newburyport, several privateers were still fitted out to prey upon the commerce of the enemy" (Currier I, 1906, p. 650).

Currier also reported that Editor Ephraim Allen of the *Newburyport Herald* said of the six owners of the privateer *Manhattan*, "they were all Democrats of the first water" (*Newburyport Herald*, July 24, 1812). When the *Decatur* set sail at the beginning of the War of 1812, Editor Ephraim Allen made the disparaging statement, "This town is disgraced with but two privateers – fitted out by Democrats – one of them being the *Decatur* with Captain Nichols – and they are not likely ever to 'set the river on fire'" (*Newburyport Herald*, August 11, 1812).

The previous week, when providing an account of another privateer, the *Manhattan*, Editor Allen remarked, "The privateer Manhattan returned to port Saturday, *without* prizes. We congratulate the owners that *she has saved herself*" (*Newburyport Herald*, August 4, 1812).

The Essex Junto

The roots of opposition to decisions of the federal government in the early nineteenth century trace back to1778 when a powerful and radical group of Massachusetts Federalist lawyers, merchants, and politicians became organized. Twenty-seven men formed a self-appointed group that supported the Federalist Alexander Hamilton and opposed the Embargo Act and the war effort ("Essex Junto." 2012. www.legal-dictionary.thefreedictionary.com). John Hancock coined the name for his Essex County opponents at the 1778 state convention ("Essex Junto." 2014. www.britannica.com). The Junto originated in Newburyport in Essex County, Massachusetts, and then moved to nearby Ipswich, also in Essex County (Brown, 1915, p. 8).

The Essex Junto became deeply entrenched in New England, and they joined with the Federalist Party of Massachusetts (Banner, 1970, p. viii). The Junto felt that the War of 1812 was offensive and morally wrong. They indicated that the British had always been willing to make a treaty. The Federalists were emphatic in stating that there could be no peace in America as long as the federal government had the financial means to continue war (Banner, 1970, p. 93).

Prior to the War of 1812, the Embargo Act of 1807 blocked United States ships from doing any business with foreign lands. The government thought that by removing United States vessels from all danger that this would protect the vulnerable American merchant vessels. However, the embargo backfired, and the lack of trade decimated the economy as banks failed, men were out of work, and an economic depression resulted, especially in New England. The Embargo Act had the effect of redirecting New England's anger away from Britain and toward Washington DC (Ellis, 2012).

When war against Britain was declared by the United States on June 18, 1812, this action was condemned by New England's political leadership. "Federalist leaders were strongly opposed to the war and did everything this side of treason to hinder it" (Malone & Rauch, 1964, p. 135). The best example of obstruction was in Massachusetts, where Governor Caleb Strong, an avid Federalist, proclaimed a public fast after the start of the war to "atone for the administration's action" (Buckley, 1934, p. 4).

In addition, President Madison needed troops, and he asked the Massachusetts militia to be summoned. Strong refused to call the militia into federal service (Ellis, 2012). He declared that he would not send the militia out of state. Madison saw this as an unpatriotic act, and he viewed Strong as defying the war effort. In response, Madison sent no ground forces to protect New England. Governor Strong reacted to Madison's decision by saying that the federal government had abandoned Massachusetts (ibid.).

At issue was freedom that the states wanted; they wanted the right to their own independence. The young Union was still a national experiment, and a sense of united nationalism did not yet exist (Banner, 1970, p. 100). The Union of the country brought together newly independent states, but they were each reluctant to surrender their powers to a central government. National sentiment was weak in 1812 (Buckley, 1934, p. 4).

Essex Junto in Newburyport

Perhaps the most hated of all Jeffersonian doctrines among Newburyport Federalists was the idea of democracy. Federalists asserted that "whenever democracy has been in power, corruption shortly followed" (Labaree, 1962, p. 128). Labaree reported that Editor Park of the Federalist *Repertory* stated in 1803, "We hate democracy – we have opposed it and we will oppose it with all our heart, with all our soul, and with all our strength, and with all our mind … We will never submit to be governed" (ibid.).

Labaree also related that Editor Allen of the *Newburyport Herald* had little sympathy when the British captured and burned Washington in August 1814, when he asked on September 20, 1814, "Who will say that they (the Madison administration) do not richly deserve their calamity?" (Labaree, 1962, p. 193).

To many of the Federalists, the only means to preserve their independence was disunion. Secession had frequently been discussed on the floor of Congress, and it had been considered for years (Brown, 1915, p. 37). Federalists were struggling to seek a basis for separation from the Union (ibid., 43).

This discontent in New England offered an opportunity for the British to profit (Buckley, 1934, p. 5). The Essex Junto had secretly made plans with the British for an Alliance that was in response to the Embargo Act (Brown, 1915, p. 45). The Essex Junto was referred to as the "Blue Lights" during the War of 1812. They would shine blue lights to either alert the British ships blockading the harbor of escaping American ships, or to signal British ships to come ashore and smuggle goods. The Junto also attempted to block the raising of an army (ibid., 93).

Fortunately, the New England states were initially exempted from the British blockade that the Royal Navy began along the Atlantic coast (Buckley, 1934, p. 5). The British eventually did put a blockade into place along the New England coast, but they never attacked Boston or the North Shore. The British were hoping they could convince New Englanders to secede from the fragile union and break away from the United States (Ellis, 2012).

Hartford Convention

The war had not been going well. "There were strong calls for outright secession" (Banner, 1970, p. viii). There was also talk of starting a Northern Confederacy in reaction to Madison's "odious and disastrous war" (Buckley, 1934, p. 7). An assembly of twenty-six representatives from the New England states was called in Hartford, Connecticut, in December 1814 (ibid., 14).

The Hartford Convention was a partisan meeting in an attempt to hold the Federalist Party together. The convention was denounced by many as an assembly of traitors plotting to destroy the Union, while the Federalists declared that it was a "group of devoted patriots to soothe the just wrath of oppressed and outraged New England and thus saving the Union" (Buckley, 1934, p. 1).

Sessions of the Hartford Convention took place from December 15, 1814 to January 3, 1815. The War of 1812 had continued for two and a half years. However, the nature of the secrecy of the Hartford Convention session led to a charge of treason (Malone & Rauch, 1964, p. 135).

Newburyporters became impatient for action by the Convention. They were disappointed in the result, as no new confederacy was formed. They wanted a new form of government that would safeguard their homes and end the war (Labaree, 1962, p. 198). The Convention decided not to secede, and their report was moderate and conciliatory in nature (Banner, 1970, p. iv). The Convention's final report was a disappointment to the extreme Federalists (Buckley, 1934, p. 25).

However, the Convention did decide to appoint commissioners to go to Washington to present their grievances and suggestions for proposed amendments to the Constitution. The Massachusetts commission representing the Hartford Convention left Boston on February 3 and arrived in Washington February 11 (Buckley, 1934, p. 25). News of the Ghent Peace Treaty had just arrived.

The commission realized that their mission was quite unnecessary (Buckley, 1934, p. 26). The group quietly returned home, marking the end of the Essex Junto and the Federalist Party. The Hartford Convention stamped the Federalists with a stigma of disloyalty from which they never recovered (Brown, 1915, p. 116).

Dr. G. William Freeman

Newburyport Votes to Secede from the Union

There had been a significant decline in the economy of Newburyport because of the three successive disasters to the town: the commercial trade restrictions from the Embargo Act in 1807, the Great Fire of Newburyport in 1811, and the War of 1812 (Smith, 1854, p. 179). Newburyporters wanted direct action. They were disappointed in the report from the Hartford Convention. Townspeople were desperate, the war was continuing, and they were concerned about their homes and the mercantile trade. The town wanted to take a step beyond the recommendations of the Hartford Convention.

On January 16, 1815, Mr. Ebenezer Moseley, Chairman of the Board of Selectman, called for a town meeting at which he was the moderator. A large number of citizens participated in that meeting, and they "adopted a long and spirited memorial to the General Court" (Currier I, 1906, p. 665). Currier provided excerpts of the letter that was sent to the Massachusetts Senate and House of Representatives:

> We have no hesitation in saying that we shall consider our State Legislature as the sole, rightful, bound judge of the course which our safety net may require, Nor have we a doubt that the citizens of the Northern States, ardently as they are attached to the Union ... would declare that our own resources shall be appropriated to our own defence, and that the laws of the United States shall be temporarily suspended in the operation of our territory, and that hostilities shall cease towards Great Britain on the part of the free, sovereign and independent states of New England.
>
> in John J. Currier
> *History of Newburyport,*
> Vol. I, 1906, p. 665

NOTE: See Full Transcription
of Letter in Appendix L

Newburyport had voted for secession! The Federalist Party had developed a stronghold in town, and the Town came to the brink of secession. News of the Ghent Peace Treaty arrived two weeks after the letter was composed.

Currier Omits Reference to Federalists

It is of note that Currier, in his two-volume *History of Newburyport*, written in 1906, omits reference to the Federalist influence in Newburyport. He simply presented the letter with no introductory remarks or comments. He did not discuss the Federalist Party, the Essex Junto, or secession in his two volumes. He merely presented excerpts from the town's letter. However, Currier immediately followed the town's letter with the two testimonials from British shipmasters written in support of Captain Nichols (Currier I, 1906, p. 663–665).

The end of the war forestalled a New England separatist movement. "Revolt was prevented only by the war's end" (Labaree, 1962, p. 199). Amid the celebration of the nation's "victory," the push toward disunion was forgotten, and the Federalist Party fell from popularity and diminished in its influence and power.

Peace Declared

The War of 1812 had continued for two and a half years from June 1812 to December 1814. However, news that peace had been declared in Ghent, Belgium, did not reach America until February 1815. Americans had expected news of disaster at New Orleans, and they responded with extreme joy from both Jackson's victory and the signing of the Treaty of Ghent.

"Cities were illuminated by thousands of candles and for all-night celebrations; there were parades and banquets, fireworks and endless toasts. The pealing of bells went on for days." Malone & Rauch, 1964, p.140.

The extravagant level of responses to the news of peace was a sign of significant relief by Americans who felt that they had been in a desperate situation and that their country was in peril.

In Newburyport, on the proclamation of peace, the rejoicings were extravagant. "Public and private buildings were illuminated, flags again floated from the mast-heads of vessels, salutes were heard from the eighteen-pounders, and on some public buildings there were both flags of the United States and England" (Smith, 1854, p. 205).

Nationalism Restored

Americans were relieved and overjoyed. Citizens felt a sense of euphoria that the war was over. People felt as if America had won, as they had immediately forgotten about the frustrations, blunders, and defeats that had previously happened during the war (Coles, 1965, p. 255).

America had experienced significant difficulties and humiliations during the war. The war was spread out, communications were slow, and distances were immense, making it very difficult to coordinate military operations (Coles, 1965, p. 259). In the previous summer of 1814, America faced invasion from the north, south, and along the eastern seacoast (Malone & Rauch, 1964, p. 140). In the fall of 1814, six months prior to the end of the war, the United States Treasury was bankrupt, and

America had been on the brink of annihilation (Coles, 1965, p. 238). It was one of the darkest periods in the history of the republic.

However, the morale of the country soared with a new sense of nationalism (*Great Ships,* DVD, 1996). The end of the war restored confidence in the newly formed republic. It confirmed American independence ("War of 1812," *Encyclopedia Britannica,* 2013). "No one imagined that the young Republic would have taken on Goliath" (Malone & Rauch, 1964, p. 124). America had moved from a Union of states to the United States, reflecting a new sense of independence and nationalism.

The British gained nothing from the war, as the boundaries of the United States and Canada remained unchanged (*Great Ships: The Frigates.* DVD, 1996). The British were indignant and insulted by the peace treaty, but their preoccupation with Napoleon shifted the focus away from America; Napoleon had escaped from the island of Elba and was building another army in Europe. Great Britain and America had both won and lost a great deal, but it was the Native Americans who lost the most—they lost their land and their culture. "It was a hot and unnatural war between kindred people" (*War of 1812,* 2011, Canadian Public TV).

Newburyport

In Newburyport, news of the war's end was hailed, "as if its Town meeting of January 16 had never been held" (Labaree, 1962, p. 199). With the return of peace, Newburyporters anticipated prosperity, but it did not appear (Smith, 1854, p. 205). People in town thought that they could pick up where they had left off before the war. However, Newburyport was never able to return to the glories of the past (Labaree, 1962, p. 200).

There was a decline of Newburyport as one of the centers for ocean-borne commerce. Taxes were heavy, and customs duties were laid on many articles of domestic manufacture in order to raise revenue for the government (Smith, 1854, p. 205). While foreign trade diminished significantly, the war did force New Englanders to look inland for their livelihood, which started the river-powered mills along the Merrimack River and hastened the American Industrial Revolution (Ellis, 2012).

Captain Nichols returned to Salem with the *Harpy* a week before the news arrived about the Ghent Peace Treaty. He had been at sea for more than four months when the celebrations occurred in town. While he was pleased at the war's outcome, Nichols was dismayed when he learned of the town meeting in Newburyport on January 16 that voted for secession.

While most of the residents in town were Federalists, Nichols was a Democrat and was in the minority. He did not understand the strong feeling of the Federalists; he had been fighting for his country with the *Harpy* following his imprisonment. He did not understand the strong antipathy of the Federalists that led to the secession letter. This made it difficult for him to relate easily with others in Newburyport, at Wolfe's Tavern, and even at the Newburyport Marine Society, where most of the shipmasters were Federalists.

Previously, Editor Allen of the *Newburyport Herald*, in August 1812 stated that Nichols had "disgraced the town" by sailing out of town on a privateer vessel. However, Nichols had surely vindicated himself and was now seen as a hero to the townspeople in Newburyport. It can only be conjectured what would have happened with Nichols, if the war had not come to an abrupt end, not only in his privateer cruises, but also in his hometown where residents had voted in favor of secession.

Chapter 12

Later Years: Merchant Mariner, Politician, and Customs Collector

Touching the character of Captain Nichols as
a citizen, a man, and a neighbor, he is modest and
unassuming, yet brave and decided; warmly attracted
to the constitutions of federal and state, of his native
country; and eager to resist and cool to defend those
rights for which the independence of this country
was established ...

As a man he is strictly moral and sincere as a
husband, parent, and neighbor, tender, indulgent, and
affable. His connections are highly respectable, and
are among the first of our citizens. Captain Nichols
is surely an honest, brave, and useful citizen.

Captain Benjamin Pierce,
in a letter to the British, advocating
Nichols' release from prison,
September 13, 1813

Returning home after the war was over, Captain Nichols felt satisfaction for the retribution he had been able to inflict on the British fleet for the cruel treatment he endured at Barbados and Chatham. He felt vindicated. He had continued to even the score with the British with the number of prizes he had captured from the British with his cruises on the *Decatur* and the *Harpy*.

Merchant Trade Business

After the close of the war, Captain Nichols was again engaged as a merchant mariner in commercial foreign trade from Newburyport. He continued sailing for many years, principally to ports in Russia, Amsterdam, and Denmark (Currier II, 1906, p. 249). He remained in the mercantile business that he and his brother, Captain Samuel Nichols, re-established after the devastating fire of 1811 and they continued doing business on Ferry Wharf as "W & S Nichols." It was the location where their father had been in the same mercantile and trading business in the mid-eighteenth century (*Newburyport Herald,* August 1, 1855).

Nichols was highly esteemed by his friends and respected by all (Bailey & Jones, 1906, p. 371). He was seen in his later years as a "straight, grave gentleman with piercing black eyes" (Chase, ca. 1920, p. 1).

Nichols' Family Life

Following his return to Newburyport after the war with his many cruises and naval encounters, he was able to finally reunite with his wife, Lydia, and his family. They had two children, Martha, who was then eight years old, and his son, William, who was three and a half. He had seen very little of his family since the war began, from his two voyages on the *Decatur,* his lengthy imprisonment in England, and his two cruises on the *Harpy.*

After the war, William and Lydia had three more daughters, Lydia Balch, born in 1818, Mary Lee in 1820, and Mary Caroline in 1823. However, tragedy struck the family a few years later in 1828, as Mary Lee suddenly died at the age of seven and a half. Captain Nichols was then forty-seven, and Lydia was forty-five. It was a sudden blow to the family. His eldest daughter, Martha, was then twenty-one, his son,

William Wallace, was a young man at seventeen, while Lydia was ten years old, and the youngest, Mary Caroline, was five at the time.

Both William and Lydia had previously experienced tragedies in their lives. When William was three years old, he lost his father as a young thirty-three-year-old man. Lydia was fourteen when she lost her mother in childbirth at age thirty-one. Lydia's father also died suddenly in 1812 at the beginning of the war at the age of fifty-one when Lydia was a young woman of twenty-nine. Having both grieved over the loss of parents at young ages, they again experienced deep mourning over the loss of their young daughter, Mary Lee. The death of a child is often the most devastating loss that a person can experience.

Recovering from his daughter's death, Captain Nichols continued as a mariner and followed the merchant service. A few years later in 1830, he retired from the sea at age forty-nine (Hurd, 1888, p. 1765). He had been active for fifteen years as a mariner since the war. He had traveled on many voyages across the high seas and around the world (Chase, ca. 1920, p. 14).

His brother, Samuel, continued to work as a merchant at the family business, and he resided in the original family home on Middle Street; Samuel became a master mariner and merchant. As a shipmaster, he was also elected a member of the Newburyport Marine Society in 1816 at age thirty-three (Wildes, 1864, p. 229).

In 1833, Nichols' daughter Martha, age twenty-six, married shipmaster Captain Francis Todd, age twenty-seven. Captain Todd had recently been elected to the Newburyport Maritime Society in 1833 (Bayley & Jones, 1906, p. 381). Captain Nichols became a grandfather to his first grandchild, William Nichols Todd, in 1836 (Newburyport Vital Records).

Purchase of Family Home at 5 Harris Street

On May 3, 1831, Captain Nichols purchased half of the house at 5 Harris Street two blocks away from downtown Newburyport and Market Square. The other half of the house was purchased on the same day by Mrs. Elizabeth Wood. She sold her half to Rev. Fredrick Gray, who, in turn, eleven years later sold it to Captain Nichols in 1842 (*Newburyport Daily News*, December 31, 1937). Nichols resided in the home for more than thirty years until his death in 1863 (Currier I, 1906, p. 66). The house remained in the family for more than one hundred years (Downs, 1948, p. 137).

In early 1805, Leonard Smith built two houses of similar construction for his two sons at the corner of Green and Harris Streets. The buildings were three-story brick, Federalist-style buildings with the identical architectural designs. Both buildings had fortunately been spared by the Great Fire of 1811 in Newburyport. The house at 5 Harris Street became popularly known in town as the "Nichols' home."

However, it later became necessary to sell the house and demolish it. Mrs. Emma Hale, owner of the home and widow of Captain Nichols' grandson, George E. Hale, sold the house in 1937. Before the home was destroyed, Mrs. Harry Benkard purchased the woodwork parlor and incorporated it into a wing constructed at her home in Oyster Bay, Long Island, New York. The room was later donated to the Metropolitan Museum of Art in New York in 1945 and has been on display in the American Wing. The room presents a "harmonious picture of the early Federalist period" (Downs, 1948, p. 137).

Residence of Captain William Nichols
5 Harris Street, Newburyport
Reproduced from <u>Architectural Heritage of the Merrimack</u>

Nichols' Son on Trial for Murder

Captain Nichols' son, William Wallace, had also become a mariner and sea captain. Nichols became very upset and dismayed in 1839, when his son was indicted and tried for the beating death of a crewman during a voyage. The young Captain Nichols and his mate, William Couch, were on a cruise from Liverpool back to Boston on the *Caravan.* After the cruise, they were charged with the "unjustifiably beating of Henry Burr with malice, hatred, and revenge" (Dana, 1840, p. 94).

Burr, a foreigner, had shipped on board as a cook only two days before the ship sailed. Early in the trip, it was found that he was incompetent as a cook, and he was reassigned as a regular seaman. However, he again showed incompetence at "reefing in the foretopsail" (Coffey, 1975, p. 85). First Mate Couch took parts of the rigging and administered a severe beating to Burr. Shortly after, young Captain Nichols resumed the beating. Burr lay bleeding on the deck as if dead, and he was taken below deck into the forecastle. The next day, the badly injured Burr was stretched out on deck and left to suffer the rain and cold. He was again taken below deck and died during the night (Coffey, 1975, p. 85).

Nichols and Couch were found guilty of murder because of the inhumane treatment they inflicted on Burr, who died as a result of the beating. A number of friends testified to the good characters of Nichols and Couch, and Judge Joseph Story was so impressed that he gave only the lightest of sentences (Coffey, 1975, p. 86). Couch was given a thirty-day sentence in jail and a ten-dollar fine, while Nichols had a ninety-day sentence and a one-hundred-dollar fine. Story said that he wanted to "make their imprisonment as easy as possible because of their youth, good character, and family responsibilities" (Glenn, 1984, p. 99).

Richard Henry Dana, maritime lawyer and author of *Two Years Before the Mast*, took strong exception to Judge Story's extraordinary lenity in his sentencing. He pointed out that a federal law enacted four years earlier in 1835, to protect seamen from cruelty, indicated that a conviction of cruelty against a crewman meant "being punished by imprisonment not exceeding five years or by a fine not exceeding one thousand dollars, or both, according to the nature and aggravation of the offense" (Dana, 1839, p. 93).

Dana determined that the only excuse Story could find for the extremely light sentence of Nichols was "the rashness, inconsiderateness, and pride of youth which demanded some allowance." Dana also implied that the judge's decision was heavily influenced because of the weight given by the testimony of some highly respectable witnesses on the good character of young Nichols (Dana, 1839, p. 96).

Confusion About Which 'Captain Nichols'

There has been confusion in recent articles about which of the two Nichols captains was indicted and convicted. Both father and son carried the same name and title as sea captains. In recent years, a number of people in Newburyport thought that it was the elder Captain Nichols that was placed on trial. However, it did seem to be definitely out of character for him to have been charged for such a crime, as the elder Captain Nichols had been held in such high esteem by both the citizens of Newburyport and British naval officers who had been his prisoners.

McNally clarified this in his 1839 book, *Evils and Abuses in the Naval Merchant Service Exposed,* when reviewing the Nichols' trial,

> "... but the young *Captain Nichols* stood at the bar, who happened to have a father who was born before him, worth thousands, which materially altered the case"
>
> McNally, 1939, p.143

Captain Nichols, the privateer, was 58 years old at the time of the trial, while young Captain Nichols was 27. The incident was an embarrassment to Captain William Nichols, the privateer father of young Captain Nichols.

Death of Nichols Son

Adding to the dismay and disappointment Captain Nichols experienced regarding his son's trial, a few years later he experienced deep agony upon hearing of the deaths of both his son and son-in-law in Havana in 1841. Captain William Wallace Nichols, only son of the elder Captain Nichols, and his friend and brother-in-law, Captain

Francis Todd, had stopped in Havana, Cuba, on a return voyage to Newburyport.

Captain Todd contracted yellow fever while on the island, and he passed away on May 8, 1841, at the age of thirty-five. The younger Captain Nichols cared for his friend until he died. He then placed Captain Todd's body in a coffin and sent it back to Newburyport for burial. However, Captain Nichols also caught yellow fever, and he died in Havana eleven days after Captain Todd's death on May 19, 1841. Because there was no one there to care for the body of young Nichols, he was buried in a mass grave beneath a cathedral in Havana. He was twenty-nine years old at the time (Woodworth, 2009, p. 166).

When the elder Captain Nichols heard of his son's death, he travelled to Havana to locate William's remains, but it was not possible to find them because of the mass grave. Captain Nichols then memorialized his son with a gravestone in the Oak Hill Cemetery. In 1882, members of the Todd family decided to move the remains of Francis from the Highland Cemetery to the Oak Hill Cemetery, just a few feet away from the memorial tombstone of his friend and brother-in-law, William Wallace Nichols (Woodworth, 2009, p. 166).

Nichols Enters Politics

Prior to his son's death, Captain Nichols, a strong Democrat in a town that was mostly Federalist, decided to enter politics in 1833. He was elected by popular vote of the townspeople to two terms as a state senator in 1833 and 1834. For two years, he participated in the legislative sessions of the Massachusetts General Court (Currier II, 1909, p. 493).

Despite enduring sorrow from the death of his young daughter and the loss of his son and son-in-law, Nichols continued with his interest in politics. He was elected by the town as a selectman for three terms in 1843, 1844, and 1845 (Currier II, 1909, p. 602). At the same time, he also served as the vice president of the Newburyport Marine Society from 1842 to 1846. Nichols was then in his early sixties.

In 1845, Nichols was appointed by newly elected President James Knox Polk as the Collector of Customs at the Newburyport Custom House. He served under the administration of Polk from 1845 to 1849 (Currier I, 1906, p. 676). President Polk was a Democrat and was elected as the eleventh president in 1845. He served for four years and died shortly after leaving office in 1849 at age fifty-three.

Nichols' appointment was a political one. He was chosen because of his extensive knowledge about maritime affairs in Newburyport. As the collector, Nichols inspected vessels arriving in Newburyport from foreign ports and collected duties from them. He worked as the manager of all work that transpired at the Customs House. Nichols authorized collection of all duties on imports and exports passing through Newburyport. He was also responsible for the security of goods stored at the Customs House. Ship captains and merchants had to file manifests and crew lists at the Customs House of all incoming and outgoing cruises.

What was most remarkable during his tenure as the collector was that he took his job quite seriously and handled business affairs in a personal manner. It is reported that,

> He transacted the public business as though it was his
> own individual interest, and that can perhaps be said
> of but very few government officers"
> > "Memorabilia," *Newburyport Herald,*
> > August 9, 1855.

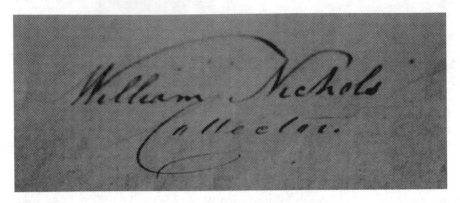

Signature of Captain William Nichols
as Collector of Customs
Custom House Maritime Museum

In 1848, while he was Collector of Customs Nichols daughter, Lydia, age thirty, married Captain Benjamin Hale, age thirty-three, a successful financier and shipmaster in Newburyport. Benjamin's father was a close friend and business associate of Captain Nichols. It was not uncommon in that time for children of friends to marry. They were now related through their children.

Benjamin and Lydia had one child, a son, George E. Hale, born in 1854, and who was Captain Nichols' second grandchild, (Newburyport Vital Records). George was this author's great-grandfather.

Absence of Memoirs

In 1863, the *Newburyport Herald* published a series of four "Memorabilia" articles on August 1, 2, 8, and 9 about the life of Nichols and his naval encounters. Nichols was seventy-four years old at the time, and he was able to hear how others understood his wartime experiences.

He left no memoirs or records of his activities during the War of 1812 or about his experiences while in prison under the British guards. He became averse to having his naval records discussed, and he disliked publicity. He destroyed his logbooks and many of the mementos from the War of 1812 (Chase, ca. 1920, p. 2). "Captain Nichols left no papers available to tell his story" (Wildes, 1864, p. 229). He provided only oral history accounts of his experiences to those who were close friends or relatives.

Toward the end of his life, some fifty years after his days as a privateer sea captain, his war stories had begun to fade from his mind. He resided in Newburyport his entire life, and he was content to live out his years without dwelling on the distant past of his naval encounters and imprisonment. His seventeen-month incarceration in England was still too painful to talk about. While he had achieved vindication for his cruel treatment by the British with his naval victories on the *Harpy,* he was unable to speak about the tortures that he suffered.

Nichols remained silent.

An additional reason for Nichols' silence was the lingering and simmering resentment he felt toward many of the townspeople in Newburyport. While he had always maintained a cordial but reserved relationship with townspeople, he could not forget the maelstrom of resistance and rejection he and his crew had endured from Newburyporters as he was preparing the *Decatur* for her first cruise during the summer shortly after the declaration of war was made in June 1812

He was hindered in every possible way from fitting out the *Decatur* by the antiwar Federalists. Townspeople were strongly opposed and resistant to Nichols and his crew, and they tried to prevent the ship from sailing out of Newburyport Harbor. He and his crew were cursed and prevented from enlisting on the *Decatur.* His men were sometimes arrested and treated like criminals. They were the victims of the prejudices of many people in town.

There was strong antipathy toward privateers fighting against the British. However, Nichols remained steadfast in his patriotic commitment to his country. He left Newburyport on his first cruise as a privateer captain on the *Decatur* in August 1812, and he returned as a hero a few weeks later. He had been personally offended, but he remained silent. However, the underlying and lingering resentment he felt toward the town was part of why he did not want to share his records and memoirs.

Nichols' silence has piqued the interest and curiosity of many. His exploits captured the minds and imagination of those who learned about him. He was not aware of how important his story would become to generations that followed him.

Death of Captain Nichols

Captain William Nichols died at his home on Harris Street on February 12, 1863. He passed away fifty years after his naval encounters and imprisonment in England during the War of 1812. He saw the start of the Civil War, but he was not alive at the time of Lincoln's assassination (Hurd, 1888, p. 1765). He was nearly eighty-two years old, and he had always regretted that his age barred him from the navy (Chase, ca. 1920, p. 1).

He was predeceased by his mother, Mary, four years earlier, who lived until the age of ninety-two and died in April 1859. He then grieved over the loss of his beloved wife, Lydia, who died two years later in March 1861 at age seventy-seven. They had been married almost fifty-six years. However, Nichols was able to see and enjoy the interaction with his two grandsons, George Hale, age 9, and William Todd, age 27.

His brother, Captain Samuel Nichols, died three years after Nichols on October 4, 1869, at age eighty-six. Samuel was the oldest member of the Newburyport Marine Society at the time of his death and had been elected to membership in the Society in 1816 at age thirty-three. He had served in the War of 1812 and was in command of the brig *Enos* that was captured by the British in 1813. He was taken to England but later released. He had also been the master of the ships *Abbie M* and *Caravan* after the war. He had also been the first officer under Captain George Coggleshall in March 1814.

Captain William Nichols was buried in the family plot at Oak Hill Cemetery. He was the oldest member of the Newburyport Marine Society at the time of his death, and twenty-three members of the Society attended his funeral. In their *History of the Newburyport Marine Society,* Bayley and Jones said of him, "Captain Nichols, although with a rough exterior as master of a privateer, was of tender sensibilities, always exhibiting the greatest affection for his mother and his family" (Bayley & Jones, 1906, p. 371).

Tribute to Captain Nichols

William Nichols grew up and lived in Newburyport his entire life. During his youth, he lived a block away from the bustling center of activity in this seaport. His father, a mariner and privateer captain in the Revolutionary War, died when William was only three years old. Shipmaster friends of his father who were also members of the Newburyport Marine Society looked after William and his family. His next-door neighbor, Captain Nichols Pierce, became a father figure to him and later became Williams' father-in-law.

He went to sea at an early age, became a merchant trading mariner, and was a shipmaster by the age of twenty-six. He grew up in a time of world turmoil during the Napoleonic Wars, the embargo, the seizure of merchant ships, and impressment of seamen. He was captured six times as a young man, escaped three times without injury, and twice placed on parole. He lived in a politically divided town that was vehemently opposed to the War of 1812, but he remained a patriot as he became a commissioned privateer captain on two cruises with the *Decatur* and two on the *Harpy*.

While capturing twenty-eight British vessels during the war, he was captured by the British and spent thirty-four days in a cage on deck and then was imprisoned in chains for one and a half years on a British prison-ship. Following his lengthy imprisonment, he spent another three months on cruises with the *Harpy* until the end of the war. He made more of the few months that he actually spent on his cruises than others could boast of in a lifetime. He captured more than six hundred prisoners and extensive merchandise and cargo goods he seized from British ships.

He was one of the most successful privateer captains in the War of 1812. His tale is one of courage, persistence, and determination, as he engaged in audacious naval encounters during the War of 1812. From his encounters at sea, he earned the name of the Holy Terror by the British. Sea captains, both British and American, admired Captain Nichols for his tenacious and indomitable spirit. He had a fierce determination to remain steadfast in the face of difficult odds.

He was an unassuming but authentic hero. He became legendary in Newburyport. Sidney Chase captured the essence of the story of Captain Nichols when he stated:

> "The extraordinary exploits of Captain William Nichols of Newburyport, privateersman in the War of 1812, are not so widely known, and they read like fiction instead of the true story of a dare-devil Yankee skipper".
>
> Sidney Marsh Chase,
> "Captain William Nichols," ca. 1920, p.2

Appendix A

Historical Perspective: A World Gone Mad

General confusion reigned in Europe after the French
Revolution and the decapitation of Louis XVI.
Emery, 1879, p. 180

The onset of the world crisis was brought about
by the French Revolution in 1793 when Louis XVI
was deposed and guillotined.
Historian Marcus Cunliffe
"Testing a Union 1788–1865"
in Schlesinger, 1983, p. 146–150

"The world seems to be on the brink of collapse"
from a newspaper clipping in the early 1800s

Part I: Prior to the War of 1812

As a young man in the merchant trading business, William
Nichols needed to have continuing knowledge about conditions in the
nation and world. From an early age, he knew about the impressment
of sailors by the British Royal Navy. As a young merchant mariner
engaged in foreign trade, he was aware of the interference of
American commercial ships by both the British and the French. He
was keenly aware of the dangers confronting him whenever he set
sail out of Newburyport Harbor.

It was a world in turmoil. From its beginning, America was continually involved in successive wars in a 'world gone mad'. There was confusion, chaos, and shifting of alliances between countries.

He grew up at a time when it was dangerous to be at sea. He had to constantly be concerned about the safety of his ships and their crews because of possible seizure and impressment by the British or French. He was sailing vessels long before the War of 1812, and he knew about the turmoil and madness that led to the war.

While he did not fully understand all of the embroilments in Europe, he remained determined to pursue his trading voyages. He kept himself abreast and informed of the foreign entanglements that were occurring in Europe. He was also attuned to what our country was doing in response to the confusion and shifting alliances happening in the world.

There was a great deal happening both before and during the War of 1812 in the United States and in the world at large. Things were not calm. It was a time when the world had, indeed, 'gone mad'. While we had won our independence in the Revolutionary War, we had not defeated the British. Some refer to the War of 1812 as our first world war. "It was a confusing and drawn-out affair" (*Great Ships: The Frigates*, DVD, 1996). Coles pointed out,

> "The real cause of trouble lay in the deranged state of the European World. It was vain to expect the world to make itself over to conform to what was proper … there were some things that could not change … we had to participate in the evil which had fallen on the community of civilized man" (Coles, 1965, p. 35).

For more than fifty years before the War of 1812, Americans had experienced a series of wars that included the French-Indian War, our own Revolutionary War, the war with the Barbary Coast pirates, and the Quasi-War with France. We were caught up in the turmoil of the Napoleonic Wars. American colonists became exhausted from all the aggression and hostilities. Adding to the confusion and anxiety of those times, a number of events occurred that created increased concern among Americans, including the Chesapeake-Leopold incident, the resulting Embargo Act, the purchase of the Louisiana Territory, the XYZ scandal, and the Little Belt incident.

In the middle of the 18th century, American colonies were embroiled in the shifting, confusing, and conflicting alliances that occurred with the major European countries. There had been centuries of Anglo-French wars occurring on a regular basis that were fought primarily on the mainland of Europe. Preceding the War of 1812, there had been thirty years of conflict between England, France, and Spain. All of this had a significant impact upon the newly formed Union of states in America.

French-Indian War (1754-1763)

Prior to our own Revolutionary War that started in 1775, the American colonies became embroiled in the French-Indian War from 1754 to 1763. This war was fought in America, but it was primarily between the British American and New France American colonies, with both sides supported by military forces from their respective parent countries, Great Britain and France.

The war resulted from ongoing frontier tensions in North America, as both the French and British colonists wanted to extend their respective country's influence in the frontier region ("French and Indian War," www.history.state.gov).

This was an imperial struggle of two countries for control over the vast expanse of land in the west. Both France and Great Britain were claiming the Ohio River valley as their territory, "They each wanted to dominate the heart of America" ("French and Indian War," www.britannica.com).

The French-Indian War was fought along the frontiers separating the New France colonies from the British colonies that extended from Virginia to Nova Scotia. Native Indians were used as allies on both sides, as both England and France sent army regiments to America to fight the war. They each attempted to capture each other's forts in the region ("French and Indian War," www.britannica.com). In addition, the British started seizing French ships and impressing seamen. This escalated into a worldwide conflict as both England and France declared war on each other in 1756 ("French and Indian War," www.state.gov).

With the signing of the Treaty of Paris in 1763, the fighting between these two countries on the North American continent officially stopped, but battles between Britain and France in Europe escalated. By the end of the war, the British controlled the entire North American frontier ("French and Indian War," www.sparknotes.com/history). Under the Treaty, France was forced to surrender all of her American possessions to the British and Spain. She had to cede Canada to the British. Spain gave up Florida but maintained possession of the Louisiana Territory to compensate for her loss of Florida to Britain (ibid.). Prior to the war, France had controlled more of present-day United States than any other European power.

The war shifted the economic, political, and social relations between the three European powers of Britain, France, and Spain and the colonies that they had established in our country. The retreat of French power from North America meant the disappearance of a strong ally against further British occupation in the American colonies. The end result of the French-Indian War was that Britain became the dominant power in the eastern half of North America ("French and Indian War," www.sparknotes.com/history).

Later, in 1796 further shifting alliances occurred as Spain allied itself with France (Schlesinger, 1983, p. 174). In 1801, Spain signed a secret treaty with France to return the Louisiana Territory to France, as Spain had taken little interest in developing the large tract of land west of the Mississippi River. This land was later purchased by the United States from France in 1803.

The war had been enormously expensive for both Great Britain and France ("French and Indian War," www.state.gov). Both countries suffered financially because of the war, with significant long-term economic consequences. France became financially burdened, which in turn weakened the monarchy and led to the French Revolution in 1789. In Great Britain, the war nearly doubled the national debt. Seeking sources to pay off this indebtedness, Great Britain attempted to impose new taxes on the American colonies. This resulted in strong resentment and resistance, which then led to the American Revolutionary War ("French and Indian War," www.sparknotes.com/history).

American Revolution (1775-1783)

American colonists, already weary from the aggression and hostilities of the previous French-Indian War, then became embroiled in our Revolutionary War with Britain in 1775. That war lasted for eight years, from 1775 to 1783. French forces once again returned to North America in 1778 to assist in America's fight against Great Britain. Fifteen years after the French-Indian War, America established a Franco-American alliance against Great Britain.

This was the one time when France was able to prevail over Great Britain through our victory of independence. France may have used our Revolutionary War as possible revenge for the loss of its holdings to Great Britain fifteen years earlier in the French-Indian War ("French and Indian War," www.sparknotes.com).

The political landscape shifted during our revolution as the colonists were now fighting against the British, who had defended them in the earlier French-Indian War. The colonies were now allies with the French with whom they had been previously fighting against. These changing allegiances were strange and confusing to many colonists who had experienced war a decade earlier with reverse alliances.

Following our Revolutionary War, a harsh depression occurred as trade with Britain shriveled. While relative calm had settled in our country for the time being, the rest of Europe remained in turmoil (Schlesinger, 1983, p. 138). The United States had not defeated the British, but we had won our independence. However, by gaining our independence, the United States was no longer part of the British Empire, and America lost the protection of the British Royal Navy on the open seas (*Great Ships: The Frigates*, DVD, 1996).

As the British Army departed at the end of the revolution in 1783, seven thousand British Loyalists fled to Canada from New York City. One hundred thousand more Loyalists had emigrated to Europe and Canada before and during the War (Schlesinger, 1983, p. 138). The British closed the British West Indies ports to American trade, and the export of United States goods was not allowed on British vessels. This forced American merchants to shift their trading, and they entered the China trade in large numbers (Schlesinger, 1983, p. 139).

Part II: Foreign Wars

Tripolitan War with Barbary Pirates

Piracy against United States commercial shipping began with the Barbary pirates after the end of the American Revolution when America lost its protection from the Britain Royal Navy. Previously, British treaties with the North Africa states had protected American ships from the Barbary corsairs. At that time, America lacked a navy to protect merchant ships from attack, and American vessels were now vulnerable to anyone who wanted to prey upon them (*Great Ships: The Frigates*, DVD, 1996).)

During the late eighteenth and early nineteenth centuries, European countries were paying annual tributes to the North African states, known collectively as the Barbary Coast. The capturing and raiding of ships was a government-supported activity as the Europeans were paying Barbary Coast states to protect their commercial shipping ("War with the Barbary Pirates," www.veteranmuseum.org).

These pirates from North Africa along the Barbary Coast became the scourge of merchant ships throughout the Mediterranean Sea and along West Africa's Atlantic coast. The corsairs seized ships on the ocean sea, enslaved and ransomed the crews, and raided European coastal towns. These marauding pirates captured and sold crews into slavery for the Muslim market in North Africa and the Middle East. Some crews were held in captivity for over a decade because the required ransom could not be paid (*Great Ships: The Frigates*, DVD, 1996).

America ended the war of Independence with an underequipped navy and was unable to protect merchant vessels from the Barbary pirates. The United States then entered into treaties with the Barbary States and provided them with tributes (Huff, 2011. www.monticello. org/site). "The new American republic adopted the common European practice of paying tribute to buy immunity from raids" ("Tripolitan War," www.infoplease.com).

For fifteen years, the United States was paying ever-increasing annual tribute and ransom prices for captured ships and crews ("First Barbary War," www.clements.umich.edu). The continuing demand for tribute to the North Africa states led to the formation of the United States Department of Navy. In March 1794, Congress established a navy to prevent further attacks on American shipping (Schlesinger, 1983, p. 165).

In 1801, newly elected President Jefferson refused to make payment to the North African states. Tripoli's Pasha had demanded a $225,000 gift (ransom) and a tribute of $25,000 annually. In retaliation, the Pasha declared war against the United States.

The Tripolitan War extended from 1801 to 1805 ("First Barbary War," www.clements.umich.edu). During the war, the United States Navy was able to execute a campaign of raids and attacks on the Barbary Coast states, and they were successful in maintaining a blockade of Tripoli Harbor and other Barbary ports (Schlesinger, 1983, p. 175).

In February 1804, Lieutenant Stephen Decatur led a courageous attack of 75 volunteers and marines to capture, burn, and sink the stranded *USS Philadelphia* in Tripoli Harbor. Following Decatur's heroic action, a force of marines and mercenaries in May marched across the desert from Egypt to the city of Derma and made a successful attack on Tripoli. Also, in July the US Navy attacked Tripoli and was able to effectively establish a blockade of Tripoli Harbor. The events of the First Barbary War are memorialized by the line in the Marine's hymn, 'to the shores of Tripoli', ("First Barbary War," 2014, www.americanhistorycentral.com/entry).

By 1805 the North African nations had significantly lowered their ransom demands and a treaty was signed with the stipulation of the $60,000 ransom for the *Philadelphia* crew and that the United States would no longer offer tributes ("First Barbary War: The Tripolitan War," www.clements.umich.edu). While Morocco had been the first nation to seize an American ship, it was also the first North African nation to stop capturing our vessels (*Great Ships: The Frigates*, DVD, 1996).

However, the treaty did not completely end the acts of piracy against American vessels ("First Barbary War" www.americanhistorycentral. com). While no ships were captured after the treaty, Barbary pirates continued their raids on American commerce for the next twenty-five years ("Barbary Wars," www.history.state.gov/milestones).

The French Revolution (July 1789)

During the early years of the United States, France experienced considerable turmoil that created a world crisis. The United States became part of the madness of the Napoleonic Wars, as we were then drawn into the Quasi-War with France.

The French Revolution began in July 1789 with the fall of the Bastille, which had been a tyrannical fortress and prison in Paris (Schlesinger, 1983, p. 154). King Louis XVI was deposed and executed along with his wife, Marie Antoinette, in January 1793 (Schlesinger, 1983, p. 162). The same year, the French revolutionary government declared war on Great Britain, Spain, and the Netherlands (Schlesinger, 1983, p. 163). France began to raid British ships and ordered seizures of ships from neutral nations carrying supplies to British ports.

In April 1793, President Washington issued a proclamation of United States neutrality in the war between France and England. He wanted to keep the United States neutral when France was at war with most of Europe (Schlesinger, 1983, p. 163). He knew that Americans were tired of wartime actions and did not want to be pulled into the European conflict.

Napoleon Bonaparte was twenty years old at the time of the French Revolution. He became a French general during that revolt. In 1795, at age twenty-six, Napoleon was made commander-in-chief of the Revolutionary forces after quelling a French rebellion in Paris. In 1799, Napoleon seized power by a coup that established him as the ruler of France (Schlesinger, 1983, p. 172). He became feared by the world. "Napoleon was a delusional genius … an outrageous megalomaniac" (Allis, 2005).

America's Proclamation of Neutrality (1794)

France had been an ally in our American Revolution, and they expected the United States to come to their aid when they declared war against Great Britain. We did not. We claimed neutrality, but France saw it as a betrayal (*Great Ships: The Frigates*, DVD, 1996). Initially, Americans felt positively toward France from their friendship during the revolution, as there was lingering animosity toward the British. However, the United States did not want to again engage in open warfare with the British. They thought that France would do that (Potter, 1981, p. 85).

When President Washington issued a proclamation of neutrality for the United States, the French resented this. The French then began to capture and seize American maritime commerce. United States vessels began to fall into French hands in the West Indies, and several crewmembers were imprisoned and mistreated. Americans were now angry, confused, and indignant with France.

In June 1794, Congress passed the Neutrality Act, which attempted to reinforce President Washington's 1793 neutrality proclamation. This act forbade American citizens from joining military service of foreign powers and banned the fitting of foreign armed vessels in American ports (Schlesinger, 1983, p. 165). The French again resented this action and continued to seize American merchant ships. The US Congress responded by strengthening its military forces and started to construct new ships, and the turmoil of the world continued.

Then, French warships began seizing American merchant vessels that were trading with Britain. In June 1793, Great Britain responded to these actions by the French and ordered the seizure of neutral vessels carrying supplies to French ports and the French West Indies.

While the United States attempted to maintain its
neutrality, it was caught up in the middle of two
warring nations. America was drawn into the fury
and turmoil of the Napoleonic Wars (Schlesinger,
1983, p. 163).

Attitudes shifted with Americans feeling more positively toward
Great Britain. The United States ratified the Jay Treaty in 1796
with Great Britain. That treaty resolved some of the remaining
issues between Great Britain and the United States left over from
the Revolutionary War (Labaree, 1962, p. 112). However, the treaty
neglected to address British impressment of American sailors, which
continued to be a major issue with the Americans.

The Jay Treaty increased French anger at the United States.
France saw the United States as a hostile nation, and they continued
to capture American merchant ships. By June 1797, more than three
hundred American vessels had been captured by the French on
the high seas. Apprehension increased about a possible war with
France, and Congress called for an eighty-thousand-man militia to
be in a state of readiness if hostilities with France should break out
(Schlesinger, 983, p. 169).

William Nichols was a teenager at the time of the conflict
with France. He had twice been captured by the French and had
successfully escaped.

Quasi-War with France (1789-1800)

Adding to the confusion of these times, a scandal labeled the
XYZ Affair resulted in an undeclared war with France. This incident
involving the United States and the new French Republic was a
political affair that inflamed Americans ("XYZ Affair and Quasi-
War with France," www.history.state.gov/milestones).

In October 1797, President John Adams dispatched three envoys to France to ease French-United States relations and negotiate issues that were threatening to lead to war. The diplomatic peace commission included Elbridge Gerry, Charles Pinckney, and John Marshall. Of major concern to the United States was the French interference with American commercial shipping (ibid.).

The French Revolutionary government was having difficulty financing the Napoleonic Wars. Upon arriving in Paris, the commission was unable to meet formally with the French Foreign Minister Marquis de Talleyrand. Instead, they were approached by three agents, Jean Hottinguer (X), Pierre Bellamy (Y), and Lucien Hauteval (Z) ("XYZ Affair and Quasi-War with France," www. history.state.gov). The French agents demanded a $250,000 bribe for Talleyrand and a loan for $10 million before negotiations could start with Talleyrand (ibid.).

The three commission members were shocked, and they rejected the bribe and loan. Negotiations ended, and the commission returned to America (Schlesinger, 1983, p. 170). The commission submitted a report to President Adams, "who inserted the letters X, Y, and Z in place of the French agents' names," and forwarded the report to Congress ("XYZ Affair and Quasi-War with France," www.history. state.gov).

Congress and the public became outraged at the attempted blackmail, which led to a sharp rise in anti-French sentiment (Schlesinger, 1983, p. 170). "For their part, the British had delighted in the anti-French uproar in the United States and moved to assist the Americans against a common foe, revolutionary France" (ibid.). In May 1798, Congress annulled former treaties with France, and the United States started attacking French warships (Schlesinger, 1983, p. 171). The failure of the commission, the attempted bribe, and publication of the unsigned documents angered the American public. This led to an undeclared naval war with France.

"The (XYZ) incident created a political firestorm in
the United States"

Labaree, 1962, p. 115

From 1798 to 1800, the United States was embroiled in a Quasi-War
with France (Schlesinger, 1983, p. 171). During this time, America's
new frigates had a chance to demonstrate their power in this naval
war with France, as they captured ninety-five armed French ships and
were able to successfully protect American commerce (*Great Ships:
The Frigates*, DVD, 1996).

After two years of undeclared war between the two countries,
French Foreign Minister Talleyrand did not want to risk an all-out
war between France and the United States. The Morfontaine Treaty
was signed in 1800, and relatively normal relations were then restored
between France and America. The hostilities of the Quasi-War ended
with no trading of territory and no surrenders (*Great Ships: The
Frigates*, DVD, 1996).

Napoleonic Wars (1792-1815)

The Napoleonic Wars were a series of hostile conflicts over a
twenty-three-year period fought between France and a number of
European countries from 1792 to1815. After seizing power in France
in 1794, Napoleon continued with his march across Europe. These
wars have been considered the first world war, as they stretched
across the nations of Great Britain, Russia, Egypt, Austria, Spain,
Portugal, Sweden, and the Netherlands. They also spilled over
into America and South America (Coote, 2000). These wars had
3.5 million causalities, and they economically devastated Europe
following the wars.

In May 1803, Great Britain declared war on France. Harassment
of American neutral commercial shipping was continued by the

British, resulting in an increased level of anger in the United States toward Great Britain (Schlesinger, 1983, p. 181). This was also when France sold the Louisiana Territory to the United States, which created considerable controversy among Americans (Schlesinger, 1983, p. 181).

The following year in May 1804, Napoleon, at age thirty-five, was proclaimed emperor of France. The next year in October 1805, the French suffered a significant defeat in the Battle of Trafalgar. Admiral Lord Nelson defeated Napoleon's combined French and Spanish fleet off the coast of Spain, which established Britain as the victor of the seas. After five hours of fighting, the British won a decisive naval battle that ensured that France would never invade Great Britain ("Battle of Trafalgar," 2010, www.history.com).

Britain then blockaded all of the French ports. As a result, Napoleon had to retreat to land battles only. He also abandoned his grand scheme for a North American empire because with the resumption of war with Britain, he was unable to win any sea battles (Schlesinger, 1983, p. 184).

In response to the British blockade, however, Napoleon countered with his Berlin Decree. He declared that Britain was also in a state of blockade of all ships entering or leaving British ports, even though France had no sea power at that time! In 1807, Napoleon then announced the Milan Decree, saying that all American ships that had been searched by the British would be seized and confiscated by the French (Schlesinger, 1983, p. 186). This was at the same time of America's Embargo Act of 1807 restricting trade with all foreign countries.

Again, the United States was caught in the middle of these two hostile European nations. In 1808, Napoleon then proclaimed the Bayonne Decree that ordered the seizure of all the American vessels entering French harbors. By that time, Napoleon had engaged nearly all European nations in a bloody struggle, and he had become master of all Europe (Schlesinger, 1983, p. 187). It was a time of confusion and turmoil in the world.

Part III: War of 1812

The War of 1812 is frequently referred to as America's Second War of Independence and is sometimes considered one of our "forgotten wars" (*Great Ships: The Frigates,* DVD, 1996). It was derisively called Mr. Madison's War, but it was truly the war that won our independence. Many issues had been left unresolved at the end of the Revolutionary War, as Britain still wanted to maintain some control in America. There was a lingering fear that Great Britain wanted to reclaim America (ibid.). "Would England ruin the shaky American republic? … It was a strange and illogical war" (Taylor, 2010, p. 10).

America Declares War Because
of British Impressment

After long years of the British Royal Navy stopping neutral United States merchantmen and impressing real or alleged British deserters from their vessels, Americans became infuriated (Schlesinger, 1983, p. 182). Great Britain ignored America's sovereignty and neutrality, as they took the best men from merchant ships to build crews for their navy vessels. The British had been attacking the nation's merchant commerce for many years with no redress (Coggleshall, 1856, p. vii).

Negotiation was exhausted, and interference with American merchant ships and the impressment of Americans sailors continued. The United States was compelled to resort to war as a last alternative, even though the British Navy seemed invincible. War was declared against Great Britain by the United States in June 1812. It was paradoxical that British Parliament had just suspended orders to seize

American ships. They wanted to resolve some of the issues between the two countries. But it was too late. Before that communication from Britain was received in the United States, war had erupted (Young, www.FPY1229@aol.com).

Prior to the War of 1812, Britain and France together had seized nearly fifteen hundred American merchant vessels between 1803 and 1812. The country's slogan for the war became "Free Trade and Sailors Rights," which was often put on the flags of privateer ships (Young, www.FPY1229@aol.com).

When the United States declared war against Great Britain in 1812, our navy consisted of only seventeen vessels—nine frigates and eight smaller vessels, with only three frigates and some smaller ships that were able to get to sea. (Young, www.FPY1229@aol.com). The British Royal Navy at that time had 1,048 vessels, which included 254 ships-of-line, 247 frigates, 183 brigs, and many armed yachts and fire ships. We had very poor odds. "All logic made war foolish … a weak nation grabbed the lion by its tail" (Young, www.FPY1229@aol.com).

There were no privateers in existence when President Madison declared war in June 1812 (Garitee, 1977, p. 255). British and French privateers were continuing to harass and attack America's neutral merchant ships. The US Congress then called upon privateers to perform missions of national importance. America relied heavily on privately owned warships to compensate for its small navy.

When war was declared and at the request of the government, Americans began to fit out privateers as rapidly as possible ("Privateering: War of 1812," 2004, www.ctrivermuseum.org). There was an overnight flurry of activity in our seaports, and the United States rapidly developed a fleet of privateers. Within two months after war was declared, 150 privateers had put to sea (Vallar, 2003). It became relatively easy to convert a merchant vessel into an armed ship. Many of these vessels came from Salem, Baltimore, and Newburyport.

Political Turmoil in America

In addition to all the madness that was occurring in the world, America was a country in conflict with itself (*Great Ships: The Frigates*, DVD, 1996). While experiencing considerable impact from "a world at war," significant political turmoil was happening within the United States. There was a schism occurring in the country, and partisan politics were dividing the country (*War of 1812*, DVD, PBS, 2011).

Thomas Jefferson and his Democratic-Republicans initially supported the French, while Alexander Hamilton and his anti-war Federalists supported the British. The Federalists were threatening secession of the New England states from the new republic. Along with a continuing residual fear that the British might attempt to reclaim America, there was a "battle for the soul of America" (*War of 1812*, DVD, 2011).

Americans were sharply divided over a number of issues, especially about United States-French relations. "The United States was undergoing an agony of political turmoil. It was a bitter time" (Jacoby, 1998). The Federalists deeply mistrusted the French revolutionaries, and there were rumors that France was planning an invasion of America.

Democratic-Republicans initially supported the French, as they identified with the French cause, which was similar to their own revolt in America, but that attitude shifted with the Quasi-War with France (*War of 1812*, DVD, 2011). Also, many new immigrants coming to the United States were anti-British. There was a significant population increase in America for the twenty years between 1790 and 1810, from 3.9 million people to 7.2 million.

Summary Appendix A: The World of William Nichols

This was the world into which William Nichols was born and grew up as a young man in Newburyport. America was involved in war throughout Nichols young adult years, as he developed a fear of impressment when on the open sea. While many of the confusing events and circumstances were often overlapping in nature, Nichols always remained quite aware of what was happening in the nation and the world.

He overheard daily news from the seamen of incoming ships, and he listened to conversations at Wolfe's Tavern when the stagecoach stopped over. He was caught up in all of the turmoil and anxiety of the times, as he lived only two blocks from Market Square, the center of downtown Newburyport.

Appendix B

Historical Perspective: Impressment

It is the duty of every American to avoid imprisonment
in a British ship of war ... It ought to be the first article of the
impressed seaman's creed, that a British vessel of war is a
Pandora's box – a nefarious floating dungeon, freighting
calamities to every part of this lower world.

Joshua Penny, 1815,
who had been press-ganged into
the Royal Navy when he was a boy
(Jenkins & Taylor, 2012, p. 9)

Estimates suggest that for the period up to 1802,
about half of the men in the British Royal Navy had
been impressed. After 1803, the proportion was even
higher, perhaps as high as 75% impressed.

(King, 1995, p. 208)

When Captain Nichols was growing up as a young man in the maritime community of Newburyport, there was always the lingering threat of seizure and impressment whenever a ship would sail out of Newburyport Harbor. It was a dangerous time for anyone venturing out to the high seas.

Nichols was always apprehensive about the threat of possible impressment from the time he began serving as a young apprentice on ships leaving Newburyport. He knew that merchant ships had no defense and were at the mercy of British frigates and warships. He had to be constantly on alert for possible boarding and impressment by either British or French ships. This was especially true, as he was a young and able seaman.

Impressment Defined

Impressment is not a familiar word in present-day English language. It is a term seldom found in current dictionaries and has not been in general use for almost two hundred years. However, it was an extremely emotionally laden word in the latter part of the eighteenth century and early nineteenth century prior to and during the War of 1812 (Schlesinger, 1983, p. 183).

Toward the end of 1796, when the Jay Treaty went into effect that ended the American Revolutionary War with Great Britain, many issues were left unresolved in order to avert a renewed conflict. Of major importance was the treaty's neglect to address the British impressment of sailors from American ships. This became a serious concern and complaint among Americans (Schlesinger, 1983, p. 183).

Impressment is the forcible seizure of able-bodied men into military service authorized by a nation. Forcible impressment was a centuries-old practice that was driven by frequent wars between nations ("Impressment," *Columbia Encyclopedia*, 1950, p. 949). Americans despised impressment because it violated the individual rights of a sailor. The practice of impressment inflamed Americans; "They had an ingrained hatred of the practice" (Jenkins & Taylor, 2012, p. 13).

However, even though it was universally condemned, no serious attempt was ever made to prohibit it. "The feeling of outrage among Americans against impressment by Great Britain reached a high pitch for the 20 years from 1790 to 1809" (Jenkins and Taylor, 2012, p. 13). They hated the British for continuing to harass and impress their seamen. The British kidnappings helped fuel the momentum that carried the nation into the War of 1812.

Impressment Sanctioned by the British

Historically, impressment had been a royally sanctioned activity used by Great Britain as a means of crewing warships. The practice of impressment began in 1664, but legal sanction for the practice of impressment goes back to the time of King Edward I, 1239–1307 ("Press Ganging," www.urbandictionary.org).

In order to maintain their naval supremacy, the British Royal Navy practiced impressment. Because of the prolonged Napoleonic Wars from 1793 to1815, the need for able seamen grew dramatically. "During the peacetime that preceded the Napoleonic Wars, the Royal Navy had about 10,000 men; by the War of 1812, the number had risen to 140,000. The overwhelming majority of these men came from impressment" ("Impressment of American Sailors," www. marinersmuseum.org).

Great Britain justified the practice of impressment because "Its national survival was at stake and victory demanded such measures" ("Press Ganging," www.urbandictionary.org).

The endless struggles for more than two decades between Great Britain and revolutionary France demanded extra manpower. The Royal Navy found that it was more productive to impress men at sea rather than laborers or farmers in Britain. Their favorite targets were neutral merchant ships, especially those from America, far out on the high seas. Recruitment figures presented to the English Parliament indicated that more than 25 percent of the seamen on British ships were pressed men (Jenkins and Taylor, 2012, p. 12).

The United States attempted to maintain its neutrality for commercial maritime shipping during the Napoleonic Wars, but British warships often stopped unarmed American merchant ships and impressed the sailors. Great Britain regarded the United States as a serious rival in commercial trade. The United States had developed the largest merchant fleet of any neutral nation. Because of their jealousy and the threat to their commercial trade, Great Britain desired nothing more than to see a decrease in the number of American ships and sailors.

As the British continued with the practice of impressment, the United States was deprived of large numbers of seamen (Zimmerman, 1925, p. 27). Under the pretext of looking for deserters, British cruisers would violate the neutrality of the United States and kidnap American citizens. British officers claimed that the seamen were British deserters from the British Royal Navy (Jenkins and Taylor, 2012, p. 13).

Desertion from British Royal Navy

There was a high turnover rate among British sailors. Working and living conditions for the average sailor in the Royal Navy in the eighteenth century were harsh. They were much worse than conditions on merchant trading ships. Their pay was half of what was paid to American merchantmen. Also, the Royal Navy often paid wages up to two years in arrears, and they always withheld six months' pay to discourage desertion. Sometimes the Royal Navy did not pay the seamen at all (Jenkins and Taylor, 2012, p. 13).

"The British Royal Navy was a notorious floating hell. The pay was low, when it came at all, shipboard conditions were miserable, and there was ever-present risk of death or injury in battle" (Zimmerman, J.F., 1925, p. 18). Many sailors deserted the British Navy as a way to escape the harsh discipline, poor food, and required lifetime service. Sometimes British sailors would incapacitate themselves by cutting off the thumb and forefinger of their right hands (ibid.).

In the eighteenth century, desertion rates on naval ships averaged 25 percent with at least 2,500 seamen deserting annually from the British Royal Navy. In a report by Admiral Lord Nelson in 1803, he noted that more than 40,000 sailors had deserted British Navy ships in the previous eight years (Jenkins and Taylor, 2012, p. 13). Many deserters would resurface on American merchant ships that provided more generous pay and better working conditions. It was also easier to pass as an American, as they had a common language, but this further justified British officers to declare the American seamen as deserters.

The British pirating of sailors from ships in the name of the public good continued, despite how criminal the acts were. The high-handed practice of impressment was maintained by Great Britain because of "their sense of entitlement, unquestioned privilege, and arrogant disregard that violated the dignity of all sailors" (Jenkins and Taylor, 2012, p. 13). The Napoleonic Wars demanded huge numbers of sailors to man British ships (King, 1995, p. 209).

British Press Gangs

When war broke out between France and England, the British Royal Navy immediately required thousands of additional seamen. The British government established the Impress Service, and press gangs were formed to force sailors to serve on British naval vessels. Impressment was the only way to continue to man the ships of Britain's huge and growing fleet. The United States was drawn into the turmoil happening in Europe because of the impressment of American sailors (Zimmerman, 1925, p. 19).

Press gangs were formed as a group of military personnel whose job it was to find men to force into military service. The practice of press gangs was the belligerent taking of members of crews of neutral merchant ships. Failure to allow oneself to be pressed was punishable by hanging or by simply being thrown overboard. Press gangs would sometimes land on the coastal towns of America and "accidently" press civilians into naval service ("Press Ganging," www.urbandictionary.org).

Press gangs would seize any able-bodied man from a merchant vessel onto a Royal Navy ship, where he might disappear for years, if not forever. The boarding press gang would claim that many of the merchant ship seamen were British deserters, and the gangs would impress them. Press gangs took American seamen by mistake or design because of the similarity of language and manners (Zimmerman, 1925, p. 19).

Even if an American had papers to prove his citizenship, such protections were swept aside, including naturalized Americans. Citizenship papers were often disregarded by the British on the ground that they had been fraudulently obtained (Jenkins and Taylor, 2012, p. 12). The practice allowed British naval officers to determine for themselves the national character of men on board American vessels (Zimmerman, 1925, p. 25).

Samuel Pepys (1633–1703), chief secretary to the British Admiralty, after witnessing a press gang tear many young men away from their families, said, "Impressment has been a great tyranny" (Jenkins and Taylor, 2012, p. 12). Robert Chambers, 1802–1871, a Scottish author in 1854, declared, "The most hateful and terrible word to a seaman was press gang" (ibid.).

Americans Outraged by British Impressment

The United States was strongly opposed to the British kidnapping of seamen from the merchant ships. Impressment inflamed Americans who had a hatred of the practice. Americans felt that the practice humiliated and dishonored United States sailors. The slogan during the War of 1812 was "Free Trade and Sailor's Rights" (Jenkins and Taylor, 2012, p. 13).

A report by the US State Department indicated that more than nine thousand American men who claimed to be American citizens were kidnapped in this way from 1796 to 1812 (Zimmerman, 1925, p.

19). At the time of the Battle of Trafalgar in 1805, which was won by a fleet of British warships against France and Spain, over half of the British Royal Navy's sailors were impressed men. A great majority of the pressed men had been taken from American merchant ships on the high seas.

In 1805, the British continued to harass American merchantmen trading in the West Indies, and then they also began to seize cargos from the ships. British press gangs also began plundering towns along the United States coastline to seize young men (Zimmerman, 1925, p. 174).

Americans were outraged in 1807 when three seamen were seized by the HMS *Leopold* from the *Chesapeake*. In the Chesapeake-Leopold Battle, the British *Leopold* fired on the American ship *Chesapeake*, killing three, wounding eighteen more, and seizing the three seamen (Zimmerman, 1925, p. 155).

This provocation resulted in a cry for war across the United States and turned public opinion strongly against Great Britain. Zimmerman stated,

> "Impressment touched every element of human sentiment and national honor and pride"
>
> (Zimmerman, 1925, p. 254)

"The British Navy was able to abduct as many as 6,000 Americans in the early 1800s" (*Impressment*, www.galafilm.com/1812).

Impressment Ends after War of 1812

The British practice of seizing sailors from neutral United States merchant vessels on the high seas continued until 1815 when the War of 1812 and the Napoleonic Wars ended. While Great Britain never formally renounced impressment, she never exercised the practice after the War of 1812, as British vessels stopped seizing merchant marine sailors (Zimmerman, 1925, p. 26).

However, during the negotiations for peace at Ghent, Belgium, the United States failed to secure the main object for which they had been fighting. There was no mention of impressment in the Treaty of Ghent that ended the War of 1812 (Zimmerman, 1925, p. 220).

Appendix C

Historical Perspective: Privateering

It is safe to say that had it not been for our
privateers, the Stars and Stripes would
have been … completely swept away.

Eastman, 1928, p. 2

Our privateers were a most important, if
not a predominating, feature of our early sea
power (Maclay, 1899, p. viii) … American
merchants found that the swift sailing vessels
proved to be the foundation stone of the
marvelous success of privateers in this War.

Maclay, 1899, p. 20

Captain William Nichols Jr. had a letter of marque and was commissioned as a privateer during the War of 1812. His father, Captain William Nichols Sr., also had a letter of marque and was a commissioned privateer in the Revolutionary War.

Captain Nichols Jr. had been a merchant mariner and shipmaster prior to the War of 1812. It was natural that he would become a privateer captain at the onset of the war. He had excellent navigational skills and was able to skillfully maneuver ships on the high seas. As a privateer captain, he was able to use his experience, seamanship, and leadership skills in his naval encounters with the British.

Privateering Defined

A privateer is a privately owned, armed vessel commissioned by a government to attack enemy ships, usually vessels of commerce ("Privateering," *Columbia Encyclopedia*, 1950, p. 1601). A privateer vessel carried no cargo and was devoted exclusively to warlike use. The primary object was to harass the enemy by disrupting maritime shipping and capturing, sinking, or burning the enemy's ships. Privateering was also practiced as a retaliatory measure. "Privateer" refers to either a sailing vessel or to the captain of that ship.

Privateering was carried on by most nations from the earliest times until the mid-nineteenth century. The greatest era of privateering was the period from 1692 to 1814 ("Privateering," *Encyclopedia Britannica*, 2013). Privateering reached its peak of effectiveness in this country during the Revolutionary War and particularly in the War of 1812 (Garitee, 1977, p. xvii).

There has been confusion in the minds of some people as to just what a privateer was. Some thought the term "privateer" meant a pirate when, in fact, it was a legally commissioned vessel (King, 1995, p. 295). Privateers were privately financed and owned. They were outfitted, crewed, and armed as private warships that were allowed under a government license to attack enemy vessels. Privateers were legitimate; pirates were simply criminals who risked the noose when committing robbery on the high seas (Lydon, 1970, p. 25).

The confusion between pirates, buccaneers, and privateers has carried over into fiction, such that many historians have often lumped them together (Lydon, 1970, p. 24). The services of honest privateersmen "have too long been obscured by the attractiveness of the heroic pirate myth of Captain Kidd, Henry Morgan, Blackbeard, and others" (Lydon, 1970, p. 23). Privateers do not fit the mold of swashbuckler, and they did not leave buried treasure or pirate maps.

There is no present-day myth or story about the patriotic privateersmen. The myth of the glorified sea robber has been inordinate, while privateers have remained obscure. (Lydon, 1970, p. 35).

The War of 1812 has not attained romance in our history books and has not become a fertile source of folklore (Coles, 1965, p. v).

Letter of Marque

A letter of marque commission that was issued by a government differentiated a privateer from a pirate craft, and private ownership is what distinguished a privateer from the nation's warships ("Privateering," *Columbia Encyclopedia*, 1950, p. 1601). A letter of marque and reprisal obtained by the ship owner from the government was the official document for a privateer to operate.

Privateers became adjuncts of our national navies during our two wars with Great Britain. They tended to avoid direct conflict with the larger frigates and warships and usually attacked English commerce. Privateers from American ports were effective in injuring the more powerful British Royal Navy.

A letter of marque was a license of reprisal upon an enemy during wartime. It was a commission issued by the United States government authorizing privateers to arm a vessel and take property of merchant ships of the enemy. The word "marque," from the French, means the right of reprisal—a pledge of seizure by inflicting similar or more serious injury to an enemy. Without a letter of marque, a private ship was guilty of piracy (Macintyre, 1975, p. 3).

Privateering involved the forcible seizure of British vessels in retaliation for the continuing seizures of neutral United States merchant ships and the impressment of seamen. The government's license authorized merchantmen to mount guns on their ships in order to attack British commerce. The holders of letters of marque and reprisal were entitled by international law to commit acts that might otherwise have constituted piracy (King, 1995, p. 231).

Captured Prizes

British ships captured by government-sanctioned privateers were referred to as prizes. When a vessel was captured, a prize crew from the victorious ship was placed on board, and they were directed to sail to the nearest safe port ("Privateering in War of 1812," www.1812privateers.org). The ship and cargo were then condemned and adjudicated in a court proceeding.

After the court judgment, the ship and cargo were sold at auction. The government usually took a substantial share of the prize money as a means of revenue, with the admiralty taking 10 percent, and the custom duties amounting to 5 percent. Federal taxes were negligible in the early years of this country, and the United States government had no income tax at that time.

Revenue was needed to produce sufficient funds for running the government (Macintyre, 1975, p. 6). Revenue was raised through land sales, on the custom duties of imported goods, and on taxes from some selected items (Cunliffe, 1983, p. 146). Privateers during the War of 1812 turned a sizeable American profit because of all the vessels captured (Young, www.FPY1229@aol.com).

The potential to earn prize money was not limited to privateers. The crews of all warships of the United States Navy also had the opportunity to earn a share of prize money from captured ships ("Privateering in War of 1812," www.1812privateers.org).

The high cost of the War of 1812 brought about the nation's first sales taxes on gold, silver, jewelry, and watches. In 1817, Congress eliminated its internal taxes. The government relied solely on tariffs of imported goods for its revenue. Income taxes were not enacted until 1862, in order to support the Civil War effort ("History of Income Tax," 2007, www.infoplease.com).

The remaining proceeds from the prize money were divided into two "moieties," or halves, with the ship owners receiving a 50 percent share, and the remaining 50 percent was distributed to the captain, officers, and crew according to an agreement that was signed by all before the voyage (Dudley and Crawford, 1985, p. 3). The captain and crew shared unequally in the proceeds of a successful capture. The captain usually received six shares and able seamen one share, with others receiving money in proportion to their rank and rating as a seaman (Maclay, 1899, p. 9).

At times, there was a loss of shares for the seamen "when punishment was inflicted for theft, desertion, cowardice, disobedience of orders, drunkenness, and profanity" (Allen, 1927, p. 13). Smith indicated that "the prizes taken by Newburyport shipmasters were few and not of great value except for those taken by Captain William Nichols" (Smith, 1854, p. 197).

Great Britain initially viewed the war with the United States as an affair of secondary and inferior importance, as they had to deal with more global and pressing battles in the Napoleonic War. (*War of 1812*, DVD, 2011). The British were contemptuous of privateers as being little more than pirates. This was a time when the oceans became battlefields.

Privateer Ships Enter the War of 1812

During the War of 1812, there were 517 commissioned privateer vessels, mainly from Massachusetts and Maryland. These ships had almost three thousand guns. This compared with a total of six hundred guns on the twenty-three ships of the US Navy. Privateers captured more than thirteen hundred enemy ships while the US Navy captured 250 (Macintyre, 1975, p. 178).

There were frequent, thrilling incidents with the privateers, and they were important in the bearing on the results of the war. Maclay, in his 1899 book, *A History of American Privateers*, recounts numerous stories of capture, recapture, seizures, and escapes by the privateers and captains during the war (pp. 225–502).

Ships could be easily interchanged for wartime, trade, or passenger purposes, and many ships were fitted out to be privateers. During the war, more than sixty ships were fitted out locally as privateers with heavy arms from Newburyport. A patriotic and enterprising group of daring captains and sailors from Newburyport, sometimes against vehement opposition from the townspeople, "put to sea to harass and do battle against both the English and the French" (Smith, 1854, p. 192).

These new, fast-sailing privateer ships were constructed with more efficient and narrower hull shapes, making them very swift and maneuverable at sea (*Great Ships: The Frigates*, DVD, 1996). These new ships were built for speed, and they were able to reduce the sailing time from England from one month to two weeks. "Within weeks there was a veritable infestation of American privateers" (Young, FPY1229@aol.com).

It was actually the aggressive British impressment on the high seas that created the development of a fleet of ships that could out-sail the British vessels (Maclay, 1899, p. 21). Most privateer ships were constructed with a view to speed, and they became a scourge to the British Navy.

The design of the American ships became the envy of shipbuilders the world over. The American vessels were generally larger and faster than the English ships. These ships were heavily armed and had a large crew. During the war, privateer vessels were constructed from a battery of ten guns requiring thirty to sixty men, to twenty to twenty-four guns needing 150 to two hundred men (*Great Ships: The Frigates*, DVD, 1996).

Characteristics of Privateer Captains

"The first and greatest element of success with a privateersman was audacity" (Maclay, 1899, p. 12). Without a sense of "audacious impudence," a captain was doomed to failure. The expectation was that a privateer would return to port having captured some prize vessels. "To return to port empty-handed was to commit the greatest sin of the profession" (Maclay, 1899, p. 12).

By necessity, a privateersman had to be a bold, daring, and intimidating captain in order to survive. "When these qualities were combined with skillful seamanship, we have the ideal privateersman" (Maclay, 1899, p. 12).

The privateer captain had to employ all of his personal resources, navigational skills, seamanship, and survival instincts in order to ensure the success of his ship and safety of his crew (*Great Ships: The Frigates*, DVD, 1996). Only the bravest and most daring men could succeed with such a responsibility. At sea, it became a win or lose situation. Retreat was not possible once engaged in battle with another ship. To lose meant to be captured or killed while their ships were often burned or sunk.

While privateers had to be bold and daring, the American privateers also exhibited commendable and gentlemanly conduct on the high seas. There were many instances of gallantry and humanity of American privateersmen (Maclay, 1899, p. 14). Numerous letters attesting to this quality with Nichols have been penned by the captains of captured British vessels.

Privateer Victories Over the British

The British Royal Navy was stunned with the victories of the frigate *USS Constitution* over the HMS *Guerriere* and the HMS *Java*, together with the successes of the USS *President* and the *USS United*

States frigate ships. The continued success of American privateers demoralized the British Navy and shocked the British Parliament (Young, www.FPY1229@aol.com). These privateer vessels quickly earned a reputation in the Royal Navy for the quality of their ships.

The British Royal Navy reacted to the American naval victories by shutting down American ports and blockading the merchantmen in order to stop their commerce trade (Young, www.FPY1229@aol.com). As normal trade was made quite difficult, or even impossible, merchants in most seaports turned to privateering as the only alternative for making profits with the ships and men that they had on their hands. The experienced merchant mariners had the necessary risk-taking ability and competence with navigation to be successful in naval encounters with the British ("Privateering in the War of 1812," www.1812privateers.org).

With the help of darkness and bad weather, these sleek and fast-sailing privateers were often able to slip by the British ships that were blockading the harbors (Young, www.FPY1229@aol.com). Unfortunately, however, a number of privateer vessels were captured. In Newburyport, twenty-two privateers that left that seaport were burned or sunk by British cruisers, and a hundred or more men never returned. A mystery still hangs over the fate of hundreds of these seamen. The losses of the local mercantile privateer vessels were well documented by Editor Ephraim Allen in the *Newburyport Herald*. He was a Federalist and was strongly opposed to the war (Smith, 1854, p. 194).

Privateers tried to avoid a direct naval encounter with the larger frigates and warships, and usually attacked British merchant vessels. When a British warship was spotted on the seas, a privateer would turn and out-sail the larger vessels rather than run the risk of damage or capture from an attack by a much larger and heavily armed frigate (Dudley and Crawford, 1985, p. 2).

Privateers were also ill adapted for cruising in squadrons with other ships. They failed at cooperation with regular US Navy ships and with each other. They each operated independently and seemed incapable of concerted action (Dudley and Crawford, 1985, p. 2). Privateers sailed alone, searching for and capturing enemy ships on the open seas. They became marauding predators using a type of seaborne guerilla warfare strategy (Macintyre, 1975, p. 180).

Privateers were relatively smaller vessels compared to regular naval warships, such as frigates or ships-of-the-line. They had enough armament and men to overpower more lightly armed or unarmed merchantmen, which were their primary targets. American privateers were able to slowly reduce the available British trading vessels and supplies going to Canada and to their home country (Young, www. FPY1229@aol.com).

As the nation's privateers were successful in the capture of many British trading vessels, the British fleet and commerce were slowly being reduced. *Lloyd's Register* of London announced in 1815, "500 British merchantmen and three frigates captured in the first seven months of the war" (Young, www.FPY1229@aol.com).

England Alarmed by American Privateers

Confident with their success, the privateers moved east to Britain's home waters along the coast of England where many prizes were taken. "Privateers took packet ships in the Irish Sea, sailed impudently into the Thames River, and scooted past the anchored warships with ease" (Young, www.FPY1229@aol.com).

English markets began to run short, especially with fish, which was a primary food staple, because so few British trawlers were left. British mariners needed to have an armed escort when making even short voyages along the coast of England. Insurance on vessels skyrocketed and sometimes was unavailable. Insurers met a number of times in London and announced that they could not accept any more risks with the British merchant ships (Young, www.FPY1229@ aol.com).

There was great alarm by the residents along the English coastline from the exploits of the American maritime forces. English people became apprehensive that American privateers would invade their homeland. One English resident declared, "God knows, if this American war continues much longer we shall all die from hunger" (Maclay, 1899, p. xiii). Great Britain was not adequately protecting its merchant ships. The real fight the British Royal Navy had was with the American privateers.

Land vs. Sea Forces

Historians have traditionally seen the feats of heroic encounters on the high seas as being of secondary importance in the War of 1812. They have perceived that land battles were of primary importance (Maclay, 1899, p. x). Maclay indicates that "The American people have been taught for generations that our independence in that war was achieved almost entirely by the efforts of our land forces" (Maclay, 1899, p. ix). People think that the War of 1812 was brought to a close principally by the operations of our armies.

However, a comparison of the work done on sea and land "will prove a matter of surprise" (Maclay, 1899, p. ix). While fewer than six thousand prisoners were taken by American land forces in the War of 1812, fully thirty thousand prisoners were captured by our sea forces (Maclay, 1899, p. x). The English themselves regarded our maritime forces, rather than our armies, as the dominant factor in the war (Maclay, 1899, p. xvii).

Prior to the impending war, British merchants had looked forward to the war with some degree of complacency. The British had not anticipated that American privateers would cross the Atlantic and throw their coasts into alarm, or that their shipping, even in their own harbors, would be in danger. British maritime commerce was almost annihilated with sixteen thousand British seamen and eight hundred vessels taken from them (Maclay, 1899, p. xi).

This created an unprecedented devastation of the British economy. The Americans were seen as being a different sort of enemy at sea than the French had been. American privateers had considerable nautical knowledge and bold enterprise. In the estimation of the British, land forces in America played an insignificant part of the war, while sea forces were constantly on their minds (Maclay, 1899, p. x).

Meetings of British merchants and ship owners were held in Liverpool and Glasgow in 1814 because of their concerns about the economy. At a meeting in Glasgow in September 1814, it was unanimously resolved:

> The number of American privateers with which our channels are infested, the audacity with which they have approached our coasts, have proved ruinous to our commerce, humbling our pride and discreditable to the British Navy; that 800 vessels have been taken by that Power, whose maritime strength we have inpolitically held in contempt, and that there is reason to anticipate still more serious suffering.
>
> Maclay, 1899, p. xvi

So loud were the protests from British merchants against continuing the American war that pressure was brought to bear on Parliament to discontinue it. Toward the close of the War of 1812, English newspapers were full of articles recounting the vast amount of damage that had been inflicted on British commerce by American privateers (Maclay, 1899, p. xv). "It was the attack on England's commerce that struck the mortal blow to British supremacy, not the land forces" (Maclay, 1899, p. xi).

Ghent Peace Treaty

The success of American privateer ships with British vessels initiated formal communications between the United States and Britain about "the war that nobody wanted" (Young, www. FPY1229@aol.com). This led to the December 1814 Treaty of Ghent, where it was agreed that everything would to go back to the status quo before the war. However, the impressment issue, which was given as a reason for war by the United States, was never mentioned in the final peace agreement (Young, www.FPY1229@aol.com).

While it is often suggested that nobody really won the War of 1812, it was the success of the American privateers that forced the issue. It is not a myth that American privateers may have won the war; "Great Britain simply could no longer afford the war; privateers had become 'the money drainpipe'" (Young, www. FPY1229@aol.com).

Privateering Ends

After the war, the privateer ships were either used in commerce or destroyed. The seamen of the private armed service to the country achieved many brilliant exploits, displayed daring courage, and showed masterly seamanship. "Had these men been in national service, they would have been entitled to promotion and fame" (Coggleshall, 1856, p. v). Instead of being awarded a proud niche in our history, these brave men encountered neglect and disgrace by the public, because of the prevailing perception that they cared only for profit. "No testimonials have rewarded their victories of crippling the resources of a powerful adversary" (Coggleshall, 1856, p. v). The motives of privateersmen have been assailed, and they have been discredited because of the monetary nature of privateering.

After the war, the officers and crew of the privateers had to seek employment and were often engaged in menial service. "Their calling as sea warriors was gone and these men entered any trade or business they could, where the qualifications to be a successful privateersman were out of place" (Maclay, 1899, p. 507). Their occupation was gone, and they often lived out the rest of their lives as clerks, longshoremen, or wage earners.

Coggleshall, in the preface to his 1899 book, said that he hoped "to vindicate the characters of the privateers and record their patriotic triumphs ... their purposes were patriotic and they were most efficient in weakening the arm of our powerful adversary" (Coggleshall, 1899, p. v).

In an effort to curb the abuse of privateering, nations began to require that captures be condemned and adjudicated in Admiralty Courts. Sometimes privateers were making no distinction between friendly and enemy shipping, and they made some violations of the rules of war and even continued the practice at the conclusion of peace. Because of these abuses and new theories of naval warfare, the major European countries became concerned about the practice of privateering ("Privateering," *Encyclopedia Britannica*, 2013).

The death knell of privateering was sounded at a conference of representatives from leading nations held in Paris in 1856 ("Privateering," *Encyclopedia Britannica*, 2013). Privateering was declared illegal and was abandoned by the Declaration of Paris in 1856. However, the United States government refused to agree, saying that the small size of its navy made reliance on privateers necessary in time of war.

However, with the rise of the American Navy at the end of the nineteenth century, the United States was prompted to finally recognize the necessity of abolishing privateering. The United States government then assumed full responsibility for all ships engaged in military operations, and the practice of privateers became obsolete by the end of the nineteenth century ("Privateering," *Encyclopedia Britannica*, 2013).

Privateer sailors were always fighting against adverse odds and in great peril. There were more than five hundred privateer ships during the War of 1812. The tale of Captain William Nichols is the story of one privateer captain who commanded two privateer vessels, the *Decatur* and the *Harpy*, during the war. "The success of the American privateers was extremely great ... their daring spirit and boldness was unparalleled" (Thomas Clark in Eastman, 1814, p. 81).

Appendix D

Historical Perspective: Newburyport, MA

All history is local.

popular idiom

Newburyport, Massachusetts rose
to fleeting greatness between 1789
and 1812.

Coffey, 1975, p. iii

William Nichols was born and grew up in Newburyport. While he traveled across many oceans in his merchant trading and privateer ships, Newburyport remained home to him. He lived there his entire life, became a fixture in the community, and some two hundred years later is still regarded as a dashing hero by Newburyporters who have known of him.

Newburyport is a seaport that lies thirty miles north of Boston in Essex County in northeastern Massachusetts. It is where the Merrimack River opens into the Atlantic Ocean. The town stretches for two miles along the south bank of the river but only goes a half-mile inland from the river.

The Merrimack River flows from New Hampshire 170 miles through the mill towns of Manchester and Nashua, and then the Massachusetts towns of Lowell, Lawrence, and Haverhill. The river opens into a large, protected harbor.

The Plum Island arm provides protection of the harbor from the constant pounding of the sea. It has only one access to the island, the

Plum Island Turnpike. The expansive Joppa Flats salt marches extend beyond downtown to the south (Labaree, 1962, p. 2).

"Waterside People"

The area was settled south of the river in 1635 and was initially part of Newbury. Fishermen and farmers were the first to settle the area. Fishing flourished as the first industry in the United States, as Newburyport became the greatest port for the fishing industry for one hundred years. Shipbuilding then began to develop, and trading started. As merchants started trading around the world, they began settling along the southern bank of the Merrimack River and were referred to as the "waterside people." The main streets paralleled the riverbank, with Market Square being the center of Town (*Early Essex County,* Video, 1997).

The waterside people made their livelihood from the river and the sea, as shipbuilding and merchant maritime trade became the basis for business enterprises (Emery, 1879, p. 175). Many shipyards began to line the river, with long wharves extending out into the channel of the river. Shipbuilding flourished as a local industry because of the oak wood lumber stands along the shores of the 170-mile Merrimack River. The shipyards were connected by Merrimac Street, which ran parallel to the river and ended upriver where the riverbank merged into pine-covered bluffs (Labaree, 1962, p. 2). Dozens of tradesmen and artisans were needed for the shipbuilding.

Many of the local men became sailors and followed the sea because of the emerging maritime trade. Vessels from all over the world registered their cargoes at the Custom House. The many ships that were built in Newburyport brought wealth and prestige to their owners (Newburyport, newburyportchamber.org). Merchantmen began to export lumber, fish, and rum, while salt, tea, and molasses became primary imports (Coffey, 1975, p. 1).

Newburyport Breaks Away from Newbury

Newburyport was not a typical American community in the late eighteenth and early nineteenth century because of the maritime interests of its residents. It was more representative of some of the New England seaports (Labaree, 1962, p. viii). Those maritime interests became less compatible with the agricultural community in Newbury. In 1763, more than two hundred people along the waterside petitioned to have their part of Newbury set off as a separate town (Labaree, 1962, p. 3). On February 4, 1764, Newbury Port was incorporated.

The town had been successful in seceding from Newbury and had won their independence. A small, rectangular-shaped piece of land of 650 acres along the southern side of the river was established. About five hundred families and almost three thousand people living in 357 homes were included in this transition (Labaree, 1962, p. 3).

Newburyport Prospers in a Golden Age

When trading to other countries started with Newburyport vessels, the British in response, attempted to tax the trade. This action started the Revolutionary War. Following the Revolutionary War, there was a great depression in the country (*Essex County,* Video, 1987). By 1790, Newburyport was beginning to recover from the long depression over the previous decade. The town rapidly became an active and popular trading port. It was one of the largest ports in New England, rivaling Salem and Boston. Trade with the islands of West Indies and West Africa became the backbone of Newburyport's maritime commerce (Labaree, 1962, p. 94).

The sheltered harbor was homeport for a large merchant fleet that brought wealth to Newburyport. With the Napoleonic War taking place in Europe, Newburyport enjoyed the profits of neutral trade and experienced its greatest prosperity in the late eighteenth and early nineteenth centuries (Labaree, 1962, p. 94).

Before the War of 1812, Newburyport prospered and "rose to fleeting greatness between 1789 and 1812" (Coffey, 1975, p iii). From 1804 to 1812, Newburyport had an unprecedented level of commercial activity and prosperity. The town became nationally prominent and was one of the most elegant and influential mercantile centers in the United States. The center of the business district became Market Square, an area that was only one-quarter-mile square (Emery, 1879, p. 175).

Newburyport was alive, bustling, and affluent. Shipbuilding became the primary mercantile activity, as ships were built longer, narrower, and more seaworthy than the British ships. The period from 1795 to 1805 was the **Golden Age** of grandeur for Newburyport (Emery, 1879, p. 175).

When Newburyport was incorporated in 1764, the population was 2,882. The population significantly increased by 58 percent over the twenty-year period from1790 to 1810, as it went from 4,837 residents to 7,634.

During the same twenty-year period, the population of the United States had almost doubled from 3.9 million people to 7.2 million. While the United States population increased in the next ten years to 1820 by another 34 percent to 9.6 million, the Newburyport population decreased over the same time period by 11 percent, from 7,634 to 6,789, because of the economic depression following the War of 1812 (Currier I, 1906, p. 160).

Decline in Newburyport Trade

Trading ventures were becoming more precarious in the early 1800s, because of the interference of maritime commerce and the impressment of seamen by both the British and French. The merchants of Newburyport turned to more hospitable ports in the

West Indies and China. In 1790, 50 percent of the merchant ships from Newburyport went to Caribbean ports, and by 1793, commercial vessels to the West Indies increased to 75 percent. However, many vessels suffered great losses and hardships from the impressment of sailors by the British (Labaree, 1962, p. 97).

The Embargo Act by President Jefferson in 1807 had a disastrous effect on the maritime trade of Newburyport, as all trade with foreign ports was not allowed. While the Embargo Act was lifted two years later in 1809, the terrible Newburyport fire in 1811 and the War of 1812 set a decline in motion that ended the town's importance as a commercial port (Labaree, 1962, p. 97).

These three successive disasters in Newburyport of the Embargo Act, the Great Fire, and the War of 1812 during the early nineteenth century led to the end of the "Golden Period" of Newburyport (Smith, 1854, p. 179). Many stately Federalist-style homes built by ship owners and sea captains continue to line the main streets of Newburyport as a reminder of the Golden Period of maritime trade. That period slowly came to an end after the War of 1812.

The Newburyport Turnpike, now known as US Route 1, was first constructed as a stagecoach road in 1805. It was a straight road from Boston to Newburyport, and it still traverses the town on its way north. The first bridge across the Merrimack at Deer Island was completed in 1796, and a chain bridge was constructed to span the Merrimack River into Amesbury in 1905. It is the only suspension bridge in Massachusetts (Chain Bridge, 2001).

The railroad came to Newburyport in 1846 and was constructed directly into the center of the town and continued on to New Hampshire and Maine. The railroad to Newburyport became obsolete in the early twentieth century, and it was discontinued in 1941. There is now a commuter rail line that extends from Boston to Newburyport at its terminal point.

Dr. G. William Freeman

Newburyport Federalists

During the early 1800s, Newburyport had a strong division of partisan politics: The Federalists vs. the Jeffersonian Democrats. The split permeated through every aspect of life in Newburyport. Lines were sharply drawn, and there was considerable bitterness between neighbors (Emery, 1879, p. 239). Most of the newer, prominent merchants and professional men were Federalists. By 1807, of the twenty-five wealthiest citizens in Newburyport, sixteen were Federalists, with only two Democrats.

During this period, social prestige became very important in Newburyport. Merchants and ship owners dominated the economic and social activities in town, and many were elevated to public office, which gave them power to control the town. Many of the prominent families controlled the social institutions through friendship and marriage. These people had unchallenged political leadership, as few citizens ever dared to question the traditions of this maritime community (Labaree, 1962, p. 5).

The most prominent social club was the Newburyport Marine Society, established in 1772. Membership was restricted to shipmasters. "Captain" became a title of considerable distinction, and they had great authority in the maritime community. More than half of the merchants and professional men in Newburyport were shipmasters (Labaree, 1962, p. 4).

It became possible for a young man to become a captain at age nineteen and to own a ship at twenty-four. Captain Nichols, his father, his brother, his father-in-law, and his son-in-law were all members elected into the Marine Society.

These men also formed the Marine Fire Society in 1775 to look after its members in case of fire (Bayley and Jones, 1906, p. 10). Each member was required to have two leather water buckets hanging by their front door to assist other members in case of fire. In addition, the Newburyport Marine Society provided funds to needy members or their dependents if a shipmaster was lost at sea (Labaree, 1962, p. 10). After the war, many shipmasters retired from the sea at an early age to open their own mercantile business or counting houses (Labaree, 1962, p. 5).

Most of the men in the Marine Society were devoted to the Federalist Party. However, with the Embargo Act and the War of 1812, many of their fortunes significantly waned, and these Newburyport merchants stood on the brink of secession. They favored a narrow sectionalism instead of a new nationalism (Labaree, 1962, p. vii). Following the war, the divisiveness ended and was eventually forgotten (Smith, 1854, p. 205).

Appendix E

Letter from Captain Nicholas Pierce to His Son, Nathaniel Pierce, in a British Prison

Newburyport February 19th, 1812

Nath. Pierce

This is to inform you that we received your letter of the 24th of September and were sorry to hear of you being on board of a gard ship in England while we are here enjoying every luxury and liberty of life in this country as I wish to impress on your mind that you are an American born which is a land of Liberty and freedom but I think I have no occasion to say more for I think you have seen enough to Know and to Revere your own country America.

Me and your mother is well, and your brothers and sisters but troubled to think you are there but they are as I am will take care of yourself although you are young you have seen some of the things in life which will enable you to go through life with fortitude and on better prospects in future.

Your dear little Mary is every day talking of you and regrets that you are in the hands of John Bull and that if she had him here in Newburyport, she would do something bad to him for keeping you from coming home.

My son you are young but be not discouraged you will have your liberty shortly. I have sent documents with this enclosed to M. Dickeson March in London clarifying who you are and your nativity here under the seal of the governed of this Commonwealth which is better that any protection from the customhouse.

When you receive this you may be sure of the other documents having arrived as they go by the same conveyance but I think you will be liberated before and if you should receive this my letter before your with the other Boys write a polite letter to Mr. Dickeson and let him know where you are and your wish to be liberated and to return to your own country (America) and who you taken with as soon as may be and if you should want money he will supply you with some by the order of Captain Benjamin Pierce as I am not known there but on my acct. here.

Be sure to gard against going into any service but your own country's and return as soon as possible for every one of your friends wants to see you so no more.

From your loving father
and mother
Nic. & M Pierce

Nic. Nathaniel Pierce
On board his Majesties Ship
Roy William Portsmouth
Spithead England

See Chapter 8

NOTE: This transcribed letter was written by Nathaniel's father, Captain Nicholas Pierce, in an effort to have Nathaniel released from the HMS Prison-Ship *Roy William* in England.

The letter is located in the Historical Collection of the Custom House Maritime Museum in Newburyport, Massachusetts.

Appendix F

Letter to Captain William Nichols
from Nathaniel Pierce

December 1, 1813

to Captain William Nichols
on board the Nassau Prison Ship, Chatham, England

Dear Brother

Writing to you a few lines, knowing they will be acceptable to you in your dreadful confinement. Your wife is in good health and your children enjoy the same blessing and improve fast. Your mother's health is as good as usual. Your brother Samuel had got home in good health and still remains at home not having been exchanged.

Capt. Swasey has got home in good health and has purchased a farm of wetland and is to move his family on it in a few days, expecting to live more at ease on the land than on the sea. All of the crew of the Brig has arrived at home in good health. Things have remained the same as when you left.

Your Governor not Deaf to the Calls of its Subjects had retaliated for you with detention of two British subjects rank equal to yours and they are confined for you and will not be released till you are at liberty.

All friends are well and send their respects to you and hope that you will soon be restored to your native land and family. Wishing that these lines will find you in good health is the wish of your brother.

Nath. W. Pierce

I am sorry to inform you of the Death of my Father he died Dec. 20th 1812 after a short sickness.

See Chapter 8

NOTE: During the War of 1812, eighteen-year old Nathaniel Pierce wrote this letter to his brother-in-law, Captain William Nichols, who was imprisoned on the HMS Prison-Ship *Nassau* **in Chatham, England.**

This letter is located in the War of 1812 Collection at the Peabody Essex Museum in Salem, Massachusetts.

Appendix G

Letters by U.S. Commodore William Bainbridge and Lt. James Foot, of the Decatur

Navy Yard, Charlestown
June 3, 1813

HONORABLE WILLIAM JONES
Secretary of the Navy
City of Washington

Sir:

I have the honor to enclose to you a deposition respecting the inhumane treatment with Mr. Nichols, late commander of the private armed ship Decatur, belonging to Newburyport, has received from the British Government at Barbados.

I have been credibly informed that Captain Nichols is a very respectable and correct man; therefore, a fair presumption that he has not committed himself in such a manner as ought to deprive him of the established rights of a prisoner of war. Any measure which the Government of our country may see proper to adopt in consequence of this communication I shall readily attend to.

I have the honor to be,
WM. BAINBRIDGE

Dr. G. William Freeman

Commonwealth of Massachusetts, Essex County:

On this thirty-first day of May, in the year of our Lord one thousand eight hundred and thirteen, personally James Foot, the subscriber to the following deposition, and made solemn that the same is true.

JACOB GERRISH, Justice of the Peace

I, James Foot, of Newburyport, in the county of Essex and Commonwealth of Massachusetts, mariner, testify and depose that I was a prize-master on board the privateer armed brigantine *Decatur*, of Newburyport, in her late cruise, William Nichols, commander, that, on the 18th day of January now last past, the said brigantine was captured by His Britannic Majesty's frigate Surprise, commanded by Captain Cochrane, and carried into Barbados.

After our arrival in Barbados, Captain Nichols, with the other officers of the *Decatur*, were paroled. About two months after our arrival, His Britannic Majesty's frigate *Vestal* arrived in Barbados, and, through the influence of the commander of the *Vestal*, Captain Nichols, without any known or pretended cause, was arrested and held in close confinement, without liberty to speak to any of his officers, or any other American.

The place where Captain Nichols was confined was about four feet in width, and seven feet in length, on board a prison-ship, where he remained for thirty-four days, as nearly as I can recollect, and was then taken on board His Majesty's ship *Tribune* and carried to England.

What the cause of the unwarrantable and unjustifiable conduct of the enemy towards Captain Nichols was, I am unable to state.

There were several reports in circulation; one was, that he was carried to England and held as a prisoner until the release of certain men in France from whom Captain Nichols recaptured his vessel,

236

which had been taken by the British before the commencement of the present war between the two countries.

Another report was, that he was to be held until the close of the war, on account of his having been active against the enemy since the commencement of hostilities, and having been fortunate in a former cruise.

JAMES FOOT

See chapter 9

NOTE: These letters were sent to President James Madison by the United States Navy, seeking action in response to the cruel and inhumane treatment of Captain William Nichols in Barbados. The letters resulted in the President's order to hold two British shipmasters in close confinement as retaliation for the treatment of Captain Nichols.

These two letters are located in the *American State Papers*, Volume III, March 13, 1780 – March 13, 1813, "Documents, Legislative and Executive of the Congress of the United States".

Appendix H

Letter from U.S. Commissary General of Prisoners John Mason to U.S. Marshall of Massachusetts James Prince, Esq.

Office of Commissary General of Prisoners
Washington, June 21, 1813

James Prince, Esq.
U.S. Marshall of Massachusetts

Sir:

Immediately upon reception of this letter, you are requested and instructed, by command of the President, to designate two masters of private armed ships, or of merchantmen, British subjects, and prisoners of war, the first in preference, if you or the Marshall of Maine have such in your charge, to place them in close confinement, and to hold them for further orders from this office, to answer for the safety and proper treatment of Captain Nichols, late master of the private armed brigantine *Decatur,* of Newburyport.

Captain Nichols was, when a prisoner, paroled in Barbados last spring, unjustifiably and inhumanely confined on board a prison-ship at that place for more than a month, and then sent to England, in similar confinement, aboard one of the enemy's armed ships.

I shall write to the Marshall of Maine, and request him, if necessary, to act in conjunction with you on the subject

You will be pleased to communicate this letter to Commodore Bainbridge, who has been good enough to interest himself in this matter of national feeling and justice, and to concert with him the proper measures; and so soon as the order is executed, to give me the names, description, and places of confinement of the two persons designated. If there be more than two of the proper characters from whom to designate, the designation should be made by lot.

I have the honor to be,

J. Mason

See Chapter 9

NOTE: This letter from the U.S. Commissary General of Prisoners John Mason, Esq. is the result of President Madison's order to hold two British shipmasters in close confinement in retaliation for the cruel and inhumane treatment of Captain William Nichols. The British strongly objected to this order.

This letter is located in the correspondence of Commissioner John Mason from the *American State Papers*, Vol. III, March 3, 1780 – March 3, 1813, "Documents, Legislative and Executive of the Congress of the United States".

Appendix I

Letter by Benjamin Pierce Regarding Captain William Nichols

Boston, September 3, 1813

Sir,

In answer to your inquires respecting captain William Nichols, I have to state, that in eighteen hundred and eleven and I think in the month of August, captain Nichols was master of my brig, *Alert,* belonging to Newburyport, engaged in a voyage to Bordeaux, that Two of three days after sailing from that port, on his return home, he was taken by the frigate (*HMS Semiramis* taken on the 6th July 1811 as reported in *Lloyd's List,* 23rd July 1811 column 1) having a cargo of wines, brandies, silks, and nothing which could possibly be construed as contraband of war; and his vessel was (after a prize-master and six men were put on board) ordered for England.

He and his mate only, with two small boys, being permitted to remain. About three days after, he and the mate rose on the crew, tied their hands behind them, and hoisted out the long boat, being only forty miles from land, (and summer time,) rigger her, placed sails and oars, put in two barrels of bread, plenty of beef, two casks of water, a keg of wine, keg of brandy other small stores, all their clothes, and such conveniences as would be necessary; supplied them with a good compass, quadrant, and then put the six men in the boat, in which they proceeded to and safely landed in France.

Captain Nichols and the mate then called on deck the two small boys, who remained below during these transactions, and proceeded on his voyage, but six days after, he was again captured by the English frigate *Vestal,* to whom he related the foregoing circumstances, and the captain and officers of this frigate did not treat him as though they thought his conduct either criminal or reprehensible – he was carried in this vessel to Portsmouth, in England, and after being on board the frigate in harbor a few days, thence proceeded to Liverpool, and there took passage to Newburyport.

A short time after, I gave him the command of another of my vessels, namely the brig Dolphin, a new vessel, then lying in Newburyport: and he proceeded on his voyage, laden with fish for Bordeaux; but on his passage out, being at sea thirteen days, he was taken by a British frigate, in company with a sloop of war (reported in *Lloyd's List* 11th February 1812 column 1, as being taken by the *Rosamond S.W.*)

The captain of the frigate asked Nichols, if he was the person who retook the *Alert?* Captain Nichols replied in the affirmative: the British captain replied, "it was a brave act, and he should be treated as a brave man deserved:" and after experiencing the best of treatment while at sea, this office delivered, on his arrival, to captain Nichols all his private adventure, the proceeds of which passed through my hands from my correspondent in England, but was suffered to be at large and come home passenger in the ship *Aurora,* by way of New York, about six weeks prior to the declaration of war between this country and England.

Directly on the declaration of war, I purchased (with my friends) the brig *Decatur,* and captain Nichols was selected as a suitable character to take command; as he proceeded on a cruise against the British, took eleven prizes, and returned to port: the *Decatur* refitted, proceeded on a second cruise, during which he was taken by the *Surprise* frigate and carried to Barbados (*Lloyd's List* 9th March 1813, column 1, reported the capture but said Decatur was taken to Antigua) and there paroled for nearly two months, when the Vestal frigate arriving at that island, he was arrested, sent onboard the prison ship, placed in close confinement in a room, built purposely for him, of five foot broad and seven wide, and no person allowed, but his keeper, to speak to him. After remaining in this unpleasing situation nearly six weeks, he was sent on board the British frigate *Tribune,* and ordered for England, since when we have not heard from him.

Touching the character of captain Nichols as a citizen, a man, and a neighbor, he is modest and unassuming, yet brave and decided; warmly attached to his constitutions, federal and state, of his native country; eager to resist and cool to defend those rights for which the independence of his country was established, and which no unjust pretensions of the enemy will lead him to submit to, however great his personal sufferings.

As a man he is strictly moral and sincere, as a husband, parent, and neighbor, tender, indulgent, and affable. His connections are highly respectable, and are among the first of our citizens. Universal assent among all classes and parties may be had, that Captain Nichols is truly an honest, brave and useful citizen. I hope this information will be the means of restoring him to his family, his friends, and his country, and I can pledge myself for correctness of the statement.

I am, sir, your obedient servant, **BENJAMIN PIERCE**

See Chapter 9

This letter was received by the U.S. Commissary General of Prisoners, Mr. John Mason, Esq. and forwarded to the Britannic Majesty's Agent for Prisoners of War, Colonel Thomas Barclay, Esq.

The letter was used to "rebut the statements made of alleged previous escape and prosecution of Captain Nichols". Mason was making an effort to have Nichols released from prison.

The letter is located in the correspondence of Commissioner John Mason in the *American State Papers* Vol. III, March 3, 1780 – March 3, 1813, "Documents, Legislative and Executive of the Congress of the United States". It has also been reproduced on the website *War of 1812: Privateers*, www.privateers.org.

Appendix J

Statement by Lieutenant Nathaniel Swazy

I, Nathaniel Swazy, Lieutenant of the brig *Decatur*, being influenced by pure motives of truth, come forward to favour the candid public with a true statement of the treatment of Captain Nichols of Newburyport while prisoner at Barbados.

On the 16th day of January, 1813, the brig *Decatur*, commanded by Capt. Nichols was captured by his Majesty's frigate *Surprise,* commanded by Thomas Cochrane, in lat.13.44 N., long 49 W. after the *Surprise* had hailed four times, being distinctly and correctly answered every time, she fired a broadside and five rounds of musket balls from fifty-seven marines into the Decatur, which killed one man and wounded seven.

The treatment Capt. Nichols and crew received on board the Surprise is too inhuman to mention. On the 26th of January, Captain Nichols, Mr. Bray and myself were paroled on shore. On the 13th of March, Capt. Nichols, by order of the admiral was compelled to go on board the prison-ship, after being loaded with the most abusive language from the transport agent, Br. John Barker.

On board the prison-ship Capt. Nichols was confined to a berth in the poop, five feet long and four feet wide, with a sentry at each entrance. For the first twenty-four hours he was not allowed either food or drink, nor were his friends or acquaintances permitted to see or afford him with the least relief. The cruel and bad treatment Capt. Nichols received on board the prison-ship would cause humanity to shudder to hear related.

In the *New England Palladium*, I read the deposition of two (seamen), George Thomas and John Williams, who undesignedly through agency of some fiend, would seem to deceive the public and give lie to Mr. Foot, a white man and a very respectable one, who presented Capt. Nichols' hard lot in prison in the *Newburyport Herald*. I know Mr. Foot's statement to be correct, as far as he said; but he did not so fully point out the deplorable situation he might have done with the greatest propriety.

In regard to the fore mentioned seamen, they were confined in prison on shore and never saw Capt. Nichols nor the prison-ship; they might have seen the outside of the prison-ship when taking their departure from Barbados, and that was all. And further the deponent saith not.

(signed) **NATH'L SWAZY**
1st **Lieutenant,** *Decatur*
January 10, 1814

See Chapter 9

This statement was made in response to the alleged depositions by two seamen that denied the cruel treatment Captain Nichols had received in Barbados.

This statement was first published in the *Boston Patriot* on January 19, 1814, and reprinted in an article about Captain Nichols in the *Newburyport Herald* on June 23, 1905.

Appendix K

Certificate of Release from Prison
of Captain William Nichols

By the Commissioners for conducting
His Majesty's Transport Service, for
taking Care of Sick and Wounded
Seamen, and for the Care and
Custody of Prisoners of War.

THESE are to certify, That *Mr. William Nichols*
As described on the Back hereof, *an American* Prisoner of War,
late master of the Decatur, American merchant vessel, or privateer
has been released from *Chatham*
and permitted to return to *the United States of America* in exchange for
Mr. W. Barss, taken when master of the
Liverpool Packet British privateer,
late prisoner of war ---
AND WHEREAS the said *Mr. Nichols*
is permitted to proceed direct, and without Delay, from *Chatham* to
Dartmouth, where immediately upon his arrival he is to present
himself to Mr. Jon Paddecombe, the board's agent for the purpose
of being embarked on board the Saratoga cartel for America.
All and singular His Majesty's Officers, Civil and Military, are hereby
desired and required to suffer *him* to pass accordingly, without any
Hindrance or Molestation whatever, provided *he* leave this Kingdom
within *fourteen* Days from the Date hereof: but if *he* should deviate
from the Route hereby pointed out, or be found in this Country after

the Time allowed to *him, he* will be liable to immediate Apprehension and Imprisonment.

Given under our Hands and Seal of Office at London, this *twenty-fourth* Day of *June* 18*14.*

George N. George

J. Douglas

John Forbes

Name,	**William Nichols**
Rank,	**Captain**
Age,	**Thirty-Six** Years
Stature,	**Five** Feet, **Seven** Inches
Person,	**Middle**
Visage,	**Long**
Complexion,	**Sallow**
Hair,	**Black**
Eyes,	**Brown**
Marks or Wounds,	**None**

See Chapter 9

The original certificate is located in the Historical Collection at the Custom House Maritime Museum in Newburyport, Massachusetts.

It has also been reproduced in Currier, Vol. I, History of Newburyport, 1906, p. 652-653.

Appendix L

Excerpts from Letter of Secession to the Massachusetts General Court from Town of Newburyport

January 16, 1815

To the Honorable the Senate and the Honorable the House of Representatives of the Commonwealth of Massachusetts:

The Inhabitants of Newburyport in town meeting assembled beg leave respectfully to represent that they believe the time to have arrived in the disastrous course of our national policy when measures of the most firm, temperate and efficient character, on the part of our State Legislature can alone save this land ...

In the midst of these aggravated evils we find no consolation in the reports of peace which the administration contrive to circulate, whenever it suits their purposes; whenever some new chain is riveted upon us, some new act of desperation attempted.

Peace itself could not heal the wounds in which they have inflicted on their country, or atone for their sins, nor can we hope for a lasting peace while corruption is seated in our high places, and the stain of blood, wickedly and wantonly shed, is crying to heaven for vengeance ...

It was with feelings of unqualified approbation that we witnessed the appointment by your honorable body of delegates to a New England Convention ...

... And it is for the purpose of expressing our assent to all its doctrines and our willingness to support to the last hazard and extremity the measures which it proposes, that we now approach you –

To whatever consequences these measures may lead, we pledge to you our own, and we believe this whole people will pledge to you their undivided and fearless support.

And should your demands and requisitions on the national government be treated with neglect ... and still find us bending under domestic tyranny and exposed to foreign invasion,

We have no hesitation in saying that we shall consider our State Legislature as the sole, rightful and bounden judge of the course which our safety may require, without any regard to the persons still assuming to be the National Government,

Nor have we a doubt that the citizens of the Northern States, ardently as they are attached to the Union, would in that event, under the guidance of their enlightened sages, standing in the spirit and upon the extreme boundary of their constitutional privileges –

Would declare that our own resources shall be appropriated to our own defence, that the laws of the United States shall be temporarily suspended in their operation in our territory, and that hostilities shall cease towards Great Britain on the part of the free, sovereign and independent states of New England.

Ebenezer Moseley, Moderator

See Chapter 11
This secession letter from the Town of Newburyport was published in the *Newburyport Herald*, January 27, 1815.

It has also been reproduced in Currier, *History of Newburyport*, Vol. I, 1906, p. 664.

Appendix M

Captain William Nichols Jr. Genealogy

First Generation

Captain William Nichols, Jr., born July 1, 1781, Newburyport, MA, died February 12, 1863, Newburyport, MA, age 81. He married September 30, 1805, Newburyport, MA, Lydia Balch Pierce, born December 25, 1783, Newburyport, MA, died March 8, 1861, Newburyport, MA, age 77. Five children were born.

Martha Willard, daughter, born March 28, 1807, Newburyport, MA.
William Wallace, son, born September 9, 1811, Newburyport, MA, died Havana, Cuba, May 19, 1841, age 29. He was unmarried.
Lydia Balch, daughter, born January 4, 1818, Newburyport, MA.
Mary Lee, daughter, born November 10, 1820, Newburyport, MA, died July 18, 1828, Newburyport, MA, age 7 years, 8 months.
Mary Caroline, daughter, born December 10, 1823, Newburyport, MA, died 1902, Newburyport, MA, age 79. She was unmarried.

Captain Nichols and Lydia Balch Pierce were married at the new church of the First Religious Society on Pleasant Street, Newburyport.
Captain Nichols' parents were Captain William Nichols, Sr., born January 11, 1751 and Mary Batchelder, born June 21, 1757. They were married in the Meeting House of the First Religious Society church in Market Square, Newburyport, on January 11, 1778. Captain Nichols, Sr., died April 20, 1784, age 33, and Mary died April 5, 1849, age 92.

Captain Nichols, Jr., had two siblings, an older sister, Polly, born December 25, 1778, Newburyport, MA, and a younger brother, Captain Samuel, born October 11, 1783, Newburyport, MA. Polly married Duncan Nilage, March 6, 1803, in Newburyport, MA. Samuel remained unmarried and died October 4, 1869, Newburyport, MA, just before his 86th birthday.

Second Generation

Martha Willard Nichols, born March 28, 1807, Newburyport, MA, died in 1882, age 75. She married May 28, 1833, Newburyport, MA, Captain Francis Brown Todd, born October 28, 1805, Newburyport, MA, died May 8, 1841, in Havana, Cuba, age 35. They had one child.

William Nichols Todd, son, born November 5, 1836, Newburyport, MA.

Lydia Balch Nichols, born January 4, 1818, Newburyport, MA, died July 22, 1875, Newburyport, MA, age 56. She married September 7, 1848, in Newburyport, MA, Benjamin Hale, Jr., master mariner, born May 10, 1815, Newburyport, MA, died November 18, 1890, Newburyport, MA, age 84. They had one child.

George Edward Hale, son, born May 27, 1854, Newburyport, MA.

Third Generation

William Nichols Todd, born November 5, 1836, Newburyport, MA, died July 25, 1892, Melrose, MA, age 55. He married September 30, 1864, Elizabeth Johnson, born 1839 and died 1928, age 89. They had one child.

William Nichols Todd, son, born August 6, 1865, Dorchester, MA, and died November 7, 1938, age 73. He was unmarried.

George Edward Hale, born May 27, 1854, Newburyport, MA, died March 30, 1912, Newburyport, MA, age 57. He married January 31, 1889, Newburyport, MA, Emma Frances Wells, born February 18, 1867, Kennebunk, ME, died October 31, 1941, Haverhill, MA, age 74. They had one child.

Genevieve Hale, born July 16, 1889, Newburyport, MA.

Fourth Generation

Genevieve Hale, born July 16, 1889, Newburyport, MA, died September 13, 1975, Haverhill MA, age 86. She married June 17, 1911, Newburyport, MA, Robert Mark Baumgartner, born September 26, 1882, Salem, MA, died June 4, 1949, Haverhill, MA, age 66. They had five children.

Eleanor, daughter, born May 4, 1912, Newburyport, MA.
Robert Mark, son, born September 29, 1913, Haverhill, MA, died February 7, 1929, Haverhill, MA, age 15.
Donald Hale, son, born November 12, 1915, Haverhill, MA.
Nance, daughter, born March 4, 1918, Haverhill, MA.
Janet Louise, daughter, born July 26, 1920, Haverhill, MA.

Fifth Generation

Eleanor Baumgartner, born May 4, 1912, Newburyport, MA, died September 15, 2002, Kaleva, MI, age 90. She first married May 18, 1935, Haverhill, MA, Milo Harrison Buzzee, born March 25, 1912, East Hampton, MA, died October 1989, Kissimee, FL, age 77. She married again in 1973, Martin Leninger, born May 19, 1912, died in an auto accident October 12, 1976, age 64. There were five children from her first marriage and no children from her second marriage.

Myla Lee Buzzee, daughter, born July 12, 1938, Pittsfield, MA.
Sandra McPherson Buzzee, daughter, born July 1, 1940, Pittsfield, MA, died November 25, 2004, Greenville, IN, age 64.
David Harrison Buzzee, son, born March 11, 1942, Pittsfield, MA.
Robert Mark Buzzee, son, born October 28, 1943, Ft. Wayne, IN, died June 21, 2014, Laconia, IN, age 70.
Donald Wayne Buzzee, son, born August 29, 1949, Decatur, IL.

Donald Hale Baumgartner, born November 12, 1915, Haverhill, MA, died March 5, 2006, Hampstead, NH, age 91. He married December 25, 1952, Newburyport, MA, Alice Brookings, born July 12, 1906, Newbury, MA, died May 23, 1985, Hampstead, NH, age 78. There were no children.

Nance Baumgartner, born March 4, 1918, Haverhill, MA, died November 19, 1971, Groveland, MA, age 53. She first married October 16, 1937, Los Angeles, CA, George William Freeman, born November 20, 1914, Haverhill, MA, died October 11, 1942, Pittsfield, MA, age 27. She later married July 16, 19149, Haverhill, MA, Edward Tasker Stocker, born October 30, 1916, Haverhill, MA, died February 20, 2010, in Ft, Myers, FL, age 93. She had two children from her first marriage and two children from her second marriage.

George William Freeman, Jr., son, born October 14, 1939, Pittsfield, MA.
Carol Jean Freeman, daughter, born April 6, 1941, Pittsfield, MA, died April 8, 1941, Pittsfield, age 2 days.
Anne Stocker, daughter, born December 3, 1951, Haverhill, MA.
Deborah Lynne Stocker, daughter, born February 23, 1955, Haverhill, MA died November 11, 2007, age 52, Dracut, MA.

Janet Louise Baumgartner, born July 26, 1920, Haverhill, MA, died April 22, 2012, Portsmouth, NH, age 91. She first married December 21, 1941, Haverhill, MA, Lester William White, born January 7, 1916, Portsmouth, NH, died March 17, 1996, Port St. Lucie, FL, age 80. She later married December 2, 1983, Greenland, NH, Phillip Herbert Nay, born October 8, 1916, Belmont, MA, died March 6, 1985, Sebastian, FL, age 68. She had four children from her first marriage and no children from her second marriage.

Jean Humphreys White, son, born February 10, 1943, Portsmouth, NH, died May 26, 1998, Rochester, MN, age 55.
Paul Henry White, son, born October 13, 1944, Portsmouth, NH.
Leslie Louise White, daughter, born June 23, 1947, Portsmouth, NH.
Dale Clinton White, son, born April 11, 1952, Portsmouth, NH, died December 29, 2012, Florida, age 60.

Custom House Maritime Museum
Newburyport, Massachusetts
Photograph by Benjamin Hale Freeman

Bibliography

Abell, Francis. *Prisoners of War in Britain 1756 to 1815*. London: Oxford University Press, 1914. www.archive.org.

"Account of the Great Fire, Newburyport." Newburyport: Gilman, 1811. Reprinted Decorah, Iowa: Anundsen Publishing Co., 1989.

Allen, Gardiner. "The Penobscot Expedition." In *Naval History of the American Revolution*. Massachusetts Historical Society. Boston: Houghton, 1913.

_____. *Massachusetts Privateers of the Revolution*. Boston: Massachusetts Historical Society, 1927.

Allis, Sam. "Napoleon's Last Stand." *Boston Globe*. February 24, 2005.

American State Papers, Volume III, March 3, 1780–March 3, 1813. "Documents, Legislative & Executive of the Congress of the United States," 646–645.
Washington: Gales & Seaton, 1832.

Annals of America. Volume 4, 1797–1820, Encyclopedia Britannica.

Banner, James. *Hartford Conventions 1789–1815*. New York: Knopf, 1970.

"Barbary Wars." www.history.state.gove/milestones.

"Battle Fatigue." www.medicinenet.com.

"Battle of Fort McHenry." www.militaryhistory.about.com.

"Battle of New Orleans." www.history.com.

"Battle of Trafalgar October 21, 1805." 2010. www.history.com/this-day-in-history.

Bayley, Captain William and Captain Oliver Jones. *History of the Marine Society of Newburyport, Massachusetts, 1772–1906.* Newburyport: The Press of Daily News, 1906.

Biedler, John. "Stephen Decatur and the Sinking of U.S. Philadelphia." www.redecatur/com.

Black, Henry Campbell. *Black's Law Dictionary.* St. Paul, Minnesota: West Publishing Co., 1957.

"British Capture Fort Mackinac." www.galafilm.com/1812.

British Generals in the War of 1812: High command in Canada. Canada: McGill-Queens Press, 1999.

Brown, Charles Raymond. *The Northern Confederacy Plans of Essex Junto 1796–1814, a Doctoral Dissertation.* Princeton: Princeton University Press, 1915.

Buckley, William. *Hartford Convention Tercentenary Report.* Yale University Press, 1934.

Bull, Jacqui. "Prison Hulks." 2002. www.boards.ancestry.com.

"Burning of Frigate Philadelphia 16 February 1804." Naval History and Heritage Command. www.history.navy.milphotos/events.

"Burr vs. Hamilton: Behind the Ultimate Political Feud." National Constitution Center. July 2013. www.consitutioncenter.org.

Carr, Deborah Edith. *American Prisoners of War 1812–1815*. Ottawa, Canada: Genealogical Publishing Co., 1955.

"Chain Bridge." 2001. www.massroads.com.

Chase, Sidney Marsh. "A Yankee Privateer." *Scribner's Magazine*, Vol. LIII, No. 5. New York: Charles Scribner's Sons, May 1913.

Chase, Sidney Marsh. "Captain William Nichols and the Privateer Decatur." Unpublished manuscript given to the author by his grandmother, ca. 1920.

Clark, Admiral George. *A Short History of the United States Navy*. Philadelphia: Lippincott, 1939.

Clark, Richard. "Maidstone Prison." 2002. http://www. capitalpunishmentuk.org/maidstone.html.

Coffey, Lorraine. "Rise and Decline of the Port of Newburyport, 1783–1820." Boston: Boston University Graduate School Doctoral Dissertation, 1975.

Coggleshall, Captain George. *History of American Privateers*. New York: published by the author, 1856.

Coles, Harry L. *War of 1812*. Chicago: University of Chicago, 1965.

Commonwealth of Massachusetts Archives, Vol. 165, 169.

Cooney, David M. *Chronology of the United States Navy 1775–1965*. New York: Watts, 1965.

Coote, Stephen. "Napoleon and the Hundred Days." Dugdale-Pointon, 2000. www.historyofwar.org.

Cunliffe, Marcus. "Testing a Union 1788–1805." In Schlesinger, Arthur M. *The Almanac of American History.* New York: Putnam & Sons, 1983.

Currier, John J. *History of Newburyport, Massachusetts, 1764–1905,* Volume I. Newburyport: published by the author, 1906.

_____. *History of Newburyport, Massachusetts, 1764–1909,* Volume II. Newburyport: published by the author, 1909.

Cushing, Caleb. *History and Present State of Newburyport.* Newburyport: Self-Published, 1826.

Dana, Richard. "Cruelty to Seamen." *American Jurist,* Volume 22, October 1839–January 1840, 92–107. Boston: Little-Brown, 1840.

Davis, Matthew. *The Private Journal of Aaron Burr.* New York: Harper & Brothers, 1858.

Davis, Samuel. "On Board of the Prison Ship, port of Nassau." March 10, 1814. www.blogof1812.com.

"Declaration of War of 1812." *Niles Weekly Register.* May 30, 1812. www.teachingamericanhistory.org/library.

Diagnostic and Statistical Manual of Mental Disorders, Fifth Edition (DSM-5). Washington DC: American Psychiatric Association, 2013.

Downs, Joseph. "The Benkard Room," (written by Curator of American Wing). New York: Metropolitan Museum of Art, January 1948.

Druett, Joan. "Grim Details of Life Aboard Prison Hulks." 2012. www.joan-druett.blogspot.com.

Dudley, William S. and Michael J. Crawford. "Privateering in the War of 1812." *The Naval War of 1812.* Washington: Naval Historical Center, Department of Navy, 1985.

"Duel At Dawn, 1804." Eyewitness to History. 2000. www.eyewitnesstohistory.com.

"Early Essex County." Video Presentation. Salem Historical Center, Salem, MA, 1997. www.nps.gov.

Eastman, Ralph M. *Some Famous Privateers of New England.* Boston: privately printed, State Street Trust Company, 1928.

Ellis, James. *Why New England Almost Seceded Over the War of 1812.* 2012. www.radiobostonwbur.org.

Emery, Sarah A. *Reminiscences of a Nonagenarian.* Newburyport: Huse & Co., Printers, 1879.

Emmons, George. *The Navy of the United States 1775–1853.* Washington: Gideon, 1853.

Essex County, Massachusetts Probate Index, 1638–1840. Boston: Sanborn, 1987.

"Essex Junto." 2012. www.legal-dictionary.thefreedictionary.com.

"Essex Junto." 2014. Encyclopedia Britannica. www.britannica.com.

"First Barbary War," *Encyclopedia of American History.* American History Central. www.americanhistorycentral.com.

"First Barbary War: The Tripolitan War." www.clements.umich.edu/exhibits/online.

Fitz-Eriz, David. "Chronology of the War of 1812." Washington DC: National Archives and Records Administration, 2004.

"Fort Dearborn Massacre" www.galafilm.com/1812e/events/ftdearborn.html).

"Fort Dearborn Massacre." 2000. www.prairieghosts.com/dearborn.htm.

"French and Indian War." www.britannica.com/EBchecked/topic218957.

"French and Indian War." www.history.state.gov/milestones/1750-1775.

"French and Indian War (1754–1763)." www.sparknotes.com/history.

Gabriel, Michael P., Review of Skeen, C. Edward, "Citizen Soldiers in the War of 1812." H-SHEAR, H-Net Reviews. July 1999.

Garitee, Jerome. *The Republic's Private Navy.* Connecticut: Wesleyan University, 1977.

"General Alexander Macomb." 2011. www.warof1812trail.com.

Glenn, Myra. *Campaigns Against Corporal Punishment.* Albany: State University of New York, 1984.

"Great Fire of Newburyport." www.brickandtree.wordpress.com.

"Great Fire of Newburyport." 2011. www.newburyport-today.com.

"Great Fire of Newburyport." pavementU77. 2001. www.everything2.com.

Great Ships: The Frigates. DVD. 1996. www.history.com.

Green, Aaron. "Tchaikovsky's 1812 Overture." www.classicalmusic.about.com.

Hanning, Bud. *The War of 1812: A Complete Chronology.* Jefferson, NC: McFarland & Co., Publishers, 2012.

Harris, John. "Old Ironsides." *Boston Globe.* October 16, 1977.

Hendricks, Lynne. "Landmark Event in Newburyport Past." 2011. www.newburyportnews.com.

Hickman, Kennedy. "War of 1812: Captain Thomas MacDonough." 2014. www.militaryhistory.about.com.

_____. "War of 1812: Battle of Fort McHenry." 2014. www.militaryhistory.about.com.

"History of Income Tax in the United States." 2007. www.infoplease.com.

"Historic Newburyport." 2014. www.newburyportchamber.org.

Historical Collection. Custom House Maritime Museum. Newburyport, MA.

"History of Income Tax in the United States." 2007. www.infoplease.com.

Huff, Elizabeth. "The First Barbary War." 2011. www.monticello.org/site.

Hurd, D. Hamilton. *History of Essex County, Massachusetts,* Volume II, 1763–1765. Philadelphia: J.W. Lewis Co., 1888.

"Impressment." www.galafilm.com/1812.

"Impressment of American Sailors." *Prelude to the War of 1812.* The Mariners Museum. 2000. www.marinersmuseum.org.

"Incredible Hulks: The Fearsome Prison Ships of the Former British Empire." 2012. www.urbanghostsmedia.com.

Index to Vital Records of Newburyport, MA, Volumes 1–5.

"Introduction to Newburyport History." 2012. www.nbptpreservationtrust.org.

Jacoby, Jeff. "United States Suffered Through Turmoil in 1798." *Boston Globe*. December 28, 1998.

Jenkins, Mark Collins and David A. Taylor. *The War of 1812 and the Rise of the U.S. Navy.* National Geographic Society: Boston Publishing Co., 2012.

King, Dean. *A Sea of Words*. New York: Holt & Co., 1995.

Labaree, Benjamin W. *Patriots and Partisans: The Merchants of Newburyport, 1764–1815.* Cambridge: Harvard University, 1962.

Lloyd's Register 1811–1814. Society for the Registry of Shipping, London, England reprinted London, England: Gregg International Publishers, 1969. www.lr.org.

Lydon, James. *Pirates, Privateers, and Profits.* New Jersey: Gregg, 1970.

Maclay, Edgar. *History of American Privateers.* New York: Appleton, 1899.

MacIntyre, Captain Donald. *The Privateers.* London: Elek, 1975.

Malone, Dumas and Basil Rauch. *The Republic Comes of Age, 1789–1841.* Appleton-Century-Croft. 1964.

Massachusetts Soldiers and Sailors of the Revolutionary War, Secretary of the Commonwealth. (1903) Boston: Wright & Potter Publishing Co., 1903.

McNally, William. *Evils and Abuses in the Naval Merchant Service Exposed,* 139–144. Boston: Cassidy and March, 1839.

"Medway Prison Hulks." 2011. www.medway.gov.uk.

"Napoleon," *Oxford Dictionary, 3rd Edition.* New York: Oxford University Press, 2010.

"Napoleon's Disastrous Invasion of Russia, 200 Years Ago," 2012. www.history.com.

"Newburyport." www.newburyportchamber.org.

Newburyport Daily News.
    Bartlett, H. W., "Story of Captain Nichols." September 17, 1948.
    "Bold Newburyport Privateer Who Worried John Bull." June 23, 1905.
    Brown, Ned. "Cabbages and Kings." June 13, 14, 22, and August 1, 1963.
    Somerby, Charles. "Captain Nichols Ability to Elude Foe." March 5, 1952.

_____. "Intrepid Captain Nichols Put Down Mutiny on Brig Decatur." March 11, 1952.

Newburyport Herald.
"Arrival of Harpy." February 7, 1815.
"Captain William Nichols Naval Hero." March 13, 1886.
"Cruise of Privateer Harpy." February 10, 1815.
"Herald Ship News." August 4 and 11, September 25, December 15 and 25, 1812, and February 19, March 19, June 8, July 30, 1813.
"Memorabilia." No. 7, August 1; No. 8, August 2; No. 9, August 8; and No.
10, August 9, 1855.
"Newburyport Reminiscences." March 13, 1877.
"Privateer Harpy." October 28, 1814.

Newburyport Vital Records to 1850, Vol. 1 & 2. Salem: Essex Institute, 1911.

New England Threat of Secession." *Columbian Centinel*. January 13, 1813. www.teachingamericanhistory.org/library.

New Hampshire Gazette. Portsmouth, NH, November 6, 1799.

"Nineteenth Century Justice: Prison Hulks." *Victorian Crime and Punishment*. 2006. www.vcp.e2bn.org.

O'Byrne, William. *Naval Biographical Dictionary*. London: John Murray, Publisher, 1849.

Oxford Dictionary. 3rd Edition. New York: Oxford University Press, 2010.

Peak, Elder John. *Memoir of Elder John Peak*. Boston: J. Hare, Printer, 1832.

"Penobscot Expedition, 1779." 2004. www.uswars.net.

Perkins, Bradford. *Causes of the War of 1812.* New York: Holt, 1962.

Phillips, Michael. *Ships of the Old Navy.* 2007. www.ageofnelson.org.

"Pickering." *Dictionary of American Naval Fighting Ships,* Vol. 3. 1959. www.history.naval.mil.

Pierce, Benjamin. Letter regarding Captain William Nichols (recipient unidentified), September 3, 1813. Reproduced at *War of 1812: Privateers.* www.1812privateers.org.

Pierce, Nathaniel. "Journal as a Prisoner of War at Dartmoor Prison 1814–1815." Located in the War of 1812 Collection, Series III, Peabody Essex Museum in Salem, Massachusetts.

_____. "Letter to Captain William Nichols." December 1, 1813. Located in the War of 1812 Collection, Series III, Peabody Essex Museum in Salem, Massachusetts.

Pierce, Captain Nicholas. "Letter to his son Nathaniel Pierce in a British Prison." February 19, 1812. Located in the Historical Collection, Custom House Maritime Museum of the Newburyport Maritime Society, Newburyport, Massachusetts.

Phillips, Michael. *Ships of the Old Navy.* 2007. www.ageofnelson.org.

Pitch, Anthony. "The Burning of Washington." *The British Invasion of 1814.* Annapolis, Maryland: Naval Institute Press. 1998. www.senate.gov.reference.

Potter, E.B. *Sea Power: A Naval History.* Annapolis: United States Naval Institute, 1981.

"Press Ganging." www.urbandictionary.org.

"Prison Hulks." State Library of Victoria. 2010. www.ergo@slv.vic. gov.au.

"Prison Ships." US Maritime Service Veterans. 2001. www. USMM.org.

"Privateer." *Encyclopedia Britannica.* Chicago: Encyclopedia Britannica, Inc., 2002. www.britannica.com.

"Privateer Harpy's Activities." *New York Times.* February 9, 1815. www.hillsdale.edu.

"Privateering." *Columbia Encyclopedia.* New York: Columbia University Press. 1950.

"Privateering in the War of 1812." www.1812privateers.org/United States/USgov.html

"Privateering: War of 1812." Connecticut River Museum. 2004. www.ctrivermuseum.org.

"Quasi-War with France: Ship Rose of Newburyport." www. ibiblio.org.

"Rear Admiral George Cockburn." 2012. www.destinationsouthern maryland.com/ c/378/1812rearadmiralgeorgecockburn.

Rickard, J. "Battle of Mackinac Island, 17 July 1812." November 21, 2007. www.historyofwar.org.

Rikhye, Ravi. "US Navy Fleet List War of 1812." 2002. www. orbat.com.

Robinson, John and George Francis Dow. *The Sailing Ships of New England, 1607–1907.* Salem, MA: Marine Research Society, 1922. Republished in New York by Skyhorse Publishing, 2007.

Roosevelt, Theodore. *The Naval War of 1812.* 1882. Reprinted in New York: Putnam, 1987.

Sage, Henry. "The War of 1812: the Forgotten War." 2004. www.nv.cc.va.us.

"Sailing Lore: Baltimore Clipper History: Privateers." 2005. www.intandem.com.

Salem Gazette. Volume 2, Salem, MA, September 17, 1799.

Schechner, Nathan, *Aaron Burr—A Biography, 1937.* Distributed Proofreaders Canada ebook. Posted 2014, www.pgdpcanada.net.

Schlesinger, Arthur M. *The Almanac of American History.* New York: Putnam & Sons, 1983.

Smith, E. Vale. *History of Newburyport.* Boston: Damrell & Moore, 1854.

"Some New England Sea Captains." *General Massachusetts Archives."* 2001. Farns10ᵗʰ@aol.com.

"State Organized Militia—War of 1812," 2011, www.globalsecurity.org/military/agency/army/miltia-1812).

Stein, Douglas. "Letter of Marque/Privateer Commission." Museum of America, Mystic Seaport, CT.

Stewart, William. *Admirals of the World*. Jefferson, North Carolina: McFarland & Company, 1927.

Taylor, Alan. *The Civil War of 1812*. Random House Google e-book. 2010.

The Great Republic: Naval History: War of 1812. Published in early 1900s, reprinted by Bancroft. 2004. www.publicbookshelf.com.

"The Privateer *Harpy's* Activities." *New York Times*. February 5, 1815. www.hillsdale.edu.

The War of 1812: The War That Both Sides Won. Dundorn, 2000.

"Treaty of Ghent." 2012, Columbia Electronic Encyclopedia. www.infoplease.com/enc.

"Tripolitan War." 2012, Columbia Electronic Encyclopedia. www.infoplease.com/encyclopedia/history.

"Tripolitan War of 1801–1805." 2011. www.barbarywarfare.com

Tucker, Spencer, editor. *Encyclopedia of War of 1812*. Santa Barbara, California: ABC-CLIO, 2012.

Vallar, Cindy. "Pirates and Privateers." 2003. www.cindyvallar.com.

"Vanderlyn the Artist." Friends of the Senate House. 2014. www.info@senatenousekingston.org

War of 1812. Central Canadian Public TV Association. 2011.

War of 1812. DVD. Public Broadcasting System. 2011.

War of 1812: First Invasion. DVD. 2005. www.historychannel.com.

"War with the Barbary Pirates." www.veteranmuseum.org/barbary. html).

Wildes, Rev. George D. "Memoir of Captain William Nichols of Newburyport." Historical Collections of the Essex Institute, 229– 236. Salem, MA: Essex Institute, 1864.

Woodworth, Ghlee. *Tiptoe Through the Tombstones*. Newburyport. 2009. www.tiptoethroughthetombstones@yahoo.com.

"XYZ Affair and Quasi-War with France, 1798-1800." US Department of State, Office of the Historian. www.history.state. gov/milestones/1784-1800.

Young, Frank Pierce. "Privateering During the War of 1812." Annapolis, MD. 2004. www.FPY1229@aol.com.

Zimmerman, J. F. *Impressment of American Seamen*. 1925.

Printed in the United States
By Bookmasters